We Shall Conquer or Die

Partisan Warfare in 1862 Western Kentucky

Derrick Lindow

SB
Savas Beatie
California

First edition, first printing

ISBN-13: 978-1-61121-668-4 (hardcover)
ISBN-13: 978-1-61121-669-1 (ebook)

Library of Congress Cataloging-in-Publication Data

Names: Lindow, Derrick, 1987- author.
Title: We Shall Conquer or Die: Partisan Warfare in 1862 Western Kentucky / Derrick Lindow.
Other titles: Partisan warfare in 1862 Western Kentucky
Description: El Dorado Hills, CA: Savas Beatie, [2024] | Includes bibliographical references and index. | Summary: "A deadly and expensive war within a war was waged behind the lines (and often out of the major headlines) in western Kentucky. In 1862, the region was infested with guerrilla activity that pitted brother against brother and neighbor against neighbor in a personal war that often recognized few boundaries. The partisan guerrilla fighting and efforts to bring it under control helps put the Civil War in the Western Theater in context"-- Provided by publisher.
Identifiers: LCCN 2023048584 | ISBN 9781611216684 (hardcover) | ISBN 9781611216691 (ebook)
Subjects: LCSH: Kentucky--History--Civil War, 1861-1865. | United States--History--Civil War, 1861-1865--Campaigns. | Guerrillas--Confederate States of America. | Confederate States of America. Army. Kentucky Cavalry Regiment, 10th. | Guerrilla warfare--United States--History--19th century. | United States--History--Civil War, 1861-1865--Underground movements. | Johnson, Adam Rankin, 1834-1922. | Martin, Robert M. (Robert Maxwell), 1840-1901.
Classification: LCC E474.3 .L56 2024 | DDC 973.7/469--dc23/eng/20231102
LC record available at https://lccn.loc.gov/2023048584

Printed and bound in the United Kingdom

SB
Savas Beatie
989 Governor Drive, Suite 102
El Dorado Hills, CA 95762
916-941-6896 / sales@savasbeatie.com / www.savasbeatie.com

To

Allie, Ezra, and Owen

and

Mom, Dad, and Rachel

TABLE OF CONTENTS

TABLE OF CONTENTS

(continued)

LIST OF MAPS

Photos have been placed throughout the text for the convenience of the reader.

Preface

My interest in the Civil War began in elementary school when I developed a fascination for all things historical. Both of my grandfathers fostered this curiosity. My maternal grandfather took us on car rides through the country showing us where the family came from. I used to sit with my paternal grandfather on the couch as we watched old black-and-white World War Two documentaries and read the books he gave me every year. Some of my teachers also had a way of teaching history like it was a story, and it grabbed me.

By middle school, I wore out my VHS copy of *Gettysburg* and tried to read as much as I could on the war. My parents took me to my first reenactment at Sacramento, Kentucky, in the spring of 2001, ironically Adam Johnson's and Robert Martin's first real skirmish together, and there the smell of the gunpowder ensnared me. Two years later, I started reenacting. As my dad drove us home from that first reenactment in Sacramento, we stopped at a historical marker on Highway 431. There we read about the "only" skirmish to take place in Owensboro, Kentucky, our home. Since that day, I desired to learn more about that event but never really researched it in any depth until my college years. For my Kentucky History class, I decided to write my ten-page paper on the Battle of Sutherland's Hill, also known as the Battle of Panther Creek. While researching that paper, I found some interesting sources, several of which I used in this work, but my understanding of the events that took place here on September 19-20, 1862 was still only surface level. I had yet to grasp the overarching connections and ramifications this seemingly insignificant skirmish had on the war in western Kentucky.

Years later in the fall of 2017, my curiosity for the war in my area reached an all-time high. I wanted to write something just for local consumption. Some sort of work that told the stories of my hometown and maybe the surrounding counties. As I started my research, I began with my original interest, Sutherland's Hill, and went from there. The more I researched, the more I began to realize that this was part of a much larger story. A story that stretched from western Kentucky, to Indiana, and even down to western Tennessee. I could not believe how very little had been written on the events that I researched. It also meant that this would no longer be just a local history. It mattered in the broader picture of the war. Only a few works had anything with a fair amount of research into these topics. Ray Mulesky's *Thunder From a Clear Sky: Stovepipe Johnson's Raid on Newburgh, Indiana*, focuses on the Newburgh raid itself. Benjamin F. Cooling's *Fort Donelson's Legacy: War and Society in Kentucky and Tennessee, 1862-1863*, a fascinating study into the region after Fort Donelson's fall, was an area of extreme importance to my own research. There are also several scholarly essays referenced throughout my own work and I encourage readers to enrich their understanding of the war by reading these. There was so much to the overall story in different places. Pieces here and bits there eventually turned into a complete narrative that could complete the story and put it in its proper place.

Acknowledgments

I am indebted to several people who have helped me along with this project. My friend, Tim Hubble, who was the first to read the first draft and caught many of my initial grammar errors, and suggested several ways to make it better. Greg Biggs, who has turned into a Civil War history mentor of sorts, also read the manuscript and offered suggestions and information on many additional sources. His help was extremely useful for the Tennessee portion of the book and made the story of these events much better, especially after taking me to the sites and walking the ground. Dr. Benjamin F. Cooling offered a wealth of sage advice on how to improve the manuscript, and that advice was invaluable. I also want to thank Stuart Sanders for offering lots of encouragement as I started this writing journey several years ago, and also read a version of the manuscript. My good friend and fellow teacher, Josh Bishop, stayed after school with me for several days to help plot the movements of the Partisan Rangers and the Indiana Legion on a map for the battle of Sutherland's Hill, and also offered frequent encouragement and listened while I "thought out loud." The Smith family, particularly David and Preston, introduced me to the awesome power of Newspapers.com, offered frequent encouragement, and supported me from the beginning. I also want to thank my students whom I have had the pleasure of teaching the last several years, who also offered loads of encouragement and at least pretended to lend an ear as I rambled on about the book and other historical topics.

A special thanks is in order for Theodore P. Savas and the amazing staff at Savas Beatie: David Snyder, who worked with me on the developmental edit; Rebecca Hill, who helped with the final copy edit; Ed Alexander, who produced the maps; and Veronica Kane, who designed the layout and oversaw production. Thank you for your patience in working with this first-time author and thank you for giving me a chance. I am forever grateful, and humbled, by this opportunity. I look forward to more projects in the future.

I am grateful for my parents, who nurtured my love of history in my younger years; without that, this book never would have happened, at least not by me. Most importantly, I want to thank my wife, who is my biggest cheerleader, and perhaps, the one who suffered most through this process. Her patience was saintly, and her love was unending. Allie, Ezra, and Owen, thank you for being the best. To God be the glory.

Introduction

Musket fire echoed across the Ohio River. Thousands of Union and Confederate soldiers fired as quickly as they could pull the trigger and ram home another cartridge. Thunderous artillery fire mixed with the small arms discharges. By the time the shooting ceased, some 30,000 cartridges and 1,000 rounds of artillery had been expended along the banks of the river separating North and South. The Union forces held the field, victorious, while Col. Robert Martin's Confederates fell back to their camp. Martin complimented his officers and men for their "bravery and hard work." The Union and Confederate soldiers, all of them unbloodied, shook hands to the applause of tens of thousands of spectators who had traveled to observe the 1887 Blue and Gray Reunion in Evansville, Indiana. Columns paraded up and down streets while jubilant citizens waved flags and cheered. Veterans bent with age once again marched with upright pride and patriotism. General James Shackelford, a prominent former "guerrilla hunter" in western Kentucky, just across the river from the city through which he now marched, led the column.[1]

Delegates from all over the country attended the grand reunion. One of the most prominent was former Confederate general and Kentucky governor Simon Bolivar Buckner. In his speech Buckner reflected on the peace that once again permeated throughout the nation. "I call you comrades, for today we are all comrades," proclaimed Buckner. "It gives me great pleasure to be here today and testify to my gladness that today all bitterness is gone and we recognize but one glorious flag." Shackelford echoed these sentiments when he said, "There is no North or South, but one Union." For a city that had once sat in dread of attack

1 *National Tribune*, Sep. 29, 1887, 6; *Indiana State Sentinel*, Sep. 28, 1887, 2; *Evansville Journal*, Sep. 24, 1887, 4.

Wartime image of Confederate General Simon Bolivar Buckner. *LOC*

by some of the same troops who now marched gaily through their streets, the reunion was a smashing success.[2]

Perhaps the most infamous Rebel to attend the reunion was Adam Rankin Johnson. For nearly four months in 1862 Johnson's name regularly filled the pages of the *Evansville Daily Journal*. His regiment of partisan rangers wreaked havoc in western Kentucky along the Ohio River, and he and his bold raiders even ventured onto Indiana soil.

In 1887, Johnson's name reappeared in the Indiana press but this time he arrived as a guest instead of an enemy. Even the *Indianapolis Journal* was impressed: "Of all the visitors to the city there is none with a more interesting history than Gen. Adam Johnson, who was on the staff of the famous guerrilla, John Morgan." Veterans of the 65th Indiana, men who spent a large part of their early service chasing Johnson, maintained less polite words to describe their guest. "The conspicuous presence of the noted gentleman, horse thief and robber, Adam Johnson, who was never a confederate soldier in any true sense, did not enthuse the boys who had worn the blue," declared one of the regiment's publications.[3]

Kentucky proved ripe for the sort of warfare that the soldiers of the 65th Indiana endured in the fall of 1862. Though the main armies marched away after the Union army broke Confederate Gen. Albert Sydney Johnston's line in Kentucky and western Tennessee at Forts Henry and Donelson, a divided population remained behind and the war continued. The partisan warfare pursued by Johnson differed from the bloodiness and brutality of guerrilla warfare. Instead of fighting a

2 *Indianapolis Journal*, Sep. 21, 1887, 2; Sep. 23, 1887, 4.

3 *Indianapolis Journal*, Sep. 21, 1887, 2; Jacob V. Admire, *Memoranda: Company E, 65th Regiment, Indiana Infantry Volunteers* (Osage City, KS, 1888), 56.

bloody war devoid of the common rules of war and without any Confederate army attachment, like most guerrillas, Johnson followed army orders and attempted to command his men as a regular army unit that happened to operate behind enemy lines. Yet partisan warfare created a challenge for the Confederates that joined these regiments, the Union soldiers tasked with eradicating it, and for the civilians stuck in the middle, often burdened with mixed loyalties. Kentucky, a border slave state that remained loyal to the Union, saw its population deeply divided over slavery, emancipation, secession, and the ultimate aims of the war. The Lincoln administration carefully navigated this complicated mix, but it would prove impossible to tame Kentucky.

Though a loyal state, the experience of thousands of Union soldiers marching through and garrisoning their communities embittered many Kentuckians, especially those with familial ties to the Confederacy. Even with a large portion of the population remaining loyal to the government, many Kentuckians sided with the South. The protection of hearth and home, or even the peculiar institution, presented only two of the many reasons for this sympathy. Because of this reality, the Union military operated in Kentucky as an occupying force out of necessity. An unstable environment such as this, as historians have noted, required the Union to "[establish] garrisons throughout occupied territory" to tamp down incipient secessionism and to protect valuable communications and supply lines. As will be seen, the Union took time to learn this lesson in the western part of Kentucky and even northwest Tennessee in the summer and fall of 1862. Johnson and his partisan rangers embodied what William T. Sherman believed about the war behind the lines, expressed in a letter to his brother in 1861: "[Union] armies pass across and through the land, the war closes behind and leaves the same enemy behind."[4]

In time, the war drastically changed in Kentucky, especially in 1864 and 1865. The armies moved even further away, allowing the cruelty to increase behind the lines. Such wars are "particularly messy, and it was clear that many leading Confederates were too humane to inflict the requisite bloodshed and terror on either their enemies or fellow southerners," suggest some historians. During the Civil War Kentucky became infamous for accommodating Rebel leaders, at least those who found the Confederate moniker convenient during the time, who operated in small bands away from the main armies, and who operated at times with extreme brutality. Such leaders included William Quantrill, Marcellus Jerome Clarke (also known as Sue Mundy), Champ Ferguson, "Bloody Handed" Bill Davison, and a long list of others who caused serious trouble in the state as the war

4 Robert E. Beringer, et al., *Why the South Lost the Civil War* (Athens, GA and London, 1986), 246-247; William T. Sherman, *The Sherman Letters: Correspondence Between General and Senator Sherman, 1837 to 1891*, ed. Rachel Sherman Thorndike (New York, 1894), 166.

Confederate guerrilla Champ Ferguson surrounded by guards during his trial in 1865. Charged with 53 murders, Ferguson admitted to killing over 100 men during the war and was found guilty and hanged on October 20, 1865. *LOC*

dragged on. The murder of civilians, executions of Union soldiers, and property theft and destruction were common. Though guerrilla leaders such as these spread chaos and terror across the state in 1864 and 1865, partisan [sic] leaders who operated earlier insisted that their operations were militarily and morally different.[5]

The distinction is important. Adam Johnson and his partisan rangers scoffed at the idea of the guerrilla label. Johnson vehemently denied being a guerrilla and responded to such accusations in 1862 by assuring his enemies that "every man on our side who fired a gun upon that occasion was a Confederate soldier, and had special orders not to interrupt in any way any citizen on account of his politics." This is perhaps one reason why Johnson enjoyed the support of many Kentucky Southern sympathizers in a way that the late war guerrillas did not. Never a fool, Johnson realized that barbaric treatment of Unionists could cause major trouble for his base of support.[6]

Western Kentucky in 1862 also offered unique war aims for the Confederates who fought there. Historians Herman Hattaway and Archer Jones argue that the Confederates did not necessarily need to "conquer" territory, but successful raids

5 Beringer, et al., *Why the South Lost the Civil War*, 246-247.

6 Ibid., 343.

A fortified railroad bridge across the Cumberland River in Nashville, Tennessee. To safeguard its rear and lines of supply, the Union army constructed many fortifications near important river crossings to thwart Confederate raids. *LOC*

behind the lines disrupted Union operations. Lincoln lamented, "In no other way does the enemy give us so much trouble, at so little expense to himself, as by the raids of rapidly moving small bodies of troops . . . supplying themselves with provisions . . . surprising and capturing small detachments of our forces, and breaking our communications." The Union army's lack of appreciation for mounted forces early in the war provided opportunities for a force like Johnson's to slice through Union controlled territory. The remedy to this problem required significant time and money. Consequently, a lack of equipment, arms, and a clear doctrine governing the use of cavalry and infantry behind the lines plagued Union efforts to eliminate Johnson's partisan rangers and those like him. By 1863, 56,000 Union soldiers guarded Kentucky and West Virginia from a significantly smaller number of Confederate cavalry, raiders, partisan rangers, and guerrillas. The Union had finally learned its lesson, but not before Johnson and the partisans in other parts of the south exacted a heavy toll.

Though distinct differences existed between these four classifications of fighting men, the 1862 sources used various terms such as raider, guerrilla, cavalry, and partisan indiscriminately to describe Adam Rankin Johnson and his men. The public did not always understand the differentiation between a cavalryman, raider, partisan ranger, or guerrilla at the time. Even the veterans of the 65th Indiana showed this lack of understanding years following the war.[7]

During the reunion, the now blind Johnson met with his old friend and fellow partisan, Robert Martin. A reporter from the *Evansville Journal* chatted with Martin about his and Johnson's experiences in the western Kentucky region in 1862, 25 years earlier. Martin explained to the reporter that "the Confederate Congress became alarmed" with the state of the war and authorized partisan warfare to be established "for the purpose of harassing the Union forces and retarding their movements." On their success Martin commented, we "gave the Union forces considerable trouble."[8]

7 Herman Hattaway and Archer Jones, *How the North Won: A Military History of the Civil War* (Chicago, 1983), 323, 356-357.

8 *Evansville Journal*, Sep. 17, 1887, 5.

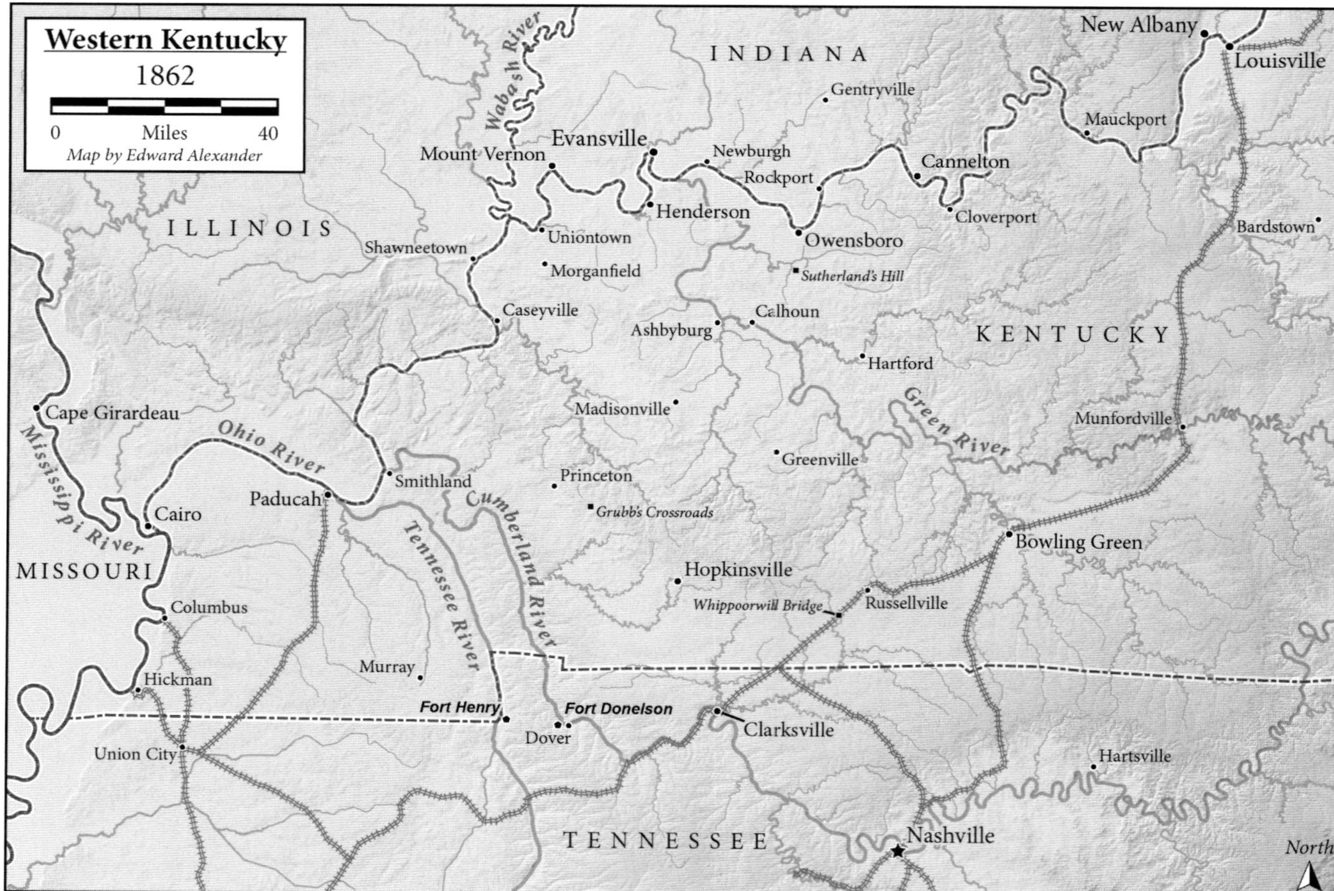

Western Kentucky
1862
0
Miles
40
Map by Edward Alexander
INDIANA
ILLINOIS
KENTUCKY
MISSOURI
TENNESSEE
Wabash River
Ohio River
Mississippi River
Green River
Cumberland River
Tennessee River
New Albany
Louisville
Gentryville
Mauckport
Evansville
Mount Vernon
Newburgh
Rockport
Cannelton
Henderson
Cloverport
Bardstown
Uniontown
Owensboro
Shawneetown
Morganfield
Sutherland's Hill
Caseyville
Calhoun
Ashbyburg
Hartford
Cape Girardeau
Madisonville
Munfordville
Greenville
Smithland
Princeton
Paducah
Cairo
Grubb's Crossroads
Bowling Green
Hopkinsville
Columbus
Whippoorwill Bridge
Russellville
Murray
Hickman
Fort Henry
Fort Donelson
Dover
Clarksville
Union City
Hartsville
Nashville
North

Chapter 1

"If you can equal him as a scout I will have a good team"

Robert Martin hurried the wagonloads of weapons, supplies, sundries, and even some looted items to the riverbank, while his comrade and commander, Adam Johnson, kept the locals of Newburgh, Indiana, occupied. On July 18, 1862, with a force of less than 40 men, they had accomplished something that no other Southerner had been able to do: capture a town on Union soil. The Confederate partisans bluffed Newburgh citizen, and local commander of the Indiana Legion, or state militia, Union Bethell, with a dangerous threat by positioning two pieces of artillery to shell the town if trouble came to the raiders. The bluff worked.[1]

Soon Martin landed on the Kentucky side of the Ohio with the captured, or stolen, supplies. They expected Federal reinforcements at any time, and already they spied the black smoke coughed out by three steamboats moving upriver. One brandished a six-pound swivel gun, the others loaded with infantry and field artillery.[2]

Johnson anxiously watched for Union activity on the Indiana shore from his small skiff. Martin led the newly recruited partisans across while Johnson made sure no attack came from the direction of Newburgh. Their landing place near the eastern side of the mouth of the Green River formed a narrow peninsula with the larger Ohio River. The position looked tactically precarious. If the steamships

1 Adam R. Johnson, *The Partisan Rangers of the Confederate States Army* (Louisville, KY, 1904), 105-107.

2 *Evansville Daily Journal*, July 21, 1862, 2.

made it to the Green before Johnson's men crossed, Union forces stood a good chance of ensnaring the raiders, and the whole enterprise would end in disaster.[3]

July 18, 1862, marked the beginning of a campaign that would last more than two months and plunge western Kentucky into the uncivil business of partisan warfare and (in Union nomenclature) anti-guerrilla operations. During those fateful months of 1862, Johnson and Martin's little band would grow to nearly 800 men, capture five towns garrisoned with Union troops, and turn neighbor against neighbor.

* * *

Only 22 years old in the summer of 1862, Lt. Col. Robert Maxwell Martin hailed from Muhlenberg County, Kentucky. Few sources exist to describe his life before or after the war. Born on January 20, 1840, near Greenville, Kentucky, Martin came from a large family of seven children. His father, Hugh, labored as a bricklayer and farmer, both occupations carried on by his sons. In 1860, Hugh Martin possessed a personal value worth $5,000 and possibly owned four slaves. Son Robert eschewed his father's manual labor but maintained his father's penchant for earning money, becoming a merchant near Dixon, Kentucky, in Webster County. By 1860, he had amassed a personal value of $1,100.[4]

Despite growing up in a Union family, Martin threw in his lot with the South. Two of his brothers served in the Union army, one in the 11th Kentucky Infantry and the other in the 35th Kentucky Mounted Infantry. Both wore officer's insignias. Martin first enlisted as a private in Nathan Bedford Forrest's cavalry when it arrived in Kentucky in the fall of 1861. With his local knowledge, he proved himself an excellent scout in the areas south of the Green River. This became especially valuable as Gen. Albert Sidney Johnston's Confederate army and Gen. Thomas L. Crittenden's Union division vied for strategic position in the region. Martin quickly rose to the position of chief scout for then-Lieutenant Colonel Forrest.

Martin's impressive physical features drew the attention of soldier and civilian alike. Described as "splendidly mounted" and wearing "his hat in a long black plume," the young Kentuckian presented "a large and striking figure." His prewar familiarity with the Green River region armed him with the knowledge to help Johnson lead what would become the 10th Kentucky Partisan Rangers.

3 Johnson, *Partisan Rangers*, 107.

4 John W. Headley, *Confederate Operations in Canada and New York* (New York, 1906), 62; 1860 Webster County, KY Census, 155; 1850 Muhlenberg County, KY Census, 101-102; Otto A. Rothert, *A History of Muhlenberg County* (Louisville, KY, 1913), 318; Basil Duke, *Morgan's Cavalry* (New York, 1906), 275.

Adam Rankin Johnson's background differed greatly from Martin's but their paths crossed by the fall of 1861.[5] Juliet Spencer Rankin gave birth to a son, Adam, on February 8, 1834 in Henderson, Kentucky. His father, Dr. Thomas Jefferson Johnson, flourished as a physician and the couple amassed a personal fortune of $6,000 as influential Henderson citizens. During his childhood, Johnson became a distinguished hunter and strong swimmer. Those who knew him remembered his outsized charisma, and that he seemed always the fastest, strongest, and wittiest. For "Ad," daytime meant the outdoors; nighttime was for reading the history and literature that helped grow the boy into a well-rounded young man. As a teenager, Johnson's father assigned him to a local druggist to learn the pharmacy trade, but the appointment did not stick. By the age of 16, Johnson began work in the tobacco industry, overseeing nearly 80 "hands" for a man by the name of David Burbank, a close associate of John C. Breckinridge. This friendship would allow Johnson to raise his own regiment nearly ten years later.[6]

One of the wealthiest counties in the United States at that time, Henderson County enjoyed a prominent location on the vital Ohio River transport artery. A hub for the tobacco trade, Henderson County shipped the lucrative crop across the United States and the world via the Ohio and Mississippi Rivers, bringing enormous wealth to the county and the city of Henderson itself. A perfect region for the crop's cultivation, the county offered lowlands along the Ohio and Green Rivers and even the land away from the rivers provided superb soil for the region's many planters. Thanks to tobacco, Henderson incubated more Southern sympathy than many of the neighboring communities.

Because of the labor intensity of tobacco, Henderson County maintained the second highest rate of slave-ownership and enslaved population in the western Kentucky region. In 1850, there were 677 slave owners and 3,988 enslaved persons. By 1860, the numbers increased to 993 owners and 5,046 enslaved persons. According to the 1861 map by Edwin Hergesheimer, 40.7 percent of the county's population remained enslaved. This translated to the political climate as demonstrated by the 1860 presidential election. Constitutional Union candidate

5 Rothert, *History of Muhlenberg County*, 318-319.

6 Johnson, *Partisan Rangers*, 2; Edmund Lyne Starling, *History of Henderson County, Kentucky: Comprising History of County and City, Precincts, Education, Churches, Secret Societies, Leading Enterprises, Sketches and Recollections, and Biographies of the Living and the Dead* (Henderson, KY, 1887), 713, 804-805. Starling states that there were 5,767 in the county in his postwar history; William C. Davis, *Breckinridge: Soldier, Statesman, Symbol* (Baton Rouge, LA, 1974), 572-583. Burbank appears to have been so close with former Vice President John C. Breckinridge that he named his youngest son John Cabell Breckinridge Burbank. He also accompanied Breckinridge to the Holy Land and Europe during Breckinridge's exile. Johnson, *Partisan Rangers*, 1; 1860 Henderson County, KY Census, 48.

Adam Rankin Johnson in Confederate Uniform.

LOC

John Bell took 846 votes, while Southern Democrat John C. Breckinridge and Northern Democrat Stephen Douglas received 498 and 211 votes respectively. Republican Abraham Lincoln, who spent his boyhood years just a few miles upriver in Spencer County, Indiana, booked only five votes. The overwhelming preference for Bell's Constitutional Union platform—of maintaining the status quo on slavery—represented the region's pro-slavery attitudes. Though the leading candidates supported slavery's continuation, pro-slavery attitudes did not mean automatic support for secession. When the secession crisis erupted, Henderson County, like most other Kentucky counties, voted for the Democratic Union ticket in the Border State Convention. This suggests that Henderson's populace favored compromise rather than secession. However, when the war came, the county split, like others in that area of Kentucky.[7]

In the decade preceding the war, Johnson and two of his brothers, Ben and Thomas, made their way to the west Texas frontier. Here, Johnson lived the frontiersman's life full of danger, adventure, and ingenuity. For five years, he worked as a surveyor in hopes of securing a place to make a home for himself. The young man also drove a stage for the Butterfield Overland Mail. Johnson knew that many families would soon settle the open Texas country and the work offered job security. The stream of new settlers would need their land surveyed and mail delivered. The Kentuckian eventually purchased a plot of land that suited him and found himself neighbors with veterans of the Texas Revolution. These men filled Johnson's imagination with heroic stories of the war and frontier life—an impression that undoubtedly influenced him when he fought his own war.[8]

Johnson also experienced brushes with Native Americans who continued to fight for control of their land. In one of the first meetings, Johnson and four other men found themselves isolated from the safety of other settlements while on a surveying job. During the night, a party of Native Americans attempted to annihilate the small group, which they perceived as trespassing. The war party nearly surrounded the camp before Johnson and his companions detected their presence. Johnson instructed the others to maintain constant gunfire upon their attackers while he snuck through the tall weeds and brush to shoot at them from the

7 Starling, *History of Henderson*, 111, 193; "Henderson County (KY) Slaves, Free Blacks, and Free Mulattoes, 1850-1870," Notable Kentucky African Americans Database, https://nkaa.uky.edu/nkaa/items/show/2367, accessed Jan. 13, 2021; E. Hergesheimer, *Map showing the distribution of the slave population of the southern states of the United States compiled from the census of Washington*, Henry S. Graham, 1861, https://www.loc.gov/item/99447026/; James W. Finck, *Divided Loyalties: Kentucky's Struggle for Armed Neutrality in the Civil War* (El Dorado Hills, CA, 2012), 110-119.

8 Johnson, *Partisan Rangers*, 3; Thomas W. Cutrer, "Johnson, Adam Rankin," *Handbook of Texas Online* (Texas State Historical Association), https://www.tshaonline.org/handbook/entries/johnson-adam-rankin, accessed Jan. 13, 2022.

rear. The crossfire forced the attackers to flee. Such trickery and deception helped keep him alive through other dangerous encounters while in Texas. Sometimes he fooled Native American raiding parties into believing he commanded more men than he actually possessed, used diversions in others, or boldly rushed headlong into an unexpected raiding party. "If the enemy could thus elude me, so also I could deceive them by this and similar devices," he later expressed. "Afterward I had occasion to put this idea in practice, I always acted promptly and confidently, ever holding the conviction that the ruse resorted to, whatever it was, would succeed." In the war to come, Johnson frequently applied the stealth tactics he had learned in his frontier days.[9]

When news of Abraham Lincoln's election reached Texas, Johnson sensed the future upheaval. He immediately arranged to marry his sweetheart, fearing the coming war might prevent their union from occurring. On January 1, 1861, he married Josephine Eastland in Burnet, Texas. War and secession failed to arrive immediately, so Johnson returned to his work on the plains. When secession did come and Texas communities formed military companies, Johnson's two brothers enlisted in a Texas artillery battery. Instead of joining them, Adam traveled back home to Henderson.[10]

On his return to Kentucky in the fall of 1861, Johnson remained aware that his parents, and two of his other brothers, sided with the Union. One of those brothers, William, served as sergeant major of the 25th Kentucky before that regiment consolidated with the 17th Kentucky in early 1862. As a lieutenant in the 17th, William received a dismissal from the service along with his commanding officer, Col. John H. McHenry, for refusing to follow the order prohibiting the return of runaway slaves. William's file reports that the dismissal occurred because he "expressed sentiments of disloyalty and insubordination." The story of Johnson's brother provides a microcosm of Kentucky's political dysphoria during the Civil War. The Union they would defend, but emancipation seemed a step too far for many.[11]

While in Confederate-occupied Bowling Green, Kentucky, Johnson reunited with many of his childhood friends, now members of Graves's Kentucky Battery. The men earnestly wanted Johnson to join them, knowing his background and skills, but he declined and traveled to Hopkinsville, Kentucky. There Johnson met

9 Johnson, *Partisan Rangers*, 2-5.

10 Ibid., 35, 38.

11 Ibid., 48; William Johnson, U.S., Compiled Service Records of Volunteer Union Soldiers Who Served in Organizations from the State of Kentucky, 1861-1865, M397, Roll 0303, National Archives; Benjamin F. Cooling, *Fort Donelson's Legacy: War and Society in Kentucky and Tennessee, 1862-1863* (Knoxville, 1997), 89.

Nathan Bedford Forrest

LOC

Nathan Bedford Forrest. So struck with the man, Johnson immediately asked to join Forrest's command. He asked to be a scout and Forrest readily agreed after Johnson informed him of his background and knowledge of the region. He also asked to travel to Henderson to see his parents, to which Forrest readily assented. He also introduced Johnson to his other scout. As Johnson related in his memoirs, Forrest told him, "I wish you to meet a young man who has just came from the front, where he has been killing Yankees. If you can equal him as a scout I will have a good team." It seemed to Johnson as if all the troopers in his new company talked about this other man's merits as a Yankee killer. He met the young scout at Forrest's tent. His name: Bob Martin. The two men examined each other thoroughly before speaking, and both "were mutually pleased." Johnson described Martin as over six feet tall and slender with brown hair and blue eyes. "I met for the first time," Johnson remembered with cheerfulness, "a man who all through the war was to be my constant companion."[12]

Martin and Johnson quickly bonded and showed themselves to be excellent scouts. Within days of meeting, the two men reconnoitered the area south of the Green River, in close proximity to Gen. Thomas L. Crittenden's division in Calhoun. On December 28, 1861, they alerted Forrest to the approaching 3rd Kentucky Cavalry. Forrest prepared his men for what would be his first engagement, the battle of Sacramento in McLean County.

Forrest grabbed a weapon from one of his soldiers and fired the opening shot. The two sides skirmished until he ordered his men to charge both Union flanks and center. The battle quickly devolved into a running fight through the village of Sacramento and brutal saber battles erupted all the way back to within a few miles of the main Federal camp at Calhoun. In the chaotic fight, Johnson and Martin witnessed Forrest's aggressiveness and disregard for his own personal safety. The

12 Johnson, *Partisan Rangers*, 38-40; Scott A. Tarnowieckyi, "Branded by the Lincolnites as Guerrillas: Adam Rankin Johnson, Guerrilla Identity, and Irregular Warfare in the Lower Green River Valley in 1862," *The Register of the Kentucky Historical Society*, 2015, 648.

Confederate cavalry won a resounding and lopsided victory, one in which Martin walked away with several trophies. After the battle, Johnson saw a delighted Martin appear out of the woods with a belt full of pistols. Johnson inquired about his activities, to which Martin replied that he got "even with a fellow that stole my horse." When asked what became of the Union soldier Martin smiled and crowed, "Well, here is his horse, his pistol, and this is his gun," and that he left the soldier "over yonder in that strip of woods you see to the left of the road." Even this early in his military career Martin demonstrated his fighting talent.[13]

The duo became a formidable backstage pair, relying on their wits and not a little bit of theatrics when necessary. On one scouting mission in Daviess County, for example, Martin and Johnson managed to steal several horses originally meant for the Union's 3rd Kentucky Cavalry, the same regiment they fought at Sacramento. The scouts forged requisition documents from General Crittenden, commander of Union forces in the area at nearby Camp Calhoun, the original destination for the mounts. Johnson later revealed in his book, "Martin had agreed to act as sergeant and I as Lieutenant Johnson, personating my brother who was with Crittenden. Leaving Martin to hold the horses, I entered the house, introduced myself and told my business, and learned that Mr. Field had gone to headquarters and expected to return soon with a squad of men to drive the horses over to camp," Johnson remembered. Meanwhile, Mrs. Field had "invited me to stay for supper, and if possible, to remain all night. I accepted the first invitation and told her I would have a ride all night under my orders." Johnson next "went out and explained matters to Martin, and we arranged to fight. It was not long before Mr. Field made his appearance, riding up the lane alone. I felt very much relieved, but Martin seemed disappointed, and think he had rather had a fight than to have captured the horses."[14]

Martin and Johnson stayed for a meal, and while they ate Johnson played the part of a Union officer well. He quizzed Martin about the "Secesh" that had been stealing horses. Mrs. Field commented, "that was not any more than she could expect from people who were trying to break up the government." Martin tried to hide his amusement by "stuffing his mouth full of biscuit to keep from laughing." After dining and with horses now in their possession, they quickly retreated to Confederate lines. Amusingly, Mrs. Field visited a neighbor and commented, "that

13 Johnson, *Partisan Rangers*, 41-43; *The War of the Rebellion: A Compilation of the Official Records of the Union and Confederate Armies*, 128 vols. (Washington, D.C., 1880-1901), Series 1, vol. 7, part. 1, 56. Hereafter cited as *OR*. All references are to Series 1 unless otherwise noted. Forrest mentions in his report that a local teenage girl, Mollie Morehead, also alerted him to the nearby Union cavalry.

14 Johnson, *Partisan Rangers*, 45-46.

if the rebel army had two such men in it she would have more respect for it." At least that is how Johnson told the story in his memoir.[15]

During another expedition to acquire horses for Forrest's cavalry in January 1862, Johnson took the opportunity to travel to Union-controlled Henderson. Though they disagreed about secession, the young man yearned to see his family for the first time in over five years. After stashing his weapons on the property of some friends, Johnson rode to his home inside a carriage. Once inside, he embraced his mother whose "loving heart no difference of political sentiment could estrange." Johnson's brothers from nearby Camp Calhoun also arrived home for a few days to see their returned brother. The brothers all talked openly of their experiences in the war and vowed to protect each other if they found themselves on the same battlefield, which transpired sooner than any of them predicted.[16]

While in Henderson Johnson took the opportunity to spy on occupying Union forces. Playing the part of the prodigal son returned from the wilds of Texas and secessionism, and shielded by his family's public Unionism, Johnson easily convinced others that he shared loyalist sympathies. He gathered intelligence by attending dinner parties where he apparently met the commanding officer of the 31st Indiana, Col. Charles Cruft, and other Union officers. The "swaggering braggadocio" and "blustering boasts" of some of the officers repulsed the young Kentuckian. Friends warned the Confederate scout that Federal authorities began to suspect this "prodigal son" of ill intentions, so he began planning to make his way back to Confederate lines.[17]

Escape proved problematic as no person could leave the city without a military pass. In the January 10, 1862, edition of the *Evansville Daily Journal*, complaints mounted about the illegal smuggling of goods across the lines in the area between Henderson and Smithland, Kentucky. "Thousands of dollars worth of goods, and letters containing important information, are daily taken across the river and sent to the Southern Confederacy," the paper grumbled. Pressured to act, Union authorities began to limit traffic by increasing patrols and stopping travelers. Though Johnson knew the area well, this would be a serious obstacle.[18]

Before leaving, Johnson acquainted himself with the approximate positions of Union soldiers picketing the roads and bridges outside of town. While moving on foot a Union soldier spotted the Rebel and Johnson flew to the woods amid orders to halt. A confident Johnson believed he could outpace any man bogged

15 Ibid.

16 Ibid., 48.

17 Ibid., 47-49.

18 *Evansville Daily Journal*, Jan. 10, 1862, 2.

down by a larger weapon and infantry gear but to his surprise the Union soldier gained on him. Changing his strategy, Johnson hid in a hollow tree and as the soldier approached, Johnson brandished his pistol and pulled the trigger. The bullet entered the man's skull and "with a cry of pain and a leap into the air he sprang over the bluff into the surging waters." Uncertain what to do next, Johnson retreated to his family's home and "resolved to put on a brave front." Not only did he have to contend with the growing Federal suspicions that he was a spy, but he had also just killed a Union soldier. If caught, he believed that soldiers would riddle his body with bullets, but with the help of his family he might gain a good lawyer and avoid punishment.[19]

The following Sunday, Johnson accompanied his mother to church. While passing a group of Union soldiers he mentioned that he would hurt anyone that attempted to "jolt" his mother or any of the women present. Upon seeing his hidden pistol, his mother implored him to "leave this town tonight." Sitting through a service full of enemy soldiers, Johnson must have been planning a new way to escape. He entertained the rash idea of stealing Colonel Cruft's horse tied up outside the church. Again, his mother talked him out of such a foolish notion and he returned home.

Johnson remained in Henderson for only a day or two before making a second attempt at escape during the night, though not without one last snag. Determined to ride out with a good horse, he noticed a lone Union sergeant riding on the road. Hiding in a deep cut Johnson surprised the man and demanded his surrender. To his shock and chagrin, the sergeant spurred his horse and galloped away. Johnson fired one shot, missed, and then ran home. He settled for his brother's horse and quietly slipped out of town. He collected his weapons and rode south to rejoin Martin and Forrest.

Johnson's story concerning Cruft and his horse raises a few questions, as does Johnson's earlier attempt to escape Henderson. Johnson's memoir is known to contain embellishments and exaggerations, but enough of his wartime derring-do has been verified that even the inflated stories are not out of character for this highly ingenious, battlefield actor. In early 1862, the 31st Indiana encamped at Calhoun and South Carrollton, Kentucky, with Cruft taking the role of acting brigadier general. Several newspapers and the regiment's own history place Cruft

19 Johnson, *Partisan Rangers*, 49-50; Starling, *History of Henderson*, 714. Johnson's daring story of escape back to Confederate lines appeared in Starling's history of Henderson County and then in Johnson's own memoir several years later. However, nothing of the incident ever made it into any of the contemporary sources. The regional newspapers generally reported any violent incident, especially when it included the death of a Union solder. Though Johnson's memoir includes some clearly exaggerated derring-do, the general events often corroborate with other sources with few exceptions.

with his men and not at Henderson. However, it is possible that in his old age Johnson misremembered or mistook another officer to be Cruft. It is also possible Cruft visited Henderson for a short time.[20]

In February 1862, Gen. Ulysses S. Grant advanced into Tennessee and captured Fort Henry, rendering the Confederate line in Kentucky untenable. When the armies encountered one another at Fort Donelson, Martin and Johnson again provided good service to Forrest as he observed the Federal advance. On February 12, 1862, Johnson returned to Forrest's command after performing other solitary assignments of which no records exist. Upon reaching Dover and the Confederate fort, Johnson heard the distant crack of gunfire. The scout immediately rode to the scene and found Forrest sitting on his horse by himself while he watched two of his companies skirmish with Union infantry coming up the Pinery Road. Delighted to see the Kentuckian, Forrest remarked, "Johnson, I am glad you have come. Ride over there and bring those fellows in; they are wasting powder." Riding toward the action, Johnson noticed that a body of Union infantry was attempting to flank the Confederate right toward Hickman Creek. Contrary to Forrest's orders, Johnson commanded the two companies to redeploy to ambush the Union advance. The Confederates fired a volley and drove back the small Federal force. Forrest never mentioned the disobedience to his orders, perhaps because he himself might have done the same thing.[21]

As the Union army tightened its grip on Fort Donelson, Johnson frequently ventured between the lines. In his memoir, he claims to have discovered a ravine that allowed him to sneak between the beats of the Union pickets and hide within a few feet of the headquarters tent of Gen. Charles F. Smith. Johnson seems to have accomplished the feat on three occasions, garnering important information on impending Union movements. This included Smith's thrust on the Confederate right on February 13th, news that the Union gunboats intended to attack on the 14th, and a report that more regiments were destined to reinforce the Federal army. On the night before the Confederate breakout of February 15th, Johnson claims that he scouted the entire length of the Union line. He began at Smith's area of operation and scouted all the way to the Union right flank. Interestingly, Johnson appreciated that two of his brothers stood very near, with the 17th and 25th Kentucky Infantry regiments, and he vowed not to shoot if he came upon them.

20 Johnson, *Partisan Rangers*, 51-52; *Terre Haute Star*, Jan. 13, 1862, 2; *Dawson's Fort Wayne Daily Times*, Jan. 13, 1862, 4; John Thomas Smith, *A History of the Thirty-First Regiment of Indiana Volunteer Infantry in the War of the Rebellion* (Western Methodist Book Concern, 1900), 10-11; *Evansville Daily Journal*, Jan. 10, 1862, 2.

21 Johnson, *Partisan Rangers*, 49; Timothy B. Smith, *Grant Invades Tennessee: The 1862 Battles of Forts Henry and Donelson* (Lawrence, KS, 2021), 168, 174.

Fortunately, Johnson crept along unseen until he made it back to Confederate lines later that night.[22]

After scouting and fighting for four days and facing death multiple times, Johnson and Martin began to feel the repercussions of the taxing duty and bitter weather. One night an exhausted Martin fell asleep in "a bed of snow." Fearing for his well-being, Forrest helped Johnson carry Martin to shelter and covered him with a few warm blankets. Martin eventually returned to duty and the bond between the two men continued to grow.[23]

The situation at Fort Donelson was becoming dire for the Confederate army after a bungled breakout attempt. Most of the fighting on February 15th went well for the Southerners, but after driving Grant's right flank back several miles, the Rebels received orders to return to their original positions. Naturally, the Federals again occupied their positions from the morning and continued to grow stronger as reinforcements arrived. The Southern high command lost the nerve to continue fighting and arranged for the army's surrender.

Forrest approached his scouts and angrily informed them that the Confederate leadership intended to surrender. Johnson recalled that while he was finally getting something warm to eat he heard the clatter of horse hooves. Forrest "dashed up" and asked, "Johnson, where's Martin?" "In the tent still asleep, General," came the reply. "Rouse him up, for God's sake, rouse him up; there's work to be done." With great effort, Martin awoke. He was still wrapped in his blanket when Forrest entered the tent. Forrest fumed, "Boys, these people are talking about surrendering, and I am going out of this place before they do, or bust hell wide open. That's what these damn fools intend to do, so you boys must go at once and find some way for my regiment to get out of here, for get out they must." Shocked at such a turn of events both men sat in silence with "open-mouthed astonishment."

The scouts left at once, riding out from the defenses to find an escape route. Anxiety nearly consumed Johnson, not only about the Federals but also for the Confederate pickets, since he believed they had orders to shoot anyone who attempted to pass. Eventually, they made their way to the extreme of the Rebel picket line near the Cumberland River through which they waded to avoid the pickets of both armies, or so claims Johnson. The two Kentuckians found a route for Forrest that could take his cavalry through the swollen waters of Lick Creek and returned by wading through the icy Cumberland again. When they reached Confederate headquarters Generals Buckner, Pillow, and Floyd listened to the duo's report of the escape route. As the generals contemplated surrender or escape,

22 Johnson, *Partisan Rangers*, 60; Smith, *Grant Invades Tennessee*, 219-223.

23 Johnson, *Partisan Rangers*, 54-66.

The Dover Hotel, place where Gen. Simon B. Buckner surrendered to Gen. Ulysses S. Grant on February 16, 1862. *LOC*

Johnson and Martin warmed themselves at the stove. The night did not go well. The army would surrender and Forrest received permission to leave, but Johnson and Martin could not go with him. Removed from Forrest's command, the scouts received orders to stay at the fort with Pillow and Floyd. Martin accompanied Pillow on a small boat that crossed the Cumberland River while Johnson escaped by steamboat with Floyd and his Virginia regiments. Thus the scouts avoided the Union prison camps, making their way instead to Nashville.[24]

In Nashville, the two comrades reconnected and again found themselves aiding Forrest, this time in restoring order to the panic-stricken city. The reunion did not last long as orders arrived for the pair to travel to Texas to deliver dispatches to Governor Francis Lubbock. This journey caused them to miss the battle of Shiloh.[25]

Weeks after the Confederate defeat at Shiloh, Johnson and Martin returned to the army near Corinth, Mississippi. Here, Johnson's Henderson connection with Mr. Burbank opened the door for him to meet Gen. John C. Breckinridge. The two young Kentuckians transferred to Breckinridge's staff as scouts. After several weeks

24 *OR* 1, vol. 7, part. 1, 295, 383; Johnson, *Partisan Rangers*, 45-46, 66-70.

25 Johnson, *Partisan Rangers*, 45-46.

General John C. Breckinridge, former vice president of the United States. *LOC*

of successful scouting and intelligence gathering, the Kentucky general and former Vice President of the United States presented the pair with a challenging task. He wanted them to recruit men in western Kentucky for a partisan ranger regiment. This assignment began several months of success for Martin and Johnson behind Union lines. There is no official record from the Confederate government authorizing Johnson to raise such a regiment and the only source of this order is Johnson himself. As scouts for Forrest, Martin and Johnson held no rank and no record exists of them serving in his regiment. The men carried no authority or commissions from the Confederate government though Johnson believed his authority came from the Confederate army and Breckinridge's order. In his memoir, Johnson argued that both men indeed served as commissioned officers while on the staff of General Breckinridge. In his later report to President Jefferson Davis, Johnson asserted that he received authority to "proceed to Kentucky, to raise men, leaving discretionary powers as to my procedure."[26]

Western Kentucky had become a backwater to the war by the summer of 1862. Several western counties in the state harbored obvious sympathies for the South. After the fall of Forts Henry and Donelson and Confederate evacuations from Bowling Green to Nashville, western Kentucky hardly seemed a location of great strategic importance. No railroads of any significance ran through this region and the Green River ferried few steamboats transporting soldiers or military goods after the spring of 1862. The Union army spared few soldiers to occupy the region. Only a sprinkling of small garrisons guarded intermittent posts along the Ohio while small companies of poorly trained home guards offered desultory protection to towns in the interior. With the area no longer teeming with enemy soldiers, Johnson planned to ride into a region full of potential recruits.

26 Tarnowieckyi, "Branded by the Lincolnites," 649-650; Davis, *Breckinridge: Statesman, Soldier, Symbol*, 381; Johnson, *Partisan Rangers*, 85-86; *Houston Tri-Weekly Telegraph*, Nov. 26, 1862.

By June, Johnson and Martin slipped past the Union garrisons and patrols in Tennessee and Kentucky and arrived back near their homes. Initially, recruiting proved a difficult task. The men were only in their twenties and their relative youth did not inspire the confidence of potential soldiers. They may have impressed Forrest, but neither Johnson nor Martin had done enough to inspire their Green River peers to risk their lives in a dubious cause. One group of potential fighters, who apparently already conducted some sort of guerrilla or bushwhacking actions, told Johnson they could muster a full company for the right man. Another lukewarm fighter disparaged Johnson: "You seem to be quite a young man for such a business. What we want in Kentucky is a leader, and when one comes I will be willing to follow him, and could bring a good company to back him."[27]

Besides their age, they had nothing by which to provide for a cavalry regiment. They possessed no weapons for any potential soldiers, nor money to pay them, nor horses to ride, and no good reason why men should follow the two young scouts. The possibility remained that not only the recruits themselves, but also their property might suffer at the hands of Federal authorities or Unionist neighbors. Others wondered who would protect the families of these new Confederate soldiers from Federal retribution if they joined up. If they wanted recruits, then they had to prove themselves. Johnson and Martin did manage one follower, a seventeen-year-old by the name of Frank Owen. Owen originally served in the Confederate 8th Kentucky Infantry at Fort Donelson that had been surrendered to Grant in February. After spending time as a prisoner at Camp Morton in Indianapolis, Owen made his escape back to Kentucky. The young man zealously wanted to return to the fight and Johnson and Martin offered the promise to do just that.[28]

In his memoir, Johnson lamented the fact that many of the former Confederate soldiers they hoped to recruit seemed to enjoy the return to civilian life rather too much. "A Federal amnesty policy and local hero worship by the fair sex . . . kept a number of ex-Confederates from returning," notes historian Benjamin Cooling. Prying them from their homes and families and convincing them to return to the perilous life of soldiering would not be easy.[29]

The army of three's first opportunity to open a new theater of the war occurred in June. While discussing their first attack on the road outside of Henderson, near the small hamlet of Hebbardsville, an unexpected convenience presented itself. The surgeon of the 11th Kentucky, Lt. John F. Kimbly, and a companion enjoying a carriage ride in the country offered themselves as unsuspecting prizes.

27 Johnson, *Partisan Rangers*, 90.

28 Tarnowieckyi, "Branded by the Lincolnites," 649-651.

29 Johnson, *Partisan Rangers*, 90; Cooling, *Fort Donelson's Legacy*, 71.

Upon hearing the rattling of the carriage wheels and the steady cadence of the horses' hooves on the road, Johnson, Martin, and Owen decided to capture the Union officer. Martin sprang from the trees, grabbed the reins of the horses, and forced the buggy to stop while Johnson covered the Union officer with his weapon. Johnson asked for Kimbly's papers, which the doctor readily produced. They informed Kimbly of his new status as a prisoner and assured him that his friend, Ms. Georgia Shelby, would receive a safe escort to a friendly home.[30]

The three men never intended to keep Kimbly as a prisoner but instead wanted to impress upon him that they commanded a much larger force. If men refused to join Johnson's new regiment, then a ghost command would have to suffice. Johnson loudly began issuing orders to his invisible regiment: "Tell Captain Ray to move his company up to the forks of the road and Bennett to go at once to Slaughtersville!" Kimbly surrendered and the ghost commanders brought him to the Green River where a passing steamer took him to Louisville. Kimbly's story rapidly spread through the area. So much, in fact, that the newspapers believed Johnson, Martin, and Owen to be the shadowy guerrilla George Davidson, known only as a "notorious character" that stole horses. The Unionists in Evansville, Indiana, were furious and the staunchly pro-Union newspaper echoed their sentiments:

> This gang of land pirates arrested on Friday of last week, Dr. Kimley Surgeon of the 11th Kentucky volunteers, who was spending a few days at home on furlough—In company with a young lady, the Doctor, in a two-horse buggy, was on his way to visit some friends in Henderson county,—He was overhauled near Hebardsville, and compelled to surrender the horse and buggy, (which he proposed to redeem with $600) and was taken to Davidson's headquarters and released on what the guerrillas termed a parole. The young lady was taken to the house of a gentleman in the neighborhood and left there. The horses and buggy were carried off—the thieves claiming they had specific use for just such an establishment. That bands of outlaws should be permitted to commit such outrages on loyal citizens in the county of Henderson is a disgrace to its patriotic inhabitants. Davidson and most of his men are well known, and that they are still at large is highly discreditable to the military and peace authorities . . . We say to the Union men of those counties, unless they organize and visit speedy and summary justice upon the heads of these marauders, they will never be permitted to live in peace.[31]

Indian fighting in Texas had proved to be an excellent education for Johnson. The men seized their first prisoner and incensed the Unionists of Indiana in the process. The time to escalate now arrived. If Johnson and Martin could not

30 Johnson, *Partisan Rangers*, 92-93.

31 Ibid.; *Evansville Daily Journal*, June 28, 1862, 2.

convince Southern men to join them, then they would return to their previous commands without any recruits. For Johnson and Martin, that was not an option. Instead, they decided to provoke the potential recruits from their proverbial slumber. Johnson later confessed:

> Now my plan is to make the Yankees run these stay-at-home Confederate soldiers out of the country and to raise such a rumpus in this region that they will think all the boys are doing devilment. . . . [M]ost older men, even among our friends, would have shaken their heads in disapproval of an apparently reckless scheme which would put the country into turmoil and perhaps accomplish no useful results. . . . [T]here was work to be done that would gain fresh recruits for our hard-pressed army.[32]

The friendship between Johnson and Martin allowed them to cultivate their skill sets behind enemy lines while scouting for Forrest, and now those same skills would help raise a partisan ranger regiment. Indeed, Johnson and Martin intended to raise a serious rumpus in the region and it would bring spectacular results.

32 Johnson, *Partisan Rangers*, 91.

Chapter 2

"Play Gideon of old"

On June 29, 1862, Martin, Owen, and Johnson rode into Henderson, Kentucky, at dusk. Here, they would raise a greater rumpus than with Dr. Kimbly. Soldiers of the Louisville Provost and Battery F, 1st Michigan Light Artillery, used the National Hotel as a temporary barracks and presented a ready target. If the army of three could cause a fracas with these men, then maybe some of the Confederate sympathizers might be roused from their fence-sitting. Johnson offered a simple plan. Lay as much fire on the enemy as possible and then disappear into the darkness. With his local knowledge, Johnson led Martin and Owen to the Barrett factory where he spent a considerable amount of his youth. Knowing the property inside and out, Johnson thought it a perfect place for concealment and from which to launch the attack.[1]

The three men arranged themselves across the street behind a barrier and waited for the opportunity to strike. The Union soldiers mingled on the hotel's porch, unarmed and unaware of the lurking danger. At 10:00 p.m. the Kentuckians opened fire with their double barrel shotguns. Johnson hit Capt. John Daly and another officer, followed by shots from Martin and Owen who directed their fire toward the other soldiers now scrambling on the porch. The blasts wounded Daly, and his comrades quickly took him inside the building. Another burst also struck Lt. George Tyler. The rapid succession of six discharges sent the Union men into confusion as they hastened for the safety of the hotel. The attackers reloaded

1 Johnson, *Partisan Rangers*, 96; Mary Elizabeth Badger, "Thrilling Heroism by Confederates," *Confederate Veteran*, vol. 8, 1900, 525; *Evansville Daily Journal*, June 23, 1862, 3.

and moved to another position in the cemetery behind the building. Near the backdoor, Martin wounded a soldier with his pistol who could not retreat into the barricaded building. As quickly as they began shooting, the Rebels disappeared into the darkness. Johnson reported that he and his companions fired only 11 shots during the entire affair.[2]

The soldiers inside the building never realized that the attackers had taken flight. They turned the hotel into a makeshift fortress. Behind barricaded doors, the Federals took up positions near the windows, firing blindly the remainder of the night into a foe that had long retreated. They succeeded only in wounding an unfortunate sow. Johnson wrote in his memoirs that this caused the soldiers to believe they had wounded or killed multiple Rebels.[3]

This night attack caused such uproar and confusion among the Federal authorities that the newspapers reported erroneously that hundreds of guerrillas attacked the Union soldiers in Henderson. "Last night a party of rebel guerrillas, supposed to be about 500 in number," the *Evansville Daily Journal* reported, "attacked a company of the Louisville Provost Guard, encamped in a hotel at Henderson. One of our Lieutenants was killed and two men wounded. The rebels finally cleared out, under cover of the darkness. Federal reinforcements will reach Henderson from two points tomorrow."[4] Later, the paper updated the story by adding, "Troops for HENDERSON—A company of soldiers were sent down to Henderson last night, and further reinforcements are on their way. Gen. Boyle is determined to make short work of the marauders in that vicinity." The Indiana press latched onto the story, and Johnson and Martin quickly came to learn the value of such publicity for their recruitment efforts.[5]

The newspaper in Cannelton, Indiana, nearly sixty miles upriver, seems to have been one of the few media outlets not falling for the exaggerated reports. They stated the facts of the event about as well as possible with the available information. "We hear of a guerrilla raid upon the town of Henderson, which resulted in killing one or more of a company of artillery stationed in that place to serve the peace and protect Union citizens. We have no particulars, and hope the

2 Johnson, *Partisan Rangers*, 96; Robert M. Martin, "Service by Kentucky Cavalry," *Confederate Veteran*, vol. 6, 1898, 114; Widow's Pension application for Lieutenant George Tyler, National Archives, Civil War "Widows' Pensions," 1861-1910; *OR* 16:2, 994-995; Ray Mulesky, *Thunder From a Clear Sky: Stovepipe Johnson's Confederate Raid on Newburgh, Indiana* (Bloomington, IN, 2006), 13-16.

3 Starling, *History of Henderson*, 715; Johnson, *Partisan Rangers*, 96.

4 *Evansville Daily Journal*, July 2, 1862, 3.

5 Ibid., July 1, 1862, 3.

Sketch of the attack on the National Hotel from Johnson's memoir.
The Partisan Rangers of the Confederate States Army

accounts are exaggerated." The *Cannelton Reporter* proved correct, but it was an empty verisimilitude in the face of the raiders' budding reputation.[6]

The telegraph wires ran hot with messages. Some reports stated that guerrillas even crossed the Ohio River and threatened Indiana towns and cities, but the reports proved false. Indiana Governor Oliver P. Morton wired Gen. James E. Blythe, "What news from Henderson, do you apprehend any trouble at River Towns[?]" Blythe, a brigade commander of the Indiana Legion, replied to Morton, "There was a fight at Henderson night before last, reinforcements went down last night partly from convalescents in the hospitals. Three or four hundred mounted marauders said to be in Henderson County," and that Evansville had "two or three hundred convalescent soldiers in hospitals . . . in condition to march if the proper officer was here to order." Blythe also communicated to Morton that the few hundred guerrillas in Henderson County successfully established a friendly network within Newburgh, Indiana. Morton found this news troubling. Quartermaster A. S. Wells telegraphed that the governor should send 10,000 Enfield cartridges to the men readying for action.[7]

While the Federal authorities scrambled to face the new threat in the Henderson area, Johnson, Martin, and Owen kept themselves hidden on a farm owned by a sympathetic family. There they received the July 1st edition of the

6 *Cannelton Reporter*, July 4, 1862, 2.

7 Governor Morton to General Blythe, July 1, 1862, General Blythe to Governor Oliver P. Morton, July 4, 1862, A. S. Wells to Governor Morton, July 4, 1862, Governor Morton Telegraphs and Slips, Indiana State Archives, IUPUI University Library Digital Publication, http://ulib.iupuidigital.org/cdm/ref/collection/Telegraph/id/8100, accessed Feb. 12, 2018. Hereafter cited as "Morton Telegraphs."

Evansville Daily Journal which described their attack on the National Hotel. From the newspaper they learned of the exaggerated reports made on the size of their small band. Correct or not, Johnson and Martin now believed they possessed the credibility needed to recruit more men for their Breckinridge Guard command.[8]

Local Union forces responded with alacrity. Nearly 400 men from several units descended on the town of Henderson, most notably, the 13th Indiana Light Artillery led by Capt. Benjamin Nicklin. The *Evansville Daily Journal* reported that he commanded not only a section of six-pound Dahlgren guns, but also cavalry and infantry totaling 200 men. The remainder of the Louisville Provost, and Andrew's Michigan Battery, plus some Federal soldiers convalescing in Evansville, pushed Nicklin's numbers to nearly 400. Newly promoted Brig. Gen. Green Clay Smith, a Kentuckian, also arrived to take overall command of the post, though it is questionable how much authority he possessed over the soldiers present. No Indiana Legion units received permission to cross the Ohio River to lend assistance.[9]

Nicklin's short reign in Henderson began with a bang. Arriving on July 1st, he immediately began to fire artillery into the dark countryside throughout the night, leaving one unfortunate secessionist dead in the woods. Nicklin frequently ordered his cavalry to the countryside on guerrilla patrols, arresting civilians accused of harboring Southern sympathies. A list of those detainees incarcerated in Louisville appeared in the Evansville newspaper in early July. Nicklin's aggressive response failed to impress Unionists in Henderson. Moreover, reports filtered back to General Blythe that these new men lacked discipline, were frequently drunk, and held little respect for Henderson's citizens. Nicklin's approach, in short, alienated those whom he was sent to protect and instead inspired Union foes. Competent officers would eventually arrive, but not before Johnson's Breckinridge Guards began to reap a harvest of recruits.[10]

In the meantime, unknown gunmen continued to harass Union pickets on a regular basis throughout the Henderson region. On July 9th, the *Evansville Daily Journal* reported that someone shot at pickets in Henderson which resulted in zero injuries. "The guerrillas are growing more bold every day, and if not speedily checked may cause great trouble and damage along our borders. The property holders in this city, and in all the border towns in Indiana, are interested," complained the *Journal* in the same issue. With Johnson's small group in hiding, other independent

8 Starling, *History of Henderson County*, 715; Johnson, *Partisan Rangers*, 96-97.

9 *Evansville Daily Journal*, July 2, 1862, 3; Mulesky, *Thunder From a Clear Sky*, 22, 38; Arlington National Cemetery Website: http://www.arlingtoncemetery.net/gcsmith.htm.

10 *Evansville Daily Journal*, July 3, 1862, 3; July 7, 1862, 2; July 7, 1862, 2; General Blythe to Governor Morton, July 4, 1862, Morton Telegraphs.

General Green Clay Smith
LOC

guerrilla bands roamed the countryside. A commander of a rebel guerrilla band by the name of Captain Thompson sent Nicklin a note threatening to drive them from Henderson. Nicklin responded tersely, "Whenever I find you, I'll hang you." Fortunately for the citizens of Henderson, Nicklin and Thompson failed to follow through on their threats and the town avoided further bloodshed. For the Southern-leaning citizens of Henderson, news of Nicklin's impending departure brought relief. His battery received orders to move to Louisville, along with the remaining Louisville Provost guards. The men of Andrew's Battery also redeployed to Louisville one day later, with General Smith on board the same steamer. The departure of all Union forces from Henderson left it an open city.[11]

Even though the Federal troops had left Henderson, the *Evansville Daily Journal* found some confidence in nearby cavalry. Hundreds of troopers, belonging to a battalion of the 9th Pennsylvania Cavalry, were operating in the Madisonville, Kentucky area south of Henderson. "We are glad to see that a Pennsylvania regiment of cavalry is doing good missionary work in Hopkins county, Ky., and in adjacent counties. If they can find any clear cases, and hang a few, it will have a salutary effect." The *Journal* would be very disappointed in the coming days, as Johnson would strike again.[12]

The young Kentuckians lurked in the western Kentucky countryside for several more days to avoid the enemy in blue. Federals from the east now patrolled the region, but the Confederates had a greater familiarity with the terrain. The battalions of the 9th Pennsylvania Cavalry regiment were spread across the Commonwealth, with a portion tangling with Col. John H. Morgan's raiders in the central part of the state. Trooper Cornelius D. Waldron wrote to his mother and sister that:

11 Mulesky, *Thunder From a Clear Sky*, 39-40; *Evansville Daily Journal*, July 9, 1862, 2, July 15, 1862, 3.

12 *Evansville Daily Journal*, July 9, 1862, 2.

> [o]ur regiment is concentrating at Bowling Green and perhaps 'ere this reaches you, we will be on our march or again we remain here some time. I, for my part, am well satisfied we remain for a time yet. . . . It is reported that there are guerrilla bands forming in this state but none in this vicinity.[13]

As Waldron was soon to learn, the serenity of his station was soon to be violently broken as Johnson continued to gain publicity and recruits.

In July, the 9th's 350 troopers moved north from Bowling Green and arrived in Madisonville, Kentucky. The Pennsylvanians encamped on a hill overlooking the town and settled in to enjoy themselves. In honor of Independence Day, the troopers prepared a barbecue and read aloud the Declaration of Independence. Civilians thronged to the Federal camp to enjoy the festivities. One soldier remarked, "At noon we had a splendid dinner brought in by the citizens. We had a fine time."[14] These festivities belied the seriousness of purpose with which the regiment had arrived.

Federal anti-partisan operations began to mount in earnest. Through his local network, Johnson learned that the Easterners were on a mission of retribution against Southern sympathizers due to the activity of other small guerrilla bands in the region. Indeed, the Pennsylvanians recently partook in the destruction of property toward suspected Rebels and those who harbored them when they "ransacked the houses and searched them" in the Madisonville, Kentucky area. In fact, the military leaders in Louisville decreed, "When damage shall be done to the person or property of loyal citizens by marauding bands of guerrillas, the disloyal neighborhood will be held responsible." Johnson penned in his memoirs, "A new . . . serious peril now threatened this section of the State. The authorities in Louisville sent a cavalry regiment to Madisonville with the loose and unwarrantable instructions to destroy by fire the houses of all the citizens that were giving aid to the Confederates." Johnson concluded that these accusations of disloyalty were rooted in old grudges. Though carrying out orders, the Pennsylvanians played into his plan to use Southern anger to his advantage and gain more recruits. "I knew I could create a revolution and commenced operations," he later wrote.[15]

13 Cornelius D. Waldron, Letter to Mother and Sister, June 3, 1862, "Spared and Shared 9," https://sparedshared9.wordpress.com/2015/05/15/1862-cornelius-d-waldron-to-mother/; Johnson, *Partisan Rangers*, 100-101.

14 John W. Rowell, *Yankee Cavalrymen: Through the Civil War with the 9th Pennsylvania Cavalry* (Knoxville, 1971), 58.

15 *OR* 16:2, 994; Cornelius D. Waldron, Letter to Mother and Sister, June 3, 1862, "Spared and Shared 9," https://sparedshared9.wordpress.com/2015/05/15/1862-cornelius-d-waldron-to-mother/; Johnson, *Partisan Rangers*, 100-101; Rowell, *Yankee Cavalrymen*, 58; Cooling, *Fort Donelson's Legacy*, 72; Lovel H. Harrison, *The Civil War in Kentucky* (Lexington, KY, 1975), 34.

Unidentified trooper of the 9th PA Cavalry.
LOC

The "authorities" referenced by Johnson was Brig. Gen. Jeremiah T. Boyle. Appointed to the position of commander of all troops in Kentucky except those already belonging to the Army of the Ohio, Boyle's mission was to counter the threats posed by men like Morgan and Johnson. The confusing command structure hampered Boyle's ability to conduct operations against raiders and guerrillas, and his communications out of Louisville are evidence of the struggle. When his efforts to suppress Confederate irregulars proved fruitless, Boyle resorted to the wartime legal system. Union persecution of southern sympathizers, including those who considered themselves non-aligned, grew under Boyle's tenure. The threat of imprisonment for failure to swear allegiance to the Union, and the disruption of civil courts and elections, pushed many to support men like Johnson. Some in the Union leadership recognized the dangers of such a policy. John B. Temple, president of the Military Board, warned Lincoln: "The indiscriminate arrest making . . . is producing a dangerous state of things." Governor Robinson complained that the arrests caused only "injury to the Union cause in Kentucky." Eventually, Stanton ordered Boyle to use caution in arresting Kentuckians and to only do so with solid evidence.[16]

Johnson's attacks grew bolder. Soon after the Pennsylvanians arrived in the Madisonville area, the Union troopers reported that two men had fired upon a patrol. The shooters escaped without causing any casualties and without one of their horses. If Johnson did this, he never mentioned it. To attract more recruits Johnson had to keep up the momentum he gained from the Henderson affair. Firing on Union patrols without effect would not bring in more men. He settled for a bold and direct attack on the Pennsylvanians' camp itself, putting his frontier education to good use. To make matters more dangerous the attack would occur in the middle of the night. For this strike, Johnson had six men to command

16 Cooling, *Fort Donelson's Legacy*, 89; Gerald R. Prokopowicz, *All for the Regiment: The Army of the Ohio, 1861-1862* (Chapel Hill, NC, 2001), 129-130; Harrison, *Civil War in Kentucky*, 34.

including Martin and Owen, plus newcomers Jake Bennett, Tom Gooch, John Conelly, and Marion Myers. Johnson mused that he was about to play "Gideon of old" on the Federal camp.[17]

On the night of July 6th, the army of seven tied their horses in the woods outside of the 9th Pennsylvania's encampment at Browning Springs on the outskirts of Madisonville. The Confederates crept toward the sleeping Union soldiers without alerting the pickets. After sneaking up near the fence surrounding the camp, Johnson broke the silence with a shotgun blast that disposed of one guard near a barn. To his surprise, he discovered that the barn was full of sleeping cavalrymen. The Union troopers ran out in confusion and one soldier fired so near that the powder burned Johnson's face. He returned fire with the second tube of his shotgun into the man's back. The other six Confederates had already begun pouring their own lead into the camp and peppered several tents. All the while, they hooped and hollered to give the impression that they were a much larger force than they in fact were.

One trooper, William Thomas, recalled,

> "We were surprised in camp this morning About 2.0.clock A.M. by a party of Guerrillas [sic][.] They came up behind the camp and shot down the guard and then fired into the tents[.] Our tent is riddled with balls[.] Henry Feindt who was sleeping by my side Had a Ball to graze the top of His head But not dangerous[.] the guard Had 14 Buckshots Shot in His Leg and thigh[.] The guerillas then fled into the woods and made their escape."

Thomas remarked that the attack was "Comanche style," a compliment to Johnson's days in Texas.[18]

While the Pennsylvanians fled back to Madisonville the Breckinridge Guards made their escape. The cavalrymen regrouped and searched the area for a short time but succeeded only in arresting a few suspected sympathizers. Johnson's attack sent a surge of anxiety throughout the Union battalion, which fired wildly during the night at what turned out to be gravestones.

The attack did more than give the Pennsylvanians a thorough scare. Johnson says he gained twenty additional recruits due to his actions that night. He moved his growing command to Henderson County and a community comprised of people he could trust. In his report to Breckinridge less than two weeks later, Johnson exaggerated the size of the enemy force by doubling it to 600 men. The

17 Johnson, *Partisan Rangers*, 101; Rowell, *Yankee Cavalrymen*, 59; Ellis Merton Coulter, *The Civil War and Readjustment in Kentucky* (Chapel Hill, NC, 1926), 152-153.

18 Johnson, *Partisan Rangers*, 101; Rowell, *Yankee Cavalrymen*, 55.

9th Pennsylvania operated in the vicinity for only a few days more before receiving orders to ride for Henderson.[19]

The Pennsylvanians may have ceded the ground, but the Federals were not about to let Johnson off the hook, and Henderson was not the safe harbor Johnson may have thought. Unbeknownst to Johnson, a meeting of Henderson Unionists convened the day after the attack on the National Hotel in which Johnson's actions received strong condemnation and he and his men were labeled "thieves, robbers, and murderers." The Unionist committee drafted a resolution for print in the regional newspapers, including the *Henderson Weekly Reporter*. Their statement read:

> *Whereas*, We are in the midst of a civil and predatory war, and theft, robbery and murder are being perpetrated in our very midst by bands, styling themselves Southern Rights men; and whereas these thieves, robbers, and murders have been countenanced and harbored by citizens claiming to be sympathizers; and whereas there is no security for the lives or property of loyal citizens while the state of things is permitted to exist.
>
> *Therefore Resolved*, That it is the duty of every loyal citizen to unite in crushing this monster, and restoring community to its original state of peace and order.
>
> *Resolved*, That we will resist, and that it is the duty of the loyal citizens throughout the County to arm themselves and assist the Federal forces in capturing, killing if necessary, and driving from the County every one who has been engaged in or may engage in perpetrating these outrages, or who may aid and abet, or harbor these outlaws, and enemies of the human race.
>
> *Resolved*, That we offer our sympathy and condolence to the family and friends of Lieut. Tyler, who was murdered in our city last night by a band of these fiends, and that we deeply sympathize with the wounded officers and soldiers. On motion, the Henderson "Weekly Mail" and all other loyal papers of the Northwest are requested to copy.
>
> J. Lambert, Pres't.
> Peter Semonin and Jas. H. Halloway [sic], Secretaries
> Col. CW. Hutchen
> John G. Halloway [sic]
> Jas. B. Lyne
> Col. Jas. M. Shackelford
> Hon. Archie Dixon[20]

19 Johnson, *Partisan Rangers*, 101; Rowell, *Yankee Cavalrymen*, 55, 60; *OR* 16:2, 994.

20 *Henderson Weekly Reporter*, July 3, 1862. Several men who signed the resolution were former Union officers who would soon return to active service.

The resolution incensed Johnson when he read it days later in the Henderson newspaper. According to the honorable citizens of Henderson, the Rebels responsible for the attack on the soldiers at the hotel were little more than bushwhacking scoundrels. It must have been especially difficult to digest the article, as some of the men whose names fell underneath the resolution were family friends. If Johnson or any of his men fell into enemy hands, they seemed to be calling for the noose, a dishonor that he was coming to believe belied his station. Johnson felt compelled to refute the allegation that his command was comprised of outlaw brigands rather than the legitimate Confederate soldiers he believed himself and his confederates to be. He wrote his rebuttal, which would be hand delivered to Henderson:

> Headquarters Breckinridge Guards, July 6, 1862
>
> Noticing in one of the Henderson papers a series of resolutions condoling with the Federal troops on their loss in a recent attack made on them, and denouncing the attacking party as thieves, murderers and robbers—and declaring war on those who made that attack—I wish to thoroughly understand the position you occupy. As it was a portion of my command that made that attack and every man engaged being a sworn Confederate soldier, I conclude that your declaration is against my Government. My orders when I was sent to this department were imperative regarding citizens and their property. I was charged not to molest them in any manner unless they were engaged in war upon us. Now, gentlemen, you perceive why I wish to have a definite answer upon this point. If you are fully resolved to war against us, we will necessarily be compelled to fight you. I have repeatedly said to Union men, who are now living in Henderson, that I did not intend to molest any citizen on account of his politics. I have written to the same affect, and I now repeat it; but I contend that each and every one who signed those resolutions have placed themselves without the pale, and I await an answer to this to show you what it really means to be an enemy to us. I deprecate civil war, and have used my best endeavors to avoid coming into contact with citizens; and here I reiterate a piece of advice given to Mr. Delano, viz., for citizens to let soldiers fight their own battles. If they do not wish to see and hear the din of war in their midst, let them have their town cleared of blue coats and I will guarantee that no one of them will be molested by Confederate soldiers. I want all persons to know that we are at war with the Federal soldiers, and if they will shut themselves up in houses we will sometimes give them a little fight just for recreation.
>
> Attached to this is a list of names signed to those resolutions, all of whom I consider as having declared war against the Confederate States and each name that I do not find appended to an article denying that to be their intention, I shall hold him as an enemy and his property subject to confiscation. The said article must be published in the Reporter

by Thursday, the 17th of July 1862. All those so appearing shall not be in any manner molested by my men. I have sent a copy of the resolution to the army.

A. R. Johnson, C.S.A.[21]

As Johnson soon learned, Henderson may not have been as aghast at his operations as the resolution suggested. He had sent Martin and William Hollis to Henderson with his message, who delivered it to former Kentucky Lieutenant Governor Archie Dixon without fuss or violence. While there, Martin dined with Johnson's Unionist father and even watched the Federal force drill and parade through the town. Martin took note of the number of the enemy without arousing suspicion of spying. He and Hollis then returned to the encampment of the ever-growing Breckinridge Guards.[22]

Johnson claimed the Henderson paper issued a full retraction of the declaration made by the Union men on July 17th, though an edited statement with a clear explanation of what the signers meant is a more realistic description. Johnson made a risky gamble with his threat toward the signers, but his reputation from years earlier served him well. The men who were personally acquainted with Johnson and his family knew he was a man of his word, and who could say exactly how many men he had at his disposal?[23]

Johnson's two attacks continued to grow his ranks. Men who previously scoffed at Johnson and Martin weeks before now joined his command. Among these were Captains Andy Ray and Jake Bennett, who commanded their own small guerrilla companies in the region. After joining, Ray rode to McLean County to bring in more recruits for the growing regiment while Bennett's men remained at the main camp in Slaughtersville, Kentucky.[24]

Though Johnson insisted that his men were legitimate Confederate soldiers, some of the new recruits struggled to throw off their former guerrilla ways. After months of operating on their own and never under the authority of any true military command, the former guerrillas did not always follow orders or respect the traditional rules of civilized warfare. This is especially true when they saw opportunities to settle old scores or bring harm to Unionist civilians. One incident near Henderson in July illustrates that not all of Johnson's men were of honorable character. The story involves an old farmer, Thomas McFarland, and his "old maid sister" whose farm sat outside Henderson. In the middle of the night, twelve of

21 Johnson, *Partisan Rangers*, 98; *Evansville Daily Journal*, July 16, 1862, 2.

22 Johnson, *Partisan Rangers*, 98-99.

23 Ibid., 98-100.

24 Ibid., 100.

Two Confederate soldiers, the one on the right identified as one of Quantrill's Missouri raiders. Incidents like that at the McFarland home might be more associated with the actions of those Missouri guerrillas. *LOC*

Johnson's newest recruits surrounded the McFarland home and demanded supper and food for their horses. McFarland sent his sister out with ham and bread to appease the unexpected visitors while he locked himself in his bedroom. The visitors, disappointed that McFarland did not appear so they could kill a Unionist, burst into the house and attempted to knock down the door. After failing to do so, the leader of the gang fired his shotgun through the door, narrowly missing McFarland. The marauders believed the shot had killed him and proceeded to search the house for goods to steal. McFarland leapt out his window and fled to the woods. The riders stole $34, clothing, and his two good horses. To make sure McFarland was dead, the thieves eventually broke down the door and fired their pistols into his bed. They were disappointed to discover his escape. The pistol discharge sparked a fire in the bed and if not for the pleas of McFarland's sister to throw the bed and blankets out the window, the house and the little they had left would have been lost. The guerrillas rode off into the night within yards of McFarland's hiding place. McFarland never again slept in his home until the war ended, and when news reached him of the death of each of the attackers, he quietly rejoiced. The war in Kentucky was personal.[25]

At this stage, Johnson's efforts were outpacing the Federal attempts to suppress partisan activity in the region. Men eager to follow Johnson poured into camp, each with their own reasons for joining. Some viewed it as their first available chance to enlist in a local Confederate unit before Union authorities enforced the draft in the state. Others, incensed at real and imagined Union deprivations upon

25 Starling, *History of Henderson County*, 385-389.

Southerners, sought revenge. Yet other men desired the adventure of the partisan experience. With the Breckinridge Guards growing to a respectable size, Johnson and Martin set their sights on Henderson itself. After the Federal units that had been garrisoning the town were recalled to Louisville, the only remaining Union force in the region was the 9th Pennsylvania, but after arriving in Henderson it received orders to return to Louisville to help contain John H. Morgan's raid into Kentucky. The horsemen boarded the steamers on July 15th and disappeared upriver. Henderson lay defenseless.[26]

26 *Evansville Daily Journal*, July 15, 1862, 3, July 16, 1862, 3; Few primary sources exist from enlisted men of Johnson's regiment that describe their reasons for joining. Of two that do exist, they both mention Union activity as the driving cause.

Chapter 3

"Some wag referred to me as 'Stovepipe Johnson'"

On July 17th, just one day after the Federal forces withdrew from Henderson, Johnson led a column of 30 men into the city. With Confederate raider John H. Morgan's foray into the Bluegrass region of the state, Union leadership abandoned important posts to stop his fast-moving raid, and this mistake benefitted Johnson. Union authorities considered the Ohio River cities as strategic priorities, serving both as shipping ports for crucial supplies as well as guarding the free-flow of river traffic; their loss to Confederate partisans was not to be countenanced. For Johnson, taking such cities offered an opportunity for further recruitment. As he entered the city a delegation of "southern men," which included the mayor and county judge, met Johnson and promptly surrendered the city. They were astonished at the small size of his force, as reports had greatly exaggerated the number of men under his command. They also informed him of a Union gunboat that lay just off the riverbank, the *Brilliant*, with its guns aimed at the town. Though the *Brilliant* had not yet been officially commissioned into the United States Navy, operating under "acting volunteer" Lt. Cmdr. Charles G. Perkins, it frequently patrolled up and down the Ohio River—until orders came to steam for St. Louis after the Navy officially purchased the vessel in August. Until then, how would Perkins react to "guerrillas" holding a river town?[1]

1 Johnson, *Partisan Rangers*, 102; Starling, *History of Henderson County*, 750; The *Brilliant* was not purchased by the War Department until Aug. 1862, and is not mentioned as being in the waters of the Ohio by the *Evansville Daily Journal* until the same month; James L. Mooney, "Brilliant (Sternwheel Gunboat) 1862-1865," *Naval History and Heritage Command*, Mar. 24, 2021, https://www.history.navy.mil/content/history/nhhc/research/histories/ship-histories/danfs/b/brilliant-i.html.

Postwar image of the old Henderson County courthouse. This building no longer stands, and this image shows the several additions that were made in the years after the war. *LOC*

Upon entering Henderson, Johnson ordered a Confederate flag raised above the courthouse, symbolically holding the city for the Confederacy. Naturally, the Unionists of Henderson fretted. When asked how he would treat loyalists, Johnson reiterated the claim he made in his letter to the Union men. They should fear no ill treatment from him or his men.[2]

But there were opportunities for even greater publicity. Johnson, never one to pass on press attention, issued a proclamation published the next day in the *Evansville Daily Journal*:

> Citizens of Kentucky:
>
> It has gone forth to the world that you are a subjugated people—that the iron hell of despotism has destroyed all spirit of resistance and crushed out the last spark of patriotism. The idea has gone through the North, and they look upon you with contempt, and send their hirelings to rule over you. It has crossed the Atlantic, and the eyes of all Europe have been looking at the position of Kentucky with wonder and astonishment. Down in the sunny South, amongst those who ought to be your brothers, you have become a by-word and a scoff. The Kentucky army has turned their anxious eyes to their native State, and

2 Johnson, *Partisan Rangers*, 103.

at each new outrage would listen for the tocsin of war but they have listened and hoped until the last ray has expired. The Confederate Cabinet and Congress have looked for some movement indicating a desire for freedom; but they looked in vain and think Kentucky lost.

But there is one man who has never despaired—that man is John C. Breckinridge—the hero, the statesman and the patriot. With the same never-despairing love that a mother bears to her offspring, does he regard Kentucky with the same anxious care as he watched her. He asked his government and the world to suspend public opinion until his State should have one more opportunity to redeem her character and now, citizens of Kentucky, the opportunity has presented itself, and for the sake of your former fame and glory—for your country—for your liberties, which ought to be dearer to you than life itself—come to the field! Rally to your country's call! Rise in your majesty and might, and drive from your midst the monster of oppression.

Then prepare now to meet the enemy; send the young men to the field; let them retrieve the character of this once proud and noble State. Circulate through the country that the Confederate Government does not war against the citizens of the country. Can you, with the example set by the people of the South, tamely submit? They have, with heroic devotion, applied the torch to their property, and, with unparalleled unanimity, have they battled for their country. Will you not risk as much as they to achieve your freedom and independence?

A. R. Johnson, C.S.A.
Henderson, July 17, 1862.[3]

Adding to the drama of the day, violence in Henderson seemed likely when Perkins came ashore to speak with Johnson. Perkins demanded that the Rebels remove their flag from the courthouse or else he would shell them from the wooden gunboat. Unknown to Johnson, Perkins was most likely bluffing, as his sweetheart and future wife resided in Henderson. Johnson responded that the flag would remain as long as he held the town. An armed struggle for control of the town seemed to be in the offing, except that Johnson never intended to hold Henderson for long. He kept Perkins and his party on shore until he was ready to leave with fresh recruits and supplies that afternoon. Removed from the courthouse, the flag now flew at the head of the column as they rode east to the Soaper farm. Perkins returned to the *Brilliant*, which did not fire a gun.[4]

3 *Evansville Daily Journal*, July 18, 1862, 2; Johnson, *Partisan Rangers*, 251-252.

4 Johnson, *Partisan Rangers*, 104: Starling, *History of Henderson County*, 716.

Stored weapons at Columbus, Kentucky in 1864. The weapons Johnson hoped to find in Newburgh would have been stored in a similar manner. *LOC*

While the Breckinridge Guards encamped at the Soaper farm, three Newburgh, Indiana, residents, including the wharf master, brought Johnson interesting information. Newburgh, just across the river, possessed hundreds of stands of guns, supplies, and equipment without any serious force to guard it. The action he now contemplated against Newburgh launched Johnson and his men into national and international fame. It would be a feat admiringly recalled by at least one former enemy as "the most successful military masterstroke achieved by any military commander of high or low authority, in either army during the war."[5]

The militia (Indiana Legion) in Newburgh was not on high alert like neighboring counties, and the only Federal guards were those convalescing in the Exchange Hotel. Johnson and Martin devised a plan to capture the arms and materiel and deal with the soldiers. The plan was not without risk. Just 12 miles downriver was the large city of Evansville, Indiana, with its multitude of steamers,

5 Johnson, *Partisan Rangers*, 104; Starling, *History of Henderson County*, 715; *Evansville Daily Journal*, July 19, 1862, 2.

gunboats, soldiers, and militia. Additionally, a telegraph wire connected Newburgh to Evansville and would allow a message to reach the larger city within moments. They also had to consider the possibility of resistance from citizens and soldiers, convalescing or not.[6]

The plan called for quick movement with only a few moving parts. Martin would cross the Ohio upriver with 24 mounted men and ride into Newburgh, while Johnson and two others crossed directly to the wharf. Once ashore, Johnson and his men would secure the warehouse full of weapons and wait for Martin to arrive. Perhaps his most inspired provision was placing two guns on the Kentucky side of the river to threaten the Indiana community. These guns had not been in Henderson nor seized from the 9th Pennsylvania at Browning Springs. Rather, they materialized that morning, one out of an old stovepipe and the other from a charred log. Old wagon wheels and axles served as the carriages for these new cannons placed on the riverbank. From a distance, they looked as real and threatening as any gun. As Johnson later quipped, "they were the most formidable-looking pieces of artillery into whose gaping mouths a scared people ever looked."[7]

If things did not go as intended, Johnson and Martin devised a contingency plan: burn the warehouse and all its goods and prevent their use by the enemy. For this purpose, containers of flammable liquid were stowed in the boats. If Union forces offered resistance, the town would burn while the Rebels appropriated whatever weapons could fit in their boats.[8]

Before putting the plan into motion, Johnson first consulted his men. He wanted them to be fully aware of the risks, considering how Union authorities viewed his command. There was no guarantee that if captured they would be treated as prisoners of war instead of guerrillas. Johnson stood in front of the men and reminded them of the danger. "Soldiers, as soon as you reach the other side of the Ohio, you will be standing upon a powder magazine, and cowardice would be the match to ignite it. All who are willing and confident take a step to the front." In one motion, every man stepped forward. The Newburgh raid would proceed.[9]

Martin and his men crossed upriver with their horses via ferry. Johnson, with Frank Owen and Felix Aiken, crossed with their weapons hidden in the bottom of their skiff. The crossing was quick and the trio immediately made for the warehouse

6 Johnson, *Partisan Rangers*, 104; John P. Etter, *The Indiana Legion: A Civil War Militia* (Carmel, IN, 2006), 78-79.

7 Etter, *Indiana Legion*, 79; Johnson, *Partisan Rangers*, 105. For a longer study on the capture of Newburgh, see Mulesky, *Thunder From a Clear Sky*.

8 Johnson, *Partisan Rangers*, 104.

9 Ibid., 105.

Modern-day view from Newburgh toward the Kentucky shore, close to where Johnson and his men crossed the Ohio River. *Author*

next to the wharf. To their surprise, their target stood with its doors wide open and prized weapons in plain view, no guards in sight. Curious citizens noticed the crossing and strangers entering the warehouse. The Rebels immediately arrested citizens that wandered too close and kept them under guard in the warehouse. Johnson observed other civilians making for the hotel and temporary army hospital and assumed they were warning the soldiers. He expected Martin's arrival any minute. Owen and Aiken worked to barricade the warehouse. Luckily for the raiding party, a storm recently cut the telegraph line to Evansville, giving Johnson and his men valuable time to procure whatever they needed.[10]

Leaving the tasks to his men, Johnson rushed for the Exchange Hotel before the soldiers quartered there could react to his actions. Upon reaching the hotel, Johnson realized he might stir up a hornet's nest. Without hesitation, he entered through the double doors to find the soldiers armed and ready with muskets aimed at his body. His instinctive theatricality took over and he commanded in his loudest voice for the soldiers not to fire and ordered them to put down their weapons. Johnson confidently walked among the soldiers and used his shotgun to push the muzzles away. He declared that none of them faced harm if they surrendered before his men arrived at the hotel. In an instant, they stacked arms and Johnson moved the mass of soldiers into the dining room.

A Union orderly, in full military dress, arrived at the hotel and the sight of unarmed Union soldiers astonished him. He angrily approached Johnson, whose threat to fill him with buckshot stopped him short. Johnson instructed the orderly to obtain the muster rolls to facilitate the parole of the prisoners. Since Johnson

10 Johnson, *Partisan Rangers*, 105; *The Boonville Enquirer*, Feb. 1, 1901, 2.

Modern-day view of the Exchange Hotel.

Author

claimed to be the leader of a legitimate unit, he knew the importance of appearing to handle the surrender process and prisoner management in a lawful manner.[11]

After Martin's arrival, the raiders fanned throughout the town, picketing street corners and limiting foot traffic to prevent anyone from leaving town to sound the alarm in the countryside or neighboring communities. They commandeered wagons to transport the captured weapons back to friendly territory in Kentucky. They pressed one Newburgh citizen and his team into service for activities south of the Ohio River, but he escaped ten days later. The presence of the raiders kept many of the citizens inside the safety of their homes while more curious types wandered the streets to discern the chaos. Supposed Copperheads also ventured out to meet their guests as this was the first time Confederate forces had captured a community north of the Mason-Dixon Line, albeit for only a few hours.[12]

However, one soldier did make it out of Newburgh. He ran to a nearby farm and informed Dr. Eli Lewis of the events in town. Lewis told his son and nephew to grab axes and cut a path through the forest so he could ride to Evansville around the Confederate pickets. "Never did boys work harder than did those two on that

11 Johnson, *Partisan Rangers*, 105; *OR* 16:2, 994.

12 Johnson, *Partisan Rangers*, 105; *Evansville Daily Journal*, July 19, 1862, 2; *History of Warrick, Spencer, and Perry Counties*, 107; *The Boonville Enquirer*, Feb. 1, 1901, 2.

hot July day," the nephew beamed. Lewis rode the 12 miles to Evansville to alert the authorities of the raid on Newburgh. He pushed his horse so hard that it died of exhaustion upon reaching the courthouse after a grueling 40-minute trek. Lewis found Col. Daniel Bates of the Indiana Legion and informed him what was happening in Newburgh. Bates immediately went to work, and Evansville roared to life. Over 1,000 men and artillery mobilized and boarded transports within the hour. Three steamers, the *Courier*, *Eugene*, and the *Commercial*, immediately fired their engines for Newburgh. The paper further reported:

> The alacrity with which the citizens responded gave most cheering evidence that when convinced of danger our people are equal to any emergency. A company of infantry with a squad of artillery, with two guns, left on board the Eugene at 5 ½ o'clock for Newburg.
>
> Captain Dexter had the *Courier* fired up with all dispatch, and having armed his crew, and with a small squad of infantry steamed off up to the river. He . . . declared his determination to prevent the rebels from recrossing the river if they were found on this side, and to use the *Courier* as a ram in case of need. The saucy little Courier went out 'flying light and running for glory.'[13]

The presence of Johnson and his raiders inevitably stirred the political conflict within border communities that was barely suppressed at the best of times. While Johnson controlled Newburgh, some citizens conversed with him and perhaps even shared a drink. Such fraternization disgusted others in the community, who quietly took note of the public collaborators. Some of Johnson's men reportedly took it upon themselves to liberate the personal property of staunch Unionists, with the help of suspected Copperheads who informed the raiders of which homes to pass.[14]

A sympathetic Newburgh citizen alerted the raiders to an approaching column of the local Indiana Legion. Johnson needed to act fast: if a couple of these militia companies attempted to retake the town, they could destroy his small command. Johnson found Capt. Union Bethell, local legion commander and owner of the warehouse, on the riverbank near the building that bore his name. He approached Bethell and alerted him to the artillery pieces he had placed across the river. Johnson insisted he only came for the weapons, but if an attack fell upon his force, the guns from Kentucky would destroy the town. Johnson may have borrowed Perkins's bluff of the day before in Henderson, with no real intention of shelling anything. Johnson addressed Bethell, "I see, sir, that you have a field glass and by looking across the river you can see that I am prepared to carry out my threat." Johnson

13 Etter, *Indiana Legion*, 81; *Evansville Daily Journal*, July 19, 1862, 2; William Henry Harrison Terrell, *Indiana in the War of the Rebellion: Report of the Adjutant General* (Indianapolis, 1869), 183.

14 Etter, *Indiana Legion*, 80; *Evansville Daily Journal*, July 21, 1862, 2.

recalled that he "saw the captain glance at his house, and as it was the largest and most prominent building near the river, he probably reflected that it would be the first knocked down. Turning pale, he sent his runners at once to stop his men from coming in." To Johnson's delight, the Indianans believed the ruse. Bethell ordered all approaching Legion units to halt.[15]

Martin loaded the weapons and supplies into the boats and quickly rowed across the river to Kentucky. Colonel Daniel Bates, commander of the Warrick Legion, reported some months later that the warehouse held over 200 stands of muskets, along with 67 cavalry sabers and 134 pistols and holsters. The pistols were so new that they were still stored in their original containers. The muskets were all .69 caliber, and Johnson took them and the accompanying accouterments.

Why were so many weapons stored in a warehouse so close to the Rebels in Kentucky? Due to the number of volunteer regiments recruited in the area, the local Legion's numbers dropped so low that some companies ceased to exist, causing an arms surplus. The Warrick County Legion ordered the superfluous weapons placed into storage as there was a belief that no Rebels would dare cross the river. The arms taken from the Federal soldiers in the hospital also greatly aided Johnson and Martin as they continued to recruit their regiment in the days and weeks ahead. The *Evansville Daily Journal* later reported that the "hospital plunderers" took 200 guns and paroled 85 soldiers. Coffee, sugar, and "other articles that could be readily transported" also went South. The Confederates threw into the river any weapons that would not fit in the skiffs, and these submerged guns became trophies for young divers in the years to come.[16]

Once Bethell sent the order to stand down, Johnson and his two men followed the rest of the command back to the Kentucky side of the river. In the distance they noticed smoke from the steamers churning for Newburgh. But as soon as Johnson pushed from the wharf for Kentucky, the Indianans swarmed into Newburgh. With his threat to level the town still in effect, the Legion fired not one shot at the Kentuckians as they crossed to safety. However, shots would be fired at Newburgh residents by their fellow citizens.[17]

Loyal citizens who kept a list of collaborators gave that information to the militia. Some of the more zealous citizens took it upon themselves to right some wrongs and set an example for other suspected Copperheads. Elliott Medford and

15 Johnson, *Partisan Rangers*, 107; *The Boonville Enquirer*, Feb. 1, 1901, 2.

16 Johnson, *Partisan Rangers*, 107; *Union Army in the Civil War: Indiana Legion reports of brigade and regimental officers, 1st-4th brigades* (Indianapolis, IN, 1900), 30-31; *Evansville Daily Journal*, July 19, 1962, 2; *History of Warrick, Spencer, and Perry Counties*, 107; *The Boonville Enquirer*, Feb. 1, 1901, 2.

17 Johnson, *Partisan Rangers*, 107; Etter, *Indiana Legion*, 81.

H. H. Carney, two of Johnson's informants from the previous night, were at the top of the list. An angry mob fell upon these men; what happened next is uncertain. One story claims that the mob captured and hung both men that evening. A more likely story relates that the two men fled across the river after Johnson departed. The Legionnaires rushed to stop them as they scurried to an available boat on the wharf. Shots pierced the air and Medford received a wound to the hip and fell to the ground before reaching a boat. Carney attempted to help him regain his feet but received a shot to the chest, killing him instantly. Medford fared only a little better; a Legionnaire rushed in and plunged his bayonet into his abdomen three times. With the third thrust, he tumbled over Medford, bending the blade inside him. The shooter, Stephen Armstrong, saw several armed men approaching. Thinking they were rebels, Armstrong fled while his wife tried to prevent fellow Unionists from shooting him. One of the bullets struck her in the heel, which caused a limp for the rest of her life. Remarkably, Medford survived. The citizens apprehended him and brought him to a doctor. The mob would visit him later.[18]

* * *

Lieutenant Colonel John W. Foster stood aboard the side-wheeled steamer *Eugene* as it cruised up the Ohio River while Johnson and his men escaped back to Kentucky. Foster's mission was to destroy the Rebels before they disappeared into the border state. The raiders were now back on the Kentucky side of the Ohio River, presumably attempting to cross the Green River into an area of rebel sympathy. Two additional steamers accompanied Foster, the *Courier* and the *Commercial*, each loaded with Union soldiers and militia. Foster formulated a simple plan to eliminate the enemy band. The three steamers would chug up the Green and disembark infantry and artillery south of the expected rebel position. The combined force could then trap the Rebels on the peninsula between the Green and Ohio Rivers.[19]

Circumstances thrust Foster into this position, and it was not an assignment that he relished. In the coming months, Foster's name would become infamous to Southern sympathizers in western Kentucky, even though he characterized himself as a reluctant soldier who did not rush to join the army when hostilities first broke out. In his book, *War Stories for My Grandchildren*, Foster asserted, "I cherished no desire for military glory, and distrusted my special fitness for the life of a soldier. In my college days I had contracted a horror of war and regarded it as the most terrible and futile of human follies. Shortly before my graduation I had delivered

18 Etter, *Indiana Legion*, 82-83; *The Boonville Enquirer*, Feb. 1, 1901, 2.

19 *Evansville Daily Journal*, July 19, 1862, 3; Ibid., July 21, 1862, 2.

a public address for my literary society on peace and war. . . . I regarded myself as a peace man." The Indiana University grad and local lawyer received a major's commission in the 25th Indiana later in 1861. He distinguished himself at the battles of Fort Donelson and Shiloh, and soon expected to command his own regiment. In the meantime, Foster returned to Evansville to escort the body of his brother-in-law for burial.[20]

On July 18, 1862, a citizen from Newburgh galloped to the courthouse in Evansville with the news of Rebels on Union soil. Foster took command by default. When the raid on Newburgh occurred, Foster led the relief force directed to capture the raiders. Unfortunately for him, Johnson and Martin escaped with the weapons they captured while he steamed into position.

Foster's carefully designed plan was now ruined. Buckshot struck the lead steamer, *Commercial*, from thick brush at the mouth of the Green. The pilot thought the entire Rebel force lurked in his front, and he moved the boat back into the safety of the Ohio. Soldiers covered the hasty retreat with musket volleys into the brush. The *Courier* moved toward the spot of the attack and let loose a torrent of musketry and shots from the swivel gun. The *Eugene* followed suit and churned forward to join the barrage. Johnson stated that this shelling lasted hours and gave his men ample time to escape. It is difficult to imagine steamers firing for hours into the same area and never receiving a reply, perhaps another example of Johnson's habitual exaggeration. When Foster's infantry finally landed, the Confederates and their stolen weapons had long fled the area. Over the next several weeks and months, Foster continued to pursue the band of elusive Rebels.[21]

After this failure, Foster and his soldiers disembarked at Newburgh. By now, hundreds of armed men from the surrounding area occupied the town. The anxious and angry citizens flooded Foster with stories and rumors, and the body of H. H. Carney still lay in the street where Stephen Armstrong had gunned him down earlier that morning. Foster had to contend with a population eager for vengeance. He placed under arrest seven locals suspected of disloyalty and had them transported to Evansville during the night. A few Copperheads made Foster's job easy as arrests continued into the following days. At least four were bold enough to "shout" for Jeff Davis and behave in a "disorderly and riotous conduct." They, too, found themselves bound for Evansville.[22]

20 John W. Foster, *War Stories for my Grandchildren* (Washington, 1918), 1-3; Daniel W. Snepp, "John W. Foster, Soldier and Politician," *Indiana Magazine of History* 32, no. 3 (1936): 207-25.

21 Foster, *War Stories*, 95-96; *Evansville Daily Journal*, July 21, 1862, 2; *New Albany Daily Ledger*, July 21, 1862, 2; Snepp, "John W. Foster," 207-25.

22 John W. Foster to General John Love, July 31, 1862, Morton Telegraphs.

Main Street of Evansville, Indiana, circa 1861. *University of Southern Indiana*

After Foster returned to Evansville the following day, a mob descended on the wounded Medford. According to local legend, Newburgh citizens carried Medford in his bed to the street for an impromptu trial. Before the mob agreed on a verdict, Indiana Legion soldier Eli Duncan settled the matter by emptying his six-shot revolver into Medford's body. The mob displayed the bodies of the two alleged traitors as a warning for anyone thinking of betraying Newburgh to Rebels again. Later that day, the Ohio River became the final resting place for the disgraced corpses.[23]

When news of the raid reached further south, Southerners added it to the list of recent Confederate achievements. The *Athens Post*, in Athens, Tennessee, gloated, "Add to these brilliant victories, the glorious achievements of Morgan in the capture of eleven cities, and the capture of Newburg, Indiana, by another guerilla Confederate leader, and who will *croak* now at the inactivity of our troops? Surely the people of the Confederate States have great reason to thank God for these brilliant successes!" The *Washington Telegraph* of Washington, Arkansas, predicted, "This little expedition will be celebrated in history as the first upon the soil of the enemy. It created great excitement in Indiana, and carried much consternation into the hearts of Union men of that portion of the State." Even in faraway England, Confederate-sympathizing newspapers celebrated Johnson's

23 Etter, *Indiana Legion*, 82-83; *Evansville Daily Journal*, July 21, 1862, 2; *New Albany Daily Ledger*, July 21, 1862, 2; *The Boonville Enquirer*, Feb. 1, 1901, 2; *The Boonville Standard*, June 23, 1916, 2. Two other stories appeared nearly 50 years later by men who were teenagers at the time. In one version, some people attempted to take the wounded Medford to the hospital on a lounger, but the soldiers refused him entry. A mob demanded justice while Medford lay on the lounger in the road. The storyteller claimed, "Two or three hundred men were around and excitement was high. Some one called out, 'hang him,' others said, 'shoot him,' when Peter Berkenbah cocked his musket and attempted to shoot him; the gun snapped but did not go off; then Ira Duncan shot him with a squirrel rifle, the ball entering below the right ear, killing him instantly." Another witness claimed, "A man standing next to me was carrying a squirrel rifle. . . . [H]e pushed aside the man on his right, and me on his left, saying, 'I can kill him,' and raising his rifle fired at the helpless man on the lounge. The ball struck Medford in the right jugular vein, the blood spurted for about two feet and death was instantaneous. Of the killing, the young Lewis observed, "All the time [Medford] was begging for his life but it had no effect upon the unsympathetic crowd. It was a most brutal murder for which there was no excuse." Lewis also claimed that the mob displayed only Carney's body on a hay wagon in front of the hotel after Carney's wife refused to accept the corpse. She hung the American flag to show her loyalty to the Union cause and told the crowd, "No rebel's body can be brought into my house." Someone hurriedly buried Medford in an old field on his family's farm.

raid. "We have delightful news to-day that the town of Newburg, Indiana has been taken. . . . This is the first capture of a free state by the rebels."[24]

Armchair generals and conspiracy theorists began to let their voices ring out in the Northern papers in the aftermath of the raid. The *Nashville Daily Union* reprinted one such conspiracy from the *Louisville Daily Journal*: "No doubt the attack on Newburg was part of a system of trans-Ohio raids designed by Governor Magoffin and Senator Powell for the very purpose of inviting an indiscriminate retaliation from Indiana, and thus precipitating Kentucky into the rebellion. As all other plans of the rebels have failed this desperate expedient has been resorted to, shall it succeed?" The *New Albany Daily Ledger* accused other newspapers of trying to capitalize on the raid by pinning the Indiana collaborators as members of the Democratic Party. "Our contemporary . . . is exceedingly careful to inform readers . . . that all the persons thus accused are 'Democrats,'" the paper noted. "Why the political antecedents or associations of men accused of high crimes should be thus paraded, we can not imagine unless it be for the purpose of making political capital to be used in the coming election."[25]

The *Indianapolis Sentinel* criticized the initial inflation and exaggeration of Confederate strength operating in the area before and during the raid. It also lamented the removal of the Henderson troops by General Boyle, which opened that section of the river to Johnson. The papers seethed:

> The telegraphic reports of the guerrilla raids in Kentucky exaggerated the numbers engaged and the extent of damage committed by them. It appears that the gang which visited Henderson and Newburgh numbered only about forty. If Gen. Boyle had not taken away the troops that were stationed at Henderson, Johnson's band would not have made their appearance either there or at Newburgh. . . . The Union men of Henderson could have dispersed the company which made the foray upon that place, if they had been supplied with arms. The best way to stop this predatory warfare is to organize military companies upon the borders and supply them with the means to protect themselves and then promptly punish those engaged in such rascalitites. The invasion of the sacred soil of Indiana caused intense excitement throughout the State, and had there been occasion tens of thousands of our citizens would have been ready to meet the foe.[26]

The stovepipe cannon, one of the two imitation guns, lent its name to Johnson for the rest of his life. In his older age, he remembered, "The employment of the

24 *Athens Post*, Aug. 1, 1862, 2; *Washington Telegraph*, Aug. 20, 1862, 2; *The Standard*, Aug. 5, 1862, 6.

25 *Nashville Daily Union*, Aug. 6, 1862, 2; *New Albany Daily Ledger*, July 30, 1862, 1.

26 *Indianapolis Sate Sentinel*, July 21, 1862, 2.

sham cannon at the capture of Newburg served to amuse our people, and some wag referred to me as 'stovepipe Johnson'—a title which seemed to so tickle the fancy of the Southern sympathizers that they took it up and spread it far and wide throughout Kentucky and the South. This sobriquet, at first facetiously applied, has stuck to me, and I am distinguished by it to this day." Stovepipe Johnson set his sights for even larger targets than Newburgh in the weeks ahead.[27]

27 Johnson, *Partisan Rangers*, 302.

Chapter 4

"Annihilate and punish the harborers of these villains"

Despite his personal misgivings about war, John W. Foster possessed the leadership, fortitude, and will to take the war to Rebels in western Kentucky. The Union war effort against the partisans needed a man of his character. General Jeremiah Boyle, commander of Union forces in Kentucky, gave Foster command of a district encompassing the area between the Green and Cumberland Rivers, from Henderson to Smithland, Kentucky. Boyle ordered Foster to drive Rebels like Johnson and their bands out of the region once and for all. Foster inherited a new problem in the area. Unconventional Confederate forces had operated in the area since the early days of the war, but until Johnson entered the region, none managed to capture the public's curiosity or gain the attention of Union authorities like Johnson. Foster made his headquarters in Henderson. Yet despite his determination, none of Foster's efforts would impair Johnson's ability to sow confusion and chaos behind Union lines. It took time for the Union to give Foster what he needed, as temporary regiments and units from the Indiana Legion could do little to alleviate the problem when given only a few days to accomplish the mission. Piecemeal Union efforts resulted in disappointing results.[1]

Before Foster's arrival at the new post, operations were already underway to try to vindicate the humiliation at Newburgh. Indiana was ripe with indignation, and Governor Oliver P. Morton, a staunch Republican and one of the more active wartime governors, moved decisively when his state felt the Southern threat. Within hours of the raid, Morton ordered a specially guarded train to Evansville

1 Foster, *War Stories*, 96; Snepp, "John W. Foster," 216.

Indiana Governor Oliver P. Morton

LOC

with weapons and ammunition for 1,000 men, including a small battery of artillery. The shipment arrived in Evansville in time to arm the flood of recruits eager to defend Indiana soil and seek revenge. Colonels John T. Wilder and James Gavin helped recruit the 76th Indiana, a 30-day regiment quickly sworn into service and deployed to Evansville. A degree of calm returned to southern Indiana. Evansville, claimed the *Daily Journal,* was "full of distinguished military gentlemen, and the gleaming of bayonets and the glitter of gold lace gives the place quite a military appearance."[2]

The Union also deployed brown water navy vessels from Cairo, Illinois. Captain A. M. Pennock proceeded to Evansville on board the former Confederate ship captured earlier in the spring, the *Clara Dolsen*. He brought along the *Restless* and a battalion of the 63rd Illinois under the command of Col. Francis Moro. The *Rob Roy* also joined with a mixed force of 60 men from the 16th U.S. Regulars, 48 men from the 13th Wisconsin, and one section of Stenback's Illinois Battery. The mixed unit fell under the command of Maj. F. A. Starring. After a brief pause in Evansville, the flotilla steamed back downriver to Henderson. The troops disembarked then proceeded to picket and occupy the city until the arrival of more troops. Gen. John Love and 500 Legion troops followed. Moro received orders to hold Henderson with his Federal troops while Love ventured into the countryside to round up as many Rebels as possible. This initial expedition arrested only two men.

Over the next several days, the Union contingent focused on the area between Henderson and Uniontown, Kentucky, as rumors spread of another cross-river raid into Indiana. No action occurred except for a few arrests and the capture of all boats that could aid guerrillas in another attack. Love made Henderson his base from which he directed his efforts into surrounding environs. After only a few

2 Etter, *Indiana Legion*, 84; *Evansville Daily Journal*, July 22, 1862, 3.

days, Pennock returned to Cairo with his vessels, with the Regulars and Wisconsin troops on board.[3]

Captain Union Bethell, whose humiliation by Johnson the previous week left him the Legion commander with the most to prove, led a small cavalry expedition into the countryside just 62 hours after the Newburgh Raid. One rider in Bethell's command took charge of exacting revenge on the Rebels. During one patrol, the Union horseman rode upon an unsuspecting member of Johnson's men picketing the road. Since the Warrick County Legion did not have uniforms, the picket, John Patterson, assumed the riders were fellow Confederates. However, after realizing his mistake and firing his "Newburgh" pistols in a vain attempt to escape, Patterson fell captive. Without orders, Dr. McGill of Newburgh rode up to Patterson, leveled his pistol against his head, and pulled the trigger. The bullet did not kill Patterson but removed both his eyes. Thomas McFarland, who had joined Bethell's riders hoping to recover some of his stolen property, was the only man to offer to take Patterson to a nearby home. Supposedly, Patterson was the foster brother of Marcellus Jerome Clarke, later more widely known as Sue Mundy. Both men surrendered at Fort Donelson and joined Johnson that summer after escaping Camp Morton. Clarke discovered Patterson and the reason behind his wounds. He vowed never to take a Union soldier alive. The details are murky, but due to his newfound sense of brutality, Clarke either deserted the regiment or some officer had him removed.[4]

Although initial reports indicated that Bethell reclaimed some of the stolen weapons, including "two flags, ten or twelve horses, and a good portion of the guns and pistols," much of the immediate Federal response yielded few results. In his report to General Love, Col. Daniel Bates, Bethell's Legion commander, failed to note much success against Johnson's men in the days following the Newburgh raid. Perhaps this is because Bethell gained little except the occasional skirmish. After a week, Love returned to Indiana.[5]

Other partisan-hunters fared little better, despite auspicious beginnings. Colonel Gavin received a warm welcome from the Unionists of Henderson. Upon entering the city, citizens shouted huzzahs for the Union and its soldiers and treated Gavin and his officers to a free meal at the hotel. Gavin quickly went to

3 *Official Records of the Union and Confederate Navies in the War of the Rebellion*, Series 1, vol. 23, 310, 263-265 [hereafter cited as *ORN*].

4 Starling, *History of Henderson County*, 390; Young E. Allison, "Sue Mundy: An Account of the Terrible Kentucky Guerrilla of the Civil War Times," *The Register of the Kentucky Historical Society* 57, no. 4 (1959): 302-303.

5 Daniel Bates to Major General Love, undated, Indiana Legion Papers Box 32, Indiana State Archives; Starling, *History of Henderson County*, 388; *Evansville Daily Journal*, July 25, 1862, 2.

work securing the area. His men frequently skirmished with guerrillas that stole horses and "other war necessities" in the region. Gavin tried to root out small groups of Rebels, but like the other expeditions before him, yielded little in terms of results. While leading a small party into the interior, Gavin received a slight buckshot wound during a skirmish. Besides this, the 76th Indiana saw little action or excitement during its time in Henderson and the 30-day regiment suffered only light casualties. The lack of results led one soldier-correspondent to complain to the *Evansville Daily Journal*: "Every day and hour develops the necessity for the inauguration of a different system of fighting guerrillas—the present, will lose us two men to their one. Why do not the authorities at once delegate the power to annihilate and punish the harborers of these villains[?]"[6]

Another Indiana Legion company, the Union Rifles of Terre Haute, mounted its own expedition. The Rifles boarded the steamer *Hornet* and proceeded up the Green River. Searching the brush in vain, the company returned to Evansville empty-handed. After stopping in Newburg and Owensboro, the Rifles received orders to proceed to Henderson to supplement Foster's operations.[7]

Foster now commanded a department that included the 76th Indiana, which mustered out on August 20th, and the brand new 65th Indiana. Raised from President Lincoln's call for more volunteers, the 65th would not arrive in Henderson until the latter half of August. As a result, the two regiments did not serve together. According to Governor Morton, the 65th numbered 800 men. Along with the 65th, Foster eventually had over 1,000 men at his disposal. Companies A-D of the newly recruited 8th Kentucky Cavalry under the command of Col. James Shackelford, four companies of the newly mustered 4th Indiana Cavalry under the command of Captain (later Major) John Platter, some artillery, and the occasional force of Indiana Legion, would all eventually join Foster and the 65th in Henderson. Unfortunately, for Foster, the 63rd Illinois returned to its own district and base at Columbus, Kentucky, while the 65th arrived with only green recruits and Austrian Lorenz rifles. Private Thomas Henderson recalled, "I occupy the high position of private in Co. I, 65th Regt. Ind. Vol. Capt. Childs Commanding. We have been thrown without drill and almost without organization into the enemies [sic] country." The 65th would learn by doing.[8]

6 Starling, *History of Henderson County*, 391; *Evansville Daily Journal*, Aug. 8, 1862, 2.

7 *Evansville Daily Journal*, July 25, 1862, 2.

8 *Evansville Daily Journal*, July 28, 1862, 3; Bently, "The Civil War Memoir of Thomas Speed," 237-239; Richard J. Reid, *4th Indiana Cavalry Regiment: A History*, 9-10; Thomas D. Henderson to Jeff, Sep. 7, 1862, Bently Historical Library; 65th Indiana Infantry Ordnance Returns ending Dec. 31, 1862, M-128, Roll 4, National Archives.

Soldiers of the 134th Illinois in Columbus, Kentucky, some time in 1864. Though not involved with this story, these soldiers display some of the typical drill performed by Union troops. *LOC*

Not only piecemeal organization but bureaucratic incompetence hampered Foster's anti-partisan efforts. In the coming weeks, the 8th Kentucky's morale plummeted, and according to Kentucky's new governor, James F. Robinson, it teetered on the edge of mutiny. Though well-led and equipped, the troopers had yet to be officially mustered into Federal service. Private Thomas Speed, for example, traveled from Owensboro to Henderson to enlist on August 21st. Yet his regiment did not officially muster into service until the middle of September. An order that regiments must be mustered in at the same location kept the 8th, and soldiers like Speed, from receiving their pay—the regiment's three battalions were unfortunately dispersed throughout the state. Robinson informed Gen. Henry Halleck of the absurdity of this rule in Kentucky. He complained, "The order to muster only at regimental rendezvous is destroying our regiments. They cannot be moved from points where recruited, and unarmed, without danger of capture. They were promised pay and bounty. The failure to fulfill is demoralizing them. . . . If you will order your mustering officer to muster them I will advance the money." To this sensible suggestion, Halleck's reply showed his lack of understanding of the situation in Kentucky or, perhaps, of human nature. He rationalized, "Nearly every state is making the same application, and it would be impossible to supply mustering officers for separate detachments. If soldiers are ready to mutiny before they reach the rendezvous for mustering, they would be of little use afterward." Halleck failed to realize that other loyal states were not active war zones like Kentucky. Such a pedantic following of regulations in the Commonwealth was dangerous.[9]

The 4th Indiana Cavalry had yet to complete its organization, training, or receive its supplies when it arrived in Evansville on August 24th, over a month after the Newburgh raid. Only a lightly drilled battalion consisting of companies B, F, G, and K under the command of Capt. John A. Platter arrived in Henderson to bolster Foster's cavalry arm. Some companies in the battalion lacked basic equipment such as haversacks and canteens. The men who made up these companies might expect a terrible time in the hot and drought-stricken area.[10]

Even if the men had received ample supplies and quality drill, they still would not have been much use in a fight against partisans or guerrillas. Only 96 cavalry sabers and 79 Colt revolvers had reached the battalion. Ideal for close combat and saber charges, these weapons did not fit the fight against guerrillas who often stayed at a distance or fought from the brush. Even with this partial armament, the expectation to engage the enemy remained. With this knowledge, the recently promoted Major Platter wired Gov. Morton:

> Dear Sir: I deem it my duty to inform you of the insufficiency of our Indiana Cavalry with their present arms. We should by all means have carbines. . . . [W]e have to hunt down the enemy through thick woods and shoot them as they run often at great speed and distance for our pistols. . . . It was my understanding that the regiment was to be armed with carbines. If it is possible, Governor, send without delay carbines for my companies for I assure you we knead them now for service now in this country. Our cavalry force is insufficient. You are probably aware of this.

Platter received a response: "We have no carbines at this time, but will have them soon." According to the regiment's ordnance returns as late as December 1862, the Hoosier cavalrymen still lacked long arms.[11]

Foster eventually received better news. The raising of the 91st Indiana had begun in Evansville in August, but it would be some time before it could handle the duty in Henderson. The *Evansville Daily Journal* reported the ongoing need for supplies and equipment for the regiment. The new regiment's plight nearly mirrored that of the Hoosier cavalry in Henderson when the paper reported:

9 *OR* Series III, vol. 2, 505, 509.

10 Reid, *4th Indiana*, 9-12.

11 Reid, 4th Indiana, 9-12; 4th Indiana Cavalry Ordnance Returns ending Dec. 31, 1862, M-1281, Roll 2, National Archives.

This sketch of Lt. Colonel Francis (Frank) Erdelmeyer, drawn by 32nd Indiana soldier Adolf Metzner, depicts a typical Indiana mounted officer. *LOC*

> The supply of camp equipage is already exhausted, and the citizens will have to come forward and contribute to the support of the volunteers as they arrive until the government can make arrangements to relieve them of this charge. Would it not be well for the citizens to meet at the Library Rooms this evening in order to perfect arrangements for uniform action in the premises. The First Congressional District is in arms. Let our people show their appreciation of the gallant men who have enlisted, by promptly supplying their wants.

Though recruitment began in August, the 91st only slowly filled its companies by September. "We are requested to announce that recruiting for the 91st Regiment is to go on with advance pay and bounty until further orders," disclosed the *Evansville Daily Journal*. Weeks passed, however, before the 91st would be of any use in the field.[12]

For his part, Foster seemed to chase every rumor that arrived at his headquarters, adding reactionary leadership to a Union approach that showed a reluctance to commit sufficient forces for which his command seemed to be established. Uniontown, in Union County and west of Henderson, appeared to be a hotbed of irregular activity. The new district commander marched west with

12 The *Evansville Daily Journal*, Aug. 18, 1862, 3; The *Evansville Daily Journal*, Sep. 2, 1862, 2.

some of his infantry into the neighboring county, but his efforts were frustrated by an uncooperative populace and a disappearing enemy. The name of the small town proved to be an ironic fit. Foster later explained, "I found that a reign of terror existed in the adjoining county of Union. . . . I made an expedition into Union County with a view to overawe the rebel sympathizers . . . [b]ut it proved of no avail. The guerrillas easily got out of our way and the rebel residents denied all knowledge of them or of the [guerrilla] parties." Union county officials begged Foster to leave some of his men there to help suppress the Rebels, but the young colonel did not have men to spare. He marched back to Henderson empty-handed.[13]

Finally, in August, reliable information reached Foster that would allow him to strike a significant blow to Johnson's growing numbers. Johnson had stashed captured arms and equipment at Madisonville, only a day's march from Henderson. The new regiments joining Foster in Henderson would not have to wait long to get their first taste of action.[14]

Johnson's war was already having a strategic effect. These Henderson regiments, and the men who filled their ranks, could not aid in the larger war effort further south. Don Carlos Buell's Army of the Ohio was plodding through northern Alabama toward Chattanooga, and he would have benefitted from these extra regiments to guard sections of the Memphis and Charleston railroad, or in any future attack on the Confederate army. Trouble in his rear would complicate Buell's efforts.

13 Foster, *War Stories*, 101.

14 Terrell, Indiana in the War of the Rebellion, 149-150; Admire, Memoranda, 48.

Chapter 5

"An appearance rather unusual and romantic"

After the success of the Newburgh raid, Johnson's Breckinridge Guards grew rapidly. The press often exaggerated his accomplishments, even as far away as London. Eager recruits, swayed by the stories of "Stovepipe" Johnson, flocked to the regiment. Ironically, the Union press that despised Johnson may have aided recruitment by overstating his exploits. The early recruiting challenge no longer troubled Johnson and Martin. In fact, something rather the opposite may have been the case. Soon, he had more men than weapons.[1]

Since Johnson organized a partisan ranger regiment, he attracted more recruits than a typical cavalry regiment behind the lines. The Confederate Congress passed the Partisan Ranger Act in April 1862, a bill introduced by Kentucky Senator Henry C. Burnett which legalized recruitment of irregular forces. Though irregular, these regiments still functioned as part of the regular army. The act stipulated that commissioned Confederate officers would command the independent regiments operating behind Union lines, officers who would obey and coordinate with the regular army. The act did not give commanders the authority to create guerrilla outfits. Partisan regiments were supposed to receive uniforms, but this promise failed to materialize behind Union lines. Many potential partisans received assurances of operating in their home region with the opportunity to visit family on a semi-regular basis. In so doing, they avoided the often monotonous and

1 His own enlistment status continued to confound, however. By Aug. 1862, an official muster into Confederate service eluded Johnson. His Guards even lacked a regimental number. What he created would eventually receive the designation of the 10th Kentucky Partisan Rangers, though not until the late fall of 1862.

The look and attitude of these "Texas Rangers," drawn by Adolf Metzner, are a close comparison to that of many of Johnson's Partisan Rangers. *LOC*

strict wartime experiences of regular army soldiers. Many recruits believed that partisan life offered more chances for excitement, flexibility, and glory. Additionally, the act attempted to lure those fighters already engaged in guerrilla activity into legitimate service.[2]

However, the army did not always succeed in keeping partisan units under their control. Several examples in the Trans-Mississippi Theater show the risks in recruiting these types of units. When Gen. Earl Van Dorn vacated Arkansas for Tennessee in the spring of 1862, few conventional forces remained to defend against the Union forces moving into the state. Partisan Ranger and guerrilla units formed to the number of about 5,000 men. Technically, the partisans operated under the control of Gen. Thomas C. Hindman, but as the war progressed these units descended from following the laws of civilized warfare to the depths of "unrestrained guerrilla conflict." The situation deteriorated so badly in Arkansas that Confederate Col. Joseph Shelby received orders to destroy those guerrillas who habitually ignored army orders or preyed on civilians. In Tennessee, Confederate cavalry, such as Forrest's, moved into the western part of the state to bring independent units under their control. The longer these irregular forces operated away from the conventional army and Confederate government control, the less likely they were to remain legitimate soldiers and more likely to become brigands and thieves.[3]

Though the act designated partisans as Confederate soldiers under Confederate authority, a legal question arose as to their legitimacy as combatants. The United

2 Winthrop Rutherfurd, "The Partisan Ranger Act: The Confederacy and the Laws of War," *Louisiana Law Review*, vol. 79, no. 3 (2019), 821-824; Daniel E. Sutherland, *A Savage Conflict: The Decisive Role of Guerrillas in the American Civil War* (Chapel Hill, 2009), 93-94; Daniel E. Sutherland, "Guerrilla Warfare, Democracy, and the Fate of the Confederacy," *The Journal of Southern History* (May 2002), 260, 281; Lynn, *Company K*, 7. Several of these commands ceased to operate independently by 1864 and were absorbed into regular Confederate commands.

3 Mackey, *The Uncivil War*, 28-39.

States held a strong tradition of irregular warfare from the Revolutionary War, the War of 1812, and the various wars against Native Americans on the frontier. But in the Civil War, Union leaders, as well as Confederates to some extent, tended to believe the war should only be fought through conventional means. In 1862, Union leaders struggled with the question of how to treat partisans when captured. The debate lasted months, but by 1863, a clear definition arose from Union leadership on what it meant to be a partisan and the treatment such combatants should receive. Union leadership reluctantly agreed that partisan regiments were constituted of legitimate soldiers and officers conducting legitimate military operations. "The partisan leader commands a corps whose object is to injure the enemy by action separate from that of his own main army. The partisan acts chiefly . . . outside of or beyond the lines of operation of his own army. He is part and parcel of the army, and, as such, considered entitled to the privileges of the laws of war, so long as he does not transgress them," read General Orders No. 30.[4]

Unionists often mistook partisan rangers for outlaw guerrillas, bushwhackers, and criminal gangs. Granted, these groups did exist and often used the Confederate cause as an excuse to steal from and terrorize their Union neighbors. Unionists tended to describe any Confederate operating outside the regular army as a guerrilla, as was common in the press. However, the term *guerrilla* is not easy to define during the Civil War, especially in western Kentucky. Contemporary sources typically described a Confederate guerrilla as any irregular fighter using irregular tactics. Terms exist that factually describe irregular fighters, including raider, guerrilla, partisan ranger, bushwhacker, bandit, and even horse thief. In exploring their deeds and the makeup of their force, Johnson and Martin fall into the partisan ranger category due to their operations and the laws passed by the Confederate legal system.[5]

The nature of partisan ranger operations seems to place them, legally and morally, somewhere between illegitimate guerrilla activities and lawful cavalry actions. Many partisan ranger units tended to identify with the regular army, and eventually attached themselves to Confederate cavalry brigades. Johnson's partisan rangers are an example of this as they transitioned to regular cavalry in one of Gen. John H. Morgan's cavalry brigades in late 1862. Historian Scott Tarnowieckyi describes it best when he writes, "Partisan Rangers were essentially regular troops, recognized by the Confederate government as part of the military; they were led

4 *OR*, 33, 238; Rutherfurd, "The Partisan Ranger Act," 821-824.

5 Andrew Fialka, "Guerrillas in the Archive: Kentucky's Irregular War through the Governor's Eyes," *The Register of the Kentucky Historical Society* 116, no. 2, (2014), 212-213; Mackey, *The Uncivil War*, 5-23.

Guerrillas robbing a civilian as depicted in *Harper's Weekly*.

LOC

by commissioned officers, received pay from the government, wore proper military uniforms, followed the rules of war, and focused their attacks on legitimate military targets. Yet they fought in an irregular manner."[6]

In the late summer of 1862, Johnson and Martin's men diverged somewhat from this description, only because of their situation. No paymaster could reach them, and the majority wore no uniforms. They completely self-supplied as they attacked different Union garrisons. However, they did attempt to organize as a legitimate regiment, complete with officers, muster rolls, and some semblance of regular discipline. Yet they had not received official recognition as a part of the Confederate army by Confederate authorities due to their location behind Union lines. As partisan rangers, Johnson and Martin saw their actions and methods as irregular but viewed themselves as legitimate Confederate officers of a legitimate command carrying out attacks on military targets.[7]

In following the Confederate law, the regiment swore its soldiers into Confederate service upon enlistment. On August 19, 1862, recruit Benjamin T. Field and other men "joined the company of Captain Sam Taylor of Louisville

6 Tarnowieckyi, "Branded by the Lincolnites," 644-645.

7 Janet Hewitt, et. al., *Supplement to the Official Records of the Union and Confederate Armies* 3, Vol. 3, Part 1, 222-227; Johnson, *Partisan Rangers*, 112.

and grand nephew of General Zachary Taylor." The next day, Field properly swore into Confederate service for three years or the duration of the war. Several weeks later, another young recruit, James Munday, also took the Confederate oath. "We were drawn up in line and sworn in by Captain Merriwether [sic] many of us with dissatisfaction but all satisfied that it was our only alternative." As the regiment added more companies, the men elected officers and non-commissioned officers. Field and Munday were chosen as sergeants of their respective companies with the expectation that they would carry out the necessary duties of the rank. The experiences of these two recruits demonstrate how Johnson's partisan rangers, though operating behind Union lines, functioned nevertheless as a regular army regiment.[8]

Mustering a partisan ranger regiment proved dangerous for recruits and recruiters alike. Those men attempting to join Johnson's regiment faced a treacherous journey through multiple counties behind Union lines. One young man caught up in the thrills of Johnson's exploits was 20-year-old Benjamin T. Field. Field lived with his mother on a farm east of Owensboro in Daviess County, Kentucky. He previously served in a local company of the prewar Kentucky State Guard and now looked to ride with "Stovepipe" Johnson's Confederate regiment.[9]

Field and another young recruit, J. W. Hewitt, set out on August 12, 1862, to join the Breckinridge Guards. With Owensboro only 20 miles upriver from Newburgh, the news of that city's capture, and the subsequent drama in the region, had no doubt reached Field. Advised by one of their former teachers at the Owensboro Academy, the boys steered clear of the main public roads when traveling west to avoid capture by the local home guard or Federal soldiers in the area. They met Captain Hart, but he ordered them to go home and come back in a few days. "[T]o our horrow [sic] we had misunderstood him, as he wanted the men to know at all times to be in a state of readiness and at a moments notice meet at designated place," Field later explained. After Hart confided the details of their secret rendezvous, the boys stealthily made their way home. This incident is one example of the unconventional, secret, and unorthodox ways Johnson's Partisan Rangers often conducted their recruiting operations.[10]

8 Benjamin T. Field, *Benjamin T. Field Memoir Ca. 1912*, William W. Struck, ed. (Louisville, KY, 2013), 11.

9 Ibid., 1.

10 Ibid., 3-7. In searching the records of Johnson's 10th Kentucky Partisan Rangers, there is no record of a Captain Hart serving in the regiment. However, there is a Private Thomas Hart, and it is possible that Hart was not elected to command a company and had merely been using the rank of "captain." He is mentioned in the Nov. 10, 1862, edition of the *Evansville Daily Journal* as one of the guerrillas that entered West Franklin, Indiana on a small raid.

When the time came to meet with Hart again, just days later, Field and a few more recruits made a point to visit their sweethearts and say goodbye. Field received a handkerchief with his initials and a lock of his girl's hair. The new recruits armed themselves for the journey as there was always the chance they could run into Unionists. They were oblivious to the fact that there would be inadequate arms to distribute to the new recruits. He later wrote, "We did not succeed in getting many recruits but thought it not safe to longer remain. So getting our implements of war which consisted of a double barrel shotgun and a huge knife made by a blacksmith out of an old rasp we bid our good by to home and loved ones and started out to hunt for our little Southern Rights."[11]

Recruits attempting to join units such as Johnson's often faced the danger of finding themselves captured or killed before they even saw the regiment they wished to join. Though recruited under the Confederate Partisan Ranger Act of 1862, the Federal government and Union authorities in Kentucky still regarded fighters such as Field as little more than outlaw guerrillas and treated them as such, especially before they formally enlisted into Johnson's regiment. Like dozens of other recruits, Field was constantly at risk of capture as he moved throughout the county. One episode saw Field and his small party stop at a friendly house to rest, only to narrowly escape capture. A man alerted the recruits to the impending danger that the home guards would soon arrive to capture or kill the would-be Rebels. Field and the other men quickly fled. Ten minutes later the house was surrounded, empty of Confederates.[12]

In Daviess County, Federal authorities ruthlessly hunted down suspected guerrillas or those wishing to join them. Ella Johnson remembered one instance where her house became a scene of violence. She recalled:

> I was alone in my mother's room one day, playing with this trunk when suddenly a Confederate soldier sprang through the open window, followed quickly by two Yankees, who fired at him. They ran through the house and killed him at the door of the outside kitchen. I had run under the bed with my cherished trunk, thinking they had taken everything else and they'd take that also. I was too terrorized to answer when I heard my mother's agonized tones, "Ella! Ella! O my God! Where is Ella?" I finally gathered strength to crawl out and let her see that I hadn't been shot, but we were a shaken household that day.[13]

11 Field, *Memoir*, 7.

12 James B. Martin, "Black Flag Over the Bluegrass: Guerrilla Warfare in Kentucky, 1863-1865," *The Register of the Kentucky Historical Society* 86, no. 4 (1988): 352-75; Field, *Memoir*, 8-9.

13 Johnson, *Granny Remembers*, 18-19.

Federal antagonism of the local population, like that experienced by young Ella, continued to fuel support for irregulars such as Johnson, and spurred the enlistments of men like Field.

News of Johnson's exploits reached other young Kentucky men as well. James Munday had wanted to join the Confederate army since the beginning of the war, but his education at Georgetown College prevented him from doing so. He feared the possibility of Federal conscription, which gave him the needed excuse to enlist in Confederate service, as he did not wish to fight against his "cherished principles." Munday and a group of men from Hancock County, Kentucky, believed it would be too difficult to join the main Confederate force under Gen. Braxton Bragg, but they had heard of the now famous "Stovepipe" Johnson and his partisans, and that the regiment operated in their own region. The idea of fighting close to home sounded agreeable to many, one of the most alluring aspects of a partisan ranger regiment. Johnson's camp was their destination, as it had been for Benjamin Field a few weeks earlier in August.[14]

One night in early September, Munday and five others from Hancock County met a second group of about 40 men at Iron Hill in eastern Daviess County. At 11:00 p.m. that evening, the man who would become Munday's captain, Clay Merriwether, led the group toward the Green River, avoiding Federal patrols along the way. The trek went on without incident, though the lack of rest and sleep proved to be a challenge for the new recruits. When the sun came up the next morning, the men were exhausted. Munday recorded that the journey had "almost worn [them] out with fatigue and without a moment of time for rest. . . . [A]fter hastily refreshing ourselves with a cool drink we moved swiftly on." Along the way they skirted a small community where several of the Union Home Guards lived and searched individual houses for muskets. Though not official Union soldiers, Munday's disdain for the Home Guards rings clear in his journal. He notes that they neared a "Union Settlement well protected by those 'gallant defenders' of our life, liberty and property, the Home Guards." Other dangers revealed themselves in other ways as well. Traveling on select roads was paramount to avoid Union patrols and garrisons. The recruits came across one man who gave them directions that would have led them straight into Union forces. The civilian turned out to be an officer of the local Home Guards.[15]

Visually, Johnson's regiment, from officers down to the enlisted men, did not look spectacular. On August 29th, Field met his commander: "I had the pleasure of seeing our commander Col A. R. Johnson for the first time. We with the fources

14 James A. Munday, *Diary of James A. Munday*, L.B. Cravens, ed. (Owensboro, KY, 1940), 1.

15 Munday, *Diary*, 1-2.

[sic] he already had gave us the appearance of a formidable cavalry squadron." Another recruit recorded that the other officers of the regiment looked uninspiring and disappointing. They did not match his vision of the men who had helped Johnson win so many impressive victories. He described Robert Martin as "a man very agreeable indeed with nothing remarkable about him to be sure, but without any indication of military ability in his conduct of affairs, without even the necessary dignity of a commander." He described Major Owen as having "a countenance rather unpleasant."[16]

When Munday first reached the regiment's camp, he was similarly dismayed. What he saw did not meet his expectations after hearing of the daring exploits of the Breckinridge Guards. Instead, they were "differently dressed, variously armed, and poorly equipped, apparently without discipline, regularity or order." Munday waited all day for a high-ranking officer to appear, hoping that some sort of discipline might materialize in camp, but nothing changed. He also complained of the obvious lack of military bearing in his fellow recruits and the officers that led them. Officers were still learning how to provide rations or supplies to the men and horses, and how to get the men under control. "All day we waited the appearance of Col. Johnson, Lieut. Col. Martin or Major Scoby hoping to see the camp assume an appearance of military discipline, and wanting some provisions made for ourselves and horses. Neither of these officers came and to add to the unpleasantness of our situation but little of the provision came," he wrote.[17]

Johnson's regiment was always going to have weapon and supply challenges as long as it operated behind Union lines, but the rapid increase of recruits magnified the problem. Though the Partisan Ranger Act stipulated that partisans in Confederate service wear army uniforms, circumstances in western Kentucky produced a different reality. One captured Union soldier recorded that when he encountered the Partisan Rangers on September 1, 1862, he noticed a lack of uniformity among the men. "Johnson and his surgeon were the only men who wore anything like uniforms," he remembered; "[n]one of his men were uniformed." Another Union captive noted, "They are ununiformed."

Just as with the sporadic weapons supply, so too did uniforms arrive piecemeal, though not through regular Confederate supply channels. During the capture of one town in August 1862, for example, the women of the community gave Johnson's men the caps originally made for the 49th Tennessee. When Munday first entered Johnson's camp, he was shocked at the different ways each man was dressed. Most wore civilian clothes, while others wore pieces of pre-war militia uniforms. One

16 Ibid., 5; Field, *Memoir*, 10.

17 Munday, *Diary*, 3.

of the first officers he met was Capt. Lorenzo D. Fisher. Munday described him as "carelessly dressed, partly in the old State Guard uniform, he presented an appearance (to me) rather unusual and romantic as he slung at his side his deadly Enfield and mounted to lead the way to Sulphur Springs." Of other enlisted men, he wrote that these "Partizan Rangers attired as usual with great variety and little elegance," though he later characterized some as "dashing horsemen."[18]

Captain Fisher typified many of Johnson's Partisan Rangers, whose clothing belied the term "uniform" and who bore a hodge-podge of arms, from coveted Enfield rifles to unreliable shotguns and family squirrel guns. The regiment maintained an assortment of arms from the raids at Newburg, Hopkinsville, Clarksville, and Uniontown. One Union soldier later recounted that his captors brought their recently captured weapons to their makeshift base of supplies to convert them for use on horseback. "The arms captured at Clarksville were brought to Madisonville, and last Friday and Saturday men were at work cutting off the bands to adapt the guns to the use of cavalry. The country is swarming with mounted rebels who are armed with shotguns and captured muskets and well mounted." Many of the recruits brought their weapons from home. Confiscating weapons from Unionists became another way to procure arms. Munday's company approached an isolated home of a supposed Unionist and Home Guard captain to take his weapon. The man had hidden the gun so well the Confederates could not find it. As the recruits gave up the search and began leaving the home, a young woman appeared and "commenced a round of the grossest abuse, when she reached the climax that 'hell was our portion.'" Munday asked his new captain not to respond to the woman. The young recruit sarcastically recalled that they left with the most profound respect for Unionist women and never found the weapon.[19]

On September 8, 1862, the regiment again found itself scattered throughout the region and three companies—Merriwether's, Fisher's, and Schofield's—eventually came together somewhere west of the Green River. While encamped, a Mr. Ray from Daviess County visited their bivouac and presented the partisans with "beautiful flags made by the ladies in Daviess." Such events seem trivial, but they illustrate the differences between partisan rangers and guerrillas. Partisans, as regular soldiers, elected company officers and non-commissioned officers and swore their recruits into Confederate service as if it was the Army of Tennessee. With their flags they presented themselves as legitimate soldiers, very unlike

18 Munday, *Diary*, 2, 5; Ransom Hawley, notes in *Partisan Rangers*, no date, Vigo County Public Library (hereafter "VCPL").

19 Munday, *Diary*, 1-2; *Arms and Equipment of the Confederacy* (New York, 1991), 44-45; *Evansville Daily Journal*, Aug. 29, 1862, 2.

guerrillas. Though drill and discipline remained problematic, the regiment still functioned as an army unit.[20]

Life in the Breckinridge Guards included occasions where the men would disperse and blend in with the population to conduct improvised operations. One Union captive learned firsthand how Johnson's men operated and informed the *Evansville Daily Journal* of their frequent disappearances into the countryside to hide, rest, and refit. "They often disperse to their homes, meeting at appointed rendezvous," he reported. Sometimes the men dispersed by companies instead of by small squads or individually. Such operations often occurred before the recruits could receive proper training or drill. James Munday's small company received orders to attack Spottsville, in Henderson County, and capture a group of Federal cavalry reportedly there, only two days after his formal enlistment. Fortunately, for the untried and completely green partisans, the Union horsemen had already departed. Over the following days, his company tried its best to disrupt Union steamboat movements on the Green River. They only achieved slight damage to the lock near Spottsville, which did little to interrupt river navigation. The *Evansville Daily Journal* reported, "a ton or two of rock had been thrown in above the upper gate. As the navigation of the Green River is a matter of indifference to the Government, the people of the Green River country will be allowed to enjoy the privilege of having their trade cut off for a while." When companies tried to accomplish successes on their own, without Johnson's tactical leadership, the results were often less than stellar.[21]

The soldiering life was not a comfortable experience for Munday or Field. Plentiful orchards loaded with peaches and apples did not make up for the days of stifling heat, and there remained always the possibility of a deadly clash with the Yankees. The nights were often miserable, with many spent in the saddle. The regiment possessed few tents, except for those captured from Union soldiers and supply dumps. Munday recalled that rain fell on him more times in his first few days as a soldier than ever before in his whole life; Field remembered those rainy nights as particularly demoralizing. The partisans slept in haystacks, barns, or whatever comfortable spot they could find. Munday wrote that on one particularly wet evening they "encamped for the night in a cool fitful shower the very thoughts of which made some of the boys very sick and they went to the neighboring farm." With the constant movement of the force, it was difficult for those who became ill to keep up with the regiment. There were several instances where they had to leave sick and wounded comrades behind at friendly homes until they could

20 Munday, *Diary*, 3.

21 *Evansville Daily Journal*, Sep. 15, 1862, 2; Aug. 29, 1862, 2.

be nursed back to health. In some cases, these men fell into the hands of Union forces patrolling the area. Being away from home and separated from families for the first time also wore on some of the new soldiers. While his company moved across the countryside in September, Munday experienced the melancholy feeling of homesickness. "The day in the woods was dreary, not alone from the gloominess of the weather for short as our change had been the day brought sad recollections of a home we could not reach and sadder memories of our anxious friends," Munday recorded.[22]

Discipline varied in the regiment. Munday complained about the absence of morals amongst some of the command. As a regular church attender in civilian life, the lack of proper Sabbath observations particularly vexed him. "Our second Sunday from home was in no way distinguished from other days and we scarcely knew when it came," he wrote. Field also commented on the paucity of holiness in the regiment. His first Sunday spent as a soldier was "Quite a contrast to the way I was brought up and always to reverence the Sabbath and keep it holy."[23]

Before his election to sergeant, Field and other soldiers were tasked with obtaining supplies for the regiment, which meant procuring them from civilians. They "captured" five horses and some guns from "the quiet peacible citizens." This part of the war did not set well with Field. He had wanted to fight as a real soldier, not steal from the populace. In another similar incident, Field recorded:

> Allow me to relate here some of the doings of that eventful day which will be a black spot on my character the balance of my life. Some three men representing themselves as the red shirt gang joined our squad. One called himself Sue Monday who afterward became notorious and claimed at that time to be held in great terrow [sic] by the yankees. Greenhorns as we were we were easily duped. . . . It made no difference to him whether the people were home or not. He entered and would appropriate any old gun or any thing that suited his fancy. At one place we stopped which he said was an old Home guards house no one was at home and the faithful watch dog defied us to enter. He deliberately shot the faithful animal and broke into the house and ransacked every drawer even turned the bed up as he said looking for arms. I thought differently and refused to accompany him any further.[24]

22 Munday, *Diary*, 4.

23 Ibid., 5; Field, *Memoirs*, 7.

24 Field, *Memoir*, 11-13. Field mentions that this Sue Mundy was part of the Red Shirt gang, though the name "Sue Mundy" was not a name used for guerrilla Marcellus Jerome Clarke until later in the war. However, Clarke did serve briefly in the regiment.

This side of partisan warfare would continue to rankle Field's ethical beliefs. Even though they had joined a partisan ranger regiment, many of the men lacked horses. One day in August, an officer instructed Field to procure mounts with seven other men. "We pushed on in our unholy business and succeeded in securing 4 horses against the remonstrations of the men and the tears and entreaties of the ladies. I now began to see what the exigencies of war ment [sic]," he bemoaned. Just as the increased presence of Union troops led some Kentuckians to sympathize more with the South, the regiment's procurement practices exacerbated and inflamed local prejudice against the Confederates.[25]

Johnson struggled to shape his men into proper soldiers. While operating behind Union lines, creating a large camp for training was not practical or possible. For many new partisans, company or battalion drill was a luxury that their frequent movements would not allow; combat experience itself would have to suffice. Fights among the men broke out, accidental weapons discharges remained a constant threat, and laziness abounded. One soldier disobeyed orders, which prompted Field, as sergeant, to report the man to his officers. The soldier became upset over the accusation and threatened to fight his own sergeant. "He swore he would whip any man . . . and throwing off his coat and popping his fists in such a demonstrative way I thought a scrap was inevitable. His threats and denunciations were so noisy that the boys began to follow [us]," he recalled. No fight occurred as witnesses corroborated Field's accusations. On another occasion in August, Field fell asleep while on picket duty, during which time his own comrades stole his weapon, "which frightened me very much when I awoke." During that same month, one of the new recruits fired his weapon, wounding one man and causing the whole company to take positions to face an ambush from an enemy that was not there. Instead of caring for horses, drilling, or maintaining their weapons, the men in Field's company often visited nearby farms for food and entertainment. "After trimming the locks of a few of the boys and supper had been served we had a little dance as the old man had two or three girls. After the frollick [sic] I made my bed between two haystacks and thought it was bully," related Field.[26]

On September 15th, Munday and the other new recruits moved into a camp with several other companies after a "tiresome" ride through rough terrain. They met pickets along the road and after riding over a hillside, Munday finally saw the regiment that he joined, though still not fully concentrated. To him it was full of "lazy groups of Partizan Rangers." That night, 350 men appeared for dress parade—at least their meager attempt at one. Munday, still unsatisfied with the

25 Ibid., 11-13.

26 Field, *Memoir*, 7-8.

discipline of the regiment, complained: "to an unpracticed eye we seemed a host, but to us, in our disappointment we seemed but a handful." He also saw the cannon that the regiment captured from Union forces, soon to become famous, and remarked, "We saw our whole array of artillery (our four pounder), and we looked with some interest down the rough threat of the 'Clarksville Cannon' of more celebrity than size."[27] Munday was not alone in his dissatisfaction. How this ragtag group of Rebels had experienced so much success was a wonder to the new partisan. The first impressions of men such as Field and Munday did not match the romantic images of partisan warfare which many of them had carried. Johnson would manage to win some remarkable victories despite the obvious shortcomings. But the deficiencies in discipline, arms, and military experience would eventually tell.

27 Munday, *Diary*, 5.

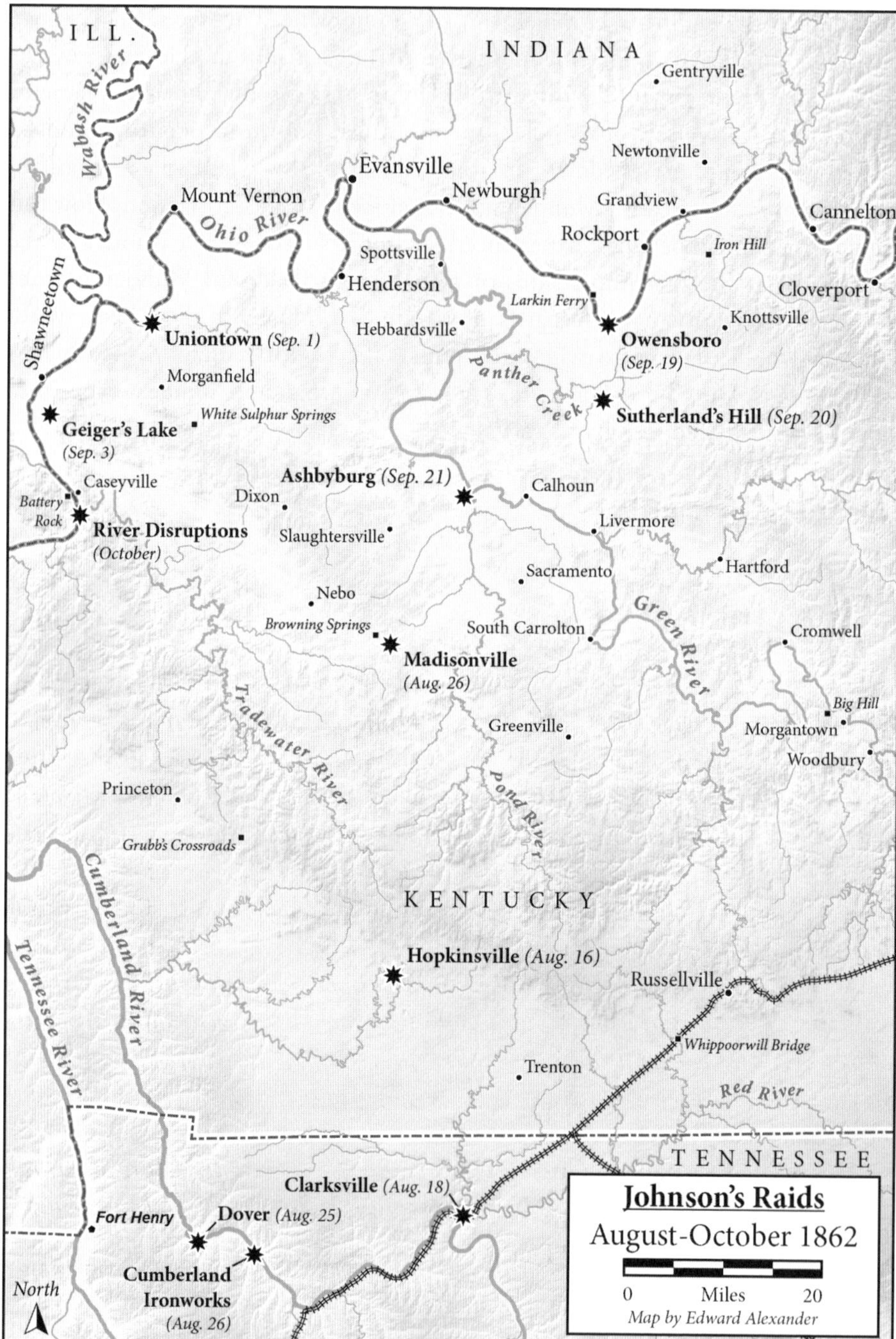

ILL.
INDIANA
Wabash River
Gentryville
Newtonville
Evansville
Mount Vernon
Newburgh
Grandview
Cannelton
Ohio River
Rockport
Iron Hill
Spottsville
Henderson
Cloverport
Shawneetown
Larkin Ferry
Knottsville
Hebbardsville
Uniontown (Sep. 1)
Owensboro
(Sep. 19)
Morganfield
Panther Creek
Sutherland's Hill (Sep. 20)
White Sulphur Springs
Geiger's Lake
(Sep. 3)
Ashbyburg (Sep. 21)
Caseyville
Calhoun
Dixon
Battery Rock
River Disruptions
(October)
Livermore
Slaughtersville
Hartford
Sacramento
Nebo
Green River
Browning Springs
South Carrolton
Cromwell
Madisonville
(Aug. 26)
Tradewater River
Big Hill
Greenville
Morgantown
Woodbury
Pond River
Princeton
Grubb's Crossroads
Cumberland River
KENTUCKY
Tennessee River
Hopkinsville (Aug. 16)
Russellville
Whippoorwill Bridge
Trenton
Red River
TENNESSEE
Clarksville (Aug. 18)
Fort Henry
Dover (Aug. 25)
Cumberland Ironworks
(Aug. 26)
North
Johnson's Raids
August-October 1862
0 Miles 20
Map by Edward Alexander

Chapter 6

"What an insignificant little cuss"

By August 1862, the Breckinridge Guards had grown to more than 300 men. Stories of Johnson's exploits against Union forces delivered more recruits than the arms and food needed to supply them. The Newburgh raid helped in this regard, yet shortages continued. Johnson looked around for another similar venture. Hopkinsville, Kentucky, located in the southwestern part of the state, presented itself as a viable target. If Johnson and Martin could surprise whatever Union troops were there, they could capture Hopkinsville's weapons, equipment, and supplies with little fighting. Johnson decided to make a move for the city.[1]

Attacking Hopkinsville was a risky gamble. Some Hopkinsville Home Guards carried the new Henry repeating rifles, which easily outclassed the medley of old shotguns, muskets, and squirrel guns the guards bore, meaning that Hopkinsville would not be easy, especially if other Union troops were present. At Newburgh, Johnson had caught convalescing soldiers with their guard down. The men of Hopkinsville, however, were in the town precisely to guard it from Rebel activity. Only Union negligence would cause a repeat of Newburgh.[2]

Once the two young commanders made the decision to move on the town, Martin ventured ahead of the column. In an 1898 issue of *Confederate Veteran Magazine,* Martin recalled the operation:

1 Johnson, *Partisan Rangers,* 112; Tarnowieckyi, "Branded by the Lincolnites," 659.

2 Martin, "Service by Kentucky Cavalry," 114.

> Col. Starling was then in command of about two hundred men at Hopkinsville, and, as they were the handiest, our column was headed for them within two hours after organization. As was a custom with me, I was soon miles on the road, with one picked man to personally look the situation over before the attack. I spent a couple of hours in the city. We left our horses a convenient distance, outside, pickets having been flanked. After a midnight lunch with a friend I set out to join Johnson.[3]

Thanks to the intelligence Martin gathered, Johnson learned that the Federal force in Hopkinsville had been ordered east toward Bowling Green. Only 200 men of the local militia remained; Union negligence would once again underwrite Johnson's success. Thanks to his growing force, and unlike Newburgh, Johnson did not need to bluff to capture the garrison. Dealing with poorly trained militia, Johnson planned to capture the enemy before they could mount an effective resistance.

At dawn on August 16, the Confederates rushed into the city and completely surprised the sleeping home guards. Hopkinsville had been even easier than Newburgh. Martin described the simplicity of the affair when he later noted, "At sunrise we had met the enemy, and 'they were ours.'" The news of Hopkinsville's capture made it into the papers three days later. The *Louisville Journal* reported, "Five or six hundred rebel guerillas entered Hopkinsville . . . on Saturday evening last. They seized all the arms they could find in the place, including fifteen Henry rifles, and then left for the south. The guerillas were commanded by 'Col. Johnson, of the Breckinridge Legion.'"[4]

The operation yielded favorable, if incomplete, results. The raiders captured 120 stands of arms, including a few Henry Rifles, plus 60 weapons from paroled militia. But sufficient stocks of ammunition continued to elude Johnson. Nor did the captured weapons alleviate the arms shortage in the ever-growing regiment. Confederate supplies could not reach him: not only were operations behind enemy lines problematic and dangerous, but the regiment never remained in one area for a substantial amount of time. And his command was not yet formally attached to a field army or complementing cavalry force, making him ineligible for supplies even if they could reach him. Johnson quickly came to realize that continued improvisation was the only solution to his logistics dilemma.[5]

Clarksville, Tennessee, offered an even more tempting prize. For the last several months, Union forces had transformed the city into one of the key supply dumps

3 Ibid., 114.

4 Martin, "Service by Kentucky Cavalry," 114; Johnson, *Partisan Rangers*, 112; *Louisville Journal*, Aug. 19, 1862, 3.

5 Johnson, *Partisan Rangers*, 112; *Houston Tri-Weekly Telegraph*, Nov. 26, 1862.

for the Department of the Ohio under the jurisdiction of Gen. Don Carlos Buell and his Army of the Ohio. Clarksville's position on the northern and eastern shore of the Cumberland River made it an ideal location for Union supplies moving toward Nashville and Buell's army. A severe drought in the summer and fall of 1862 meant that much of the Cumberland was not navigable, however, stranding large caches of stocks in Clarksville. Clarksville's burgeoning wharves presented a tantalizing target for Johnson and his ill-supplied raiders.[6]

Union commanders still had not learned their lesson. Only a few companies of the 71st Ohio, commanded by Col. Rodney Mason, guarded the town. The other companies were 40 miles away at Dover, Tennessee. The 71st Ohio did not enjoy a laudable reputation in 1862. The regiment, and Mason in particular, faced accusations of cowardice during the battle of Shiloh. Depositions eventually exonerated both unit and commander. Unfortunately for Mason, these depositions had not yet been taken in August 1862, and the affair at Clarksville would only darken his already tarnished reputation.[7]

Mason established his headquarters in the town some distance from the main camp. However, the myriad responsibilities required of his understrength regiment resulted in his men being spread over a wide area. He only had companies C, D, E, F, and K on site, a total of only 225 men present for duty in Clarksville itself. Of those 225, "22 were on river guard, 7 on telegraph guard, and 6 out on telegraph line, repairing it—in all 35; leaving those who ought to have been in camp 190; but of those only 152 were reported to me as in camp, including the camp guard of 42 men," Mason complained. "Where the other 38 were I do not know." Another officer recounted that at least 20 men were onboard the smaller supply vessels destined for Nashville, further depleting his already thin force. Aware of increasing guerrilla activity in the region, Mason requested reinforcements and artillery from several superiors. Every request was ignored, a symptom of the complicated administration of the redrawn boundaries between Grant and Buell's areas of responsibility. Though the 71st belonged to Grant's army, Buell commanded the area where they operated. Neither commander proved to be any help to Mason's unenviable situation at Clarksville. He tried to report the dire situation, but a small garrison behind the lines did not interest the army commanders.[8]

6 Martin, "Service by Kentucky Cavalry," 114.

7 Rodney Mason, *Testimony Submitted to the President of the United States by Rodney Mason, Late Colonel of 71st Ohio Volunteer Infantry, With His Application for the Appointment of a Court of Inquiry or Court Martial to Investigate Charges Against Him* (Springfield, OH, 1863), 6, 19-21.

8 *OR* 16:1, 862-865; Mason, *Rodney Mason Testimony to Abraham Lincoln*, 23-24; Martin Stewart, *Redemption: The 71st Ohio Volunteer Infantry in the Civil War* (Troy, OH, 2012), 99; Noah Andre Trudeau, "Fields Without Honor: Two Affairs in Tennessee," *Civil War Times Illustrated*, 44.

There was some virtue in Johnson's lack of formal recognition for, unlike Mason, he was not burdened by a ponderous command structure. He and his men could strike quickly, and soon, with Clarksville less than 30 miles from Hopkinsville. The city did have something that Newburgh and Hopkinsville did not—rifle pits armed with a small cannon and veteran troops with officers itching for a chance at redemption. But it would be difficult for the few companies of Ohioans to offer stout resistance from their spread-out positions if the Confederates dashed upon them quickly. Johnson could also count on the cooperation of the sympathetic population, as many of Clarksville's citizens detested life under the Yankees.[9]

Another partisan commander, Col. Thomas Woodward and his 100 Kentucky and Tennessee fighters, joined Johnson as he moved on Clarksville. Woodward had attended West Point, Harvard, and Yale, but never completed his studies at any of the schools for various disciplinary infractions. Woodward's physical stature interested contemporaries as much as his personality. He weighed no more than 110 pounds, stood well below the average height, and sported long flowing hair with a drooping mustache. One local history describes Woodward as "that gallant but ill-fated officer." Woodward faced similar challenges to Johnson, including recruitment and supply issues. In Johnson, Woodward found a kindred spirit and, for a time, a beneficial partnership.[10]

Johnson and Woodward hoped to take the entire Federal force and its crucial store of supplies in Clarksville. The plan called for Woodward to approach the town from the east, then surround the Federal camp at Stewart College and demand its surrender. Meanwhile, Johnson and some of his men planned to dash through town where Mason had his quarters and capture him. Johnson prepared to destroy the supplies on the riverbank if the Ohioans refused to surrender.[11]

On August 18, 1862, the plan went into motion. Johnson rode out of Hopkinsville at dusk the previous night and arrived on the outskirts of Clarksville near dawn, undetected. One Buckeye of Mason's regiment recalled the following year that Johnson and Woodward's horsemen quietly captured several of the Federal pickets before an alarm could be raised. Woodward sent a messenger under a flag of truce right up to the works of the camp and demanded its surrender.

9 *OR* 16:1, 865–868; Johnson, *Partisan Rangers*, 112.

10 Johnson, *Partisan Rangers*, 112; Charles Meacham, *Meacham's History of Christian County Kentucky: From Oxcart to Airplane* (Evansville, IN, 1974); Benjamin Franklin Cooling, *Fort Donelson's Legacy: War and Society in Kentucky and Tennessee, 1862-1863* (Knoxville, TN, 1997), 97; William Henry Perrin, *County of Christian* (Chicago, 1884), 174-175. In his report to President Jefferson Davis, Johnson states that Woodward only had 60 men on hand, while the claim for 100 appears in his later memoirs.

11 Johnson, *Partisan Rangers*, 112-113.

Colonel Thomas Woodward. Allegedly, Colonel Mason paid for this photograph while in Clarksville. *LOC*

Robert Martin wrote in *Confederate Veteran Magazine* that he was the one that approached the Union works:

> Without checking the column, I did not stop till uncomfortably close to the enemy. . . . In the mean time not a shot had been fired except a few scattering ones by Johnson's men in the city to clinch our bluff. I sent in a flag, demanding a surrender. Col. Mason sent for me, and I rode inside his position, where he stood. Formal salutes were passed between us. He seemed to cavil and to show fight. At this junction an immense rebel yell came from the north side, which up to that time had been quiet. Mason asked what command that was, and I told him it was Col. Woodward coming.

As the rangers awaited the reply, Johnson made it to Mason's quarters, but he had escaped moments before. Unbeknownst to Johnson and Woodward, civilian eyes friendly to the Union spotted a portion of their approaching column and gave the Federals nearly 30 minutes to prepare for an attack. Mason slipped back to Stewart College where he met with a number of his officers. What happened next differs between Union and Confederate sources.[12]

In official Union reports, the officers met inside the college before Mason returned and debated the issue of surrender. Mason claimed that with his effective troop strength at 175, he stood no chance against the 800 he believed to be surrounding his camp. Not only were there 800 Rebels, but many of them were regular army sent home to recruit, or so he believed. Mason, and nearly all the interviewed officers, also claimed that the ranks of the Southerners swelled by the presence of armed citizens coming to the scene with their own weapons. Not only did the opposing numbers seem nearly insurmountable in a firefight but the camp

12 Johnson, *Partisan Rangers*, 112; Martin, *Kentucky Cavalry*, 114.

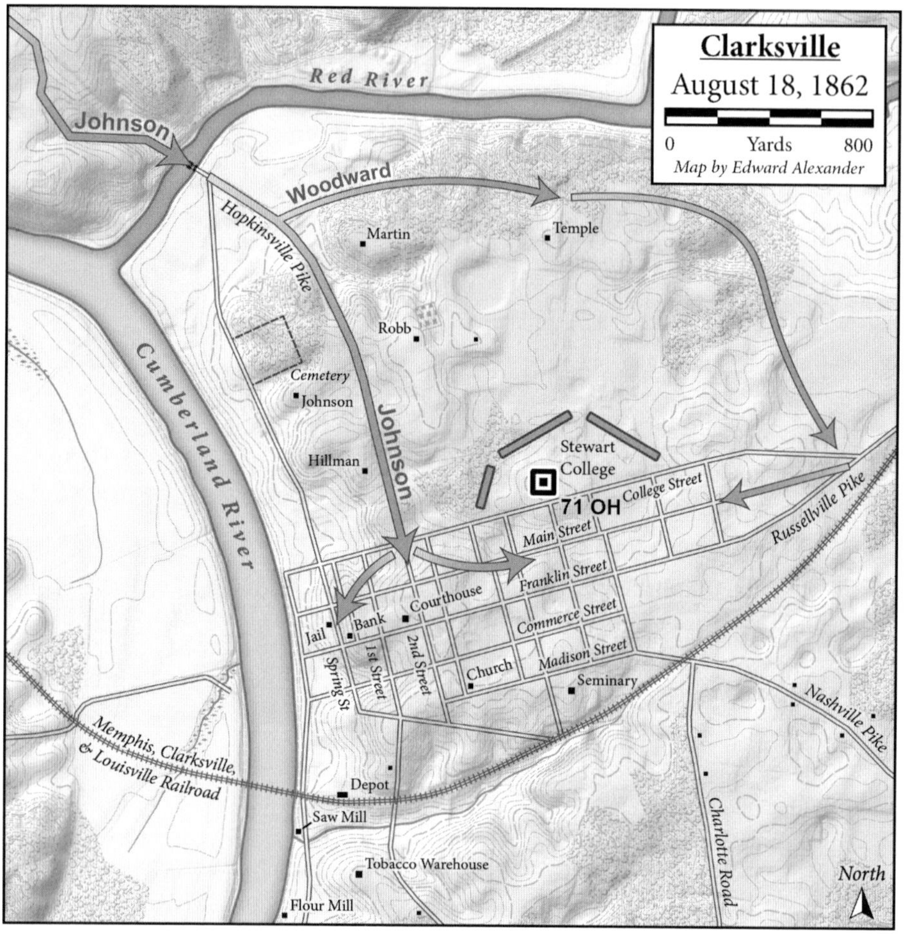

could not withstand a siege in its condition. Many officers remarked that the camp had less than a day's supply of water and only two days' worth of rations. The rangers also possessed artillery, while the Federals only had one barely serviceable piece. It is interesting that in all the depositions taken in the months following the Clarksville scandal, none of the 71st Ohio officers ever mentioned that they possessed a gun. There were scattered mentions in other sources of "a little bell-muzzled piece Col. Andrews had patched up at Donelson and brought along—a grapeshot could not be put in its chamber; we have no ammunition for that!" Mason later decried the piece as nothing more than "a little gun picked up at the rolling-mill and of no account whatever."[13]

13 *OR* 16:1, 863-865, 869; *Supplement to the Official Records of the Union and Confederate Armies*, 186, 583.

Apparently, the Confederates allowed Lt. Col. George W. Andrews to pass along their lines. He ascertained that the enemy contained over 400 cavalry drawn up in line, some armed with new 16-shot repeating rifles, the rest with a mixed array of weapons. Second Lieutenant Isaac Mann recalled:

> While the flag of truce was in camp, pending the negotiation to surrender, having had pointed out to me the location of a battery, I concluded I would go and see what there was of it. I went down to the corn-field at the right of our camp, and there found a gun. The gun squad were lying about the gun, and I asked if they had any objection to my examining the gun, and they said, 'No.' I went up to the gun and as near as I can judge it was a twelve-pound howitzer. Two limbers were standing near, and I asked where the other gun was, and they pointed it out to me across the field and further to the north. It was in sight, and was the gun that was opposite to Capt. Clark's company as mentioned in his deposition. I returned to camp, and reported to the officers what I had seen before the final vote was taken.

In recalling the discussion among the officers, T. T. More remembered Lieutenant Colonel Andrews stating that the Confederates were "the best armed body of men he ever saw."[14]

In his memoirs, Johnson portrays a livelier event:

> I decided to rush into the college, find the colonel [Mason] and compel him to surrender. Giving Captain Fisher and the other captains orders to come immediately to me, if they heard firing within the building. I sprang over the picket fence, entered the house and ran up the stairs to Colonel Mason's room. There was but one sentinel on the upper floor, and leveling my pistol at him, I ordered him to open the door to the commandant's apartment. The command was obeyed, and on entering the room, I found the colonel in his night-clothes and four of his officers gathered around him. The Union commander was very pale and excited and decidedly in favor of surrender. Three of the captains sided with him, while the other fiercely opposed the propositions. Why these belligerents were not downstairs commanding and supporting their companies who were hesitating and wavering as to what course to pursue, I do not undertake to say. But I had the drop on them, which gave me an advantage from which they could not recover, and the entire surrender was soon made without the firing of a gun inside or outside of the headquarters.[15]

Martin also related his own version years later. "He [Mason] turned to one of his staff and ordered him to place his men in line and stack arms, at the same time

14 *OR* 16:1, 867-868; Mason, *Rodney Mason Testimony to Abraham Lincoln*, 14-15, 23.

15 Johnson, *Partisan Rangers*, 113.

The Castle Building of Stewart College. The building no longer exists and is now the campus of Austin Peay State University. *The Archives at Rhodes College, Memphis, Tennessee*

handing me his sword, which I returned to him. We were not long in taking charge of the arms and reversing the muzzle of the artillery, the first we had captured. Johnson, upon receiving my message . . . was so astonished that he came himself to verify it." After the formal surrender, Mason, amused by Woodward's appearance, offered to pay to have his image captured by a local photographer so that he could "show my friends what an insignificant little cuss I surrendered to." Woodward agreed. The stories of the circumstances of the surrender by Johnson, Martin, and the Union officers are all different, and it should be assumed that Johnson's version was only first-rate storytelling.[16] Regardless of the particulars, it is clear once again that surprise and deception had allowed Johnson's Rangers to overcome and embarrass a Union regiment.

The military debacle at Clarksville, especially the apparent disgraceful behavior by Union officers whose reputations had already been compromised, became well-known throughout the nation within a few days. Only cowardice seemed to explain why a colonel in the United States service surrendered a fortified camp with nearly 300 well-armed Shiloh veterans, military stores, and artillery, and all without a shot fired.

16 Martin, *Service by Kentucky Cavalry*, 114; Stewart, *Redemption*, 102.

Johnson's exploits were becoming a serious public relations problem for the Union. The *Cleveland Daily Leader* ripped Mason for his actions. The disgusted paper wrote, "The surrender of Clarksville, Tenn., by Colonel Rodney Mason, of the 71st Ohio, was a piece of unmitigated, disgraceful cowardice. . . . Further inflaming the story was the report that Mason and Woodward made speeches complimenting each other." The *Cincinnati Commercial* reported, "Col Rodney Mason . . . has completed his career of cowardice by surrendering his whole command at Clarksville to an inferior force of guerrillas. . . . The subject is too disgusting to dwell upon. We advise Colonel Mason to keep away from Ohio." The *McArthur Democrat* of McArthur, Ohio, also slammed Mason for the surrender. "We have no language to express our feelings with reference to this disgraceful transaction. . . . Mason and Woodruff [Woodward], who commanded the guerrillas, made 'you tickle me and I'll tickle you' speeches. . . . Ohio will very gladly spare the Colonel from the ranks of her citizens."

The story of complimentary speeches made for good reading to an outraged citizenry, but Mason's officers later spoke to the "speeches" in question. Lieutenant Thomas Moore attempted to set the record straight and explained:

> At sun-down our men were drawn up in line, and the garrison flag taken down by Col. Mason and myself. We folded the flag, and Col. Mason said: 'Col. Woodard, in accordance with a stipulation in our surrender, I deliver you our garrison flag.' Col. Woodard not taking it said, 'Col. Mason, I suppose you love and regard your flag as I do my own. You will oblige me by keeping it.' Col. Mason said: 'I thank you.' These were the complimentary speeches spoken of in the newspapers.[17]

President Lincoln's judgment was the most determined. He ordered Mason cashiered from the service for repeated acts of cowardice in the face of the enemy, along with several other officers of the regiment.[18]

Some of the captured Federal soldiers of the 71st Ohio made their way north with the very men who captured them. These men traveled to Madisonville, Kentucky, and then walked the remainder of the route to Union-controlled Henderson on the Ohio River or Ashbyburg on the Green. Steamboats that would take them to Federal territory frequented both spots. One unidentified soldier of the 71st told his version of the disaster at Clarksville to the *Evansville Daily Journal*. He mentioned that Johnson's men did not have any artillery and that the Ohioans expected to make a successful defense of their position. The paper related the disappointed soldier's story:

17 *McArthur Democrat*, Aug. 28, 1862, 2; Mason, *Rodney Mason Testimony to Abraham Lincoln*, 24.

18 *OR* 16:1, 865.

> He says the rebels did not have a single field piece, as stated by Col. Mason; that the regiment was in a large building, the doors and windows barricaded with hay, and with every facility for making a successful resistance; had such a course suggested itself to the cowardly Colonel. He says further that Col. Mason was notified that the rebels were coming. . . . [T]he men expected to meet the rebels as the Ohioans have met them on many a well contested field.[19]

While Ohioans seethed in anger, the citizens of Clarksville expressed their joy. Even though Johnson did not intend to hold Clarksville for long, many believed that they had escaped Federal occupation for good and celebrated their liberation. "Clarksville was one of the truest Southern towns, and her people had suffered many impositions at the hands of Colonel Mason and his men, and on the arrival of our little Confederate command, all of its inhabitants, old and young, turned out to joyfully welcome us as their deliverers from the hated 'blue-coats'," Johnson recalled later. "There [sic] delight was shown to the boys in gray in the most extravagant ways," he added.[20]

Clarksville resident Nannie Haskins was ecstatic. She remembered, "I was wild that day with delight as I was with grief on the day of the fall of Fort Donelson. Six months since I had seen a confederate. They came dashing in on their old poor horses, dirty clothes and all sorts of arms; they had no band at all not even a bugle or a flag to show to whom they belonged but their old dirty 'grey' but 'fight was in 'um,' and they 'tuck' the place and the 'Feds' with all their blue broad cloth and brass buttons."[21] Johnson's exploits were buoying southern morale as sharply as they were depressing northern.

The ladies of the town also gave a new silk banner to Johnson and his regiment. With a large crowd of partisans and citizens gazing intently, one of the leading young women of Clarksville, Tennie Moore, presented the new flag to Johnson. Originally, the local women made the flag for the 49th Tennessee, but hid the banner after the regiment surrendered at Fort Donelson. Years later, Moore remembered that the liberating Confederates marched in line towards her large home where she addressed the crowd from her porch. As she lowered the flag from the porch, she offered a solemn peroration: "[W]e wish to present, through you, this banner to your gallant boys, who we feel, will never allow it to trail in the dust of defeat. Colonel Johnson, we place this banner of the stars and bars in your

19 *Evansville Daily Journal*, Aug. 29, 1862, 2.

20 Johnson, *Partisan Rangers*, 113.

21 Nannie Haskins Williams, *The Diary of Nannie Haskins Williams: A Southern Woman's Story of Rebellion and Reconstruction, 1863–1890,* Minoa D. Uffelman, et. al., eds. (Knoxville, TN, 2014), 2-3.

hands with the full assurance that it . . . will be a beacon to light you and your brave followers to more glorious victories." Johnson passed the new flag to Martin at his side and went to work organizing and taking stock of his growing command.[22]

Not only had Johnson captured hundreds of much-needed weapons (including the unpopular Belgian models), he had also acquired ammunition, wagons, "a million dollars in army supplies," and one 4-pound artillery piece. W. B. Albright, the man that took charge of the gun, called it a "fourth of July gun." Most valuable of all, Johnson raised a new company of Clarksville men commanded by a local, William Marr.[23]

After settling the situation in Clarksville, Woodward and Johnson next planned to capture Fort Donelson and Dover, Tennessee, where the remaining four companies of the 71st Ohio held the town. Before this plan could come to fruition, a messenger reached Johnson that Col. John W. Foster and his 65th Indiana had begun an advance with a sizable Federal force from Henderson toward Johnson's main base of supplies at Madisonville, less than 40 miles south of Henderson.[24]

Johnson responded quickly. The planned raid on Dover would not proceed as originally imagined. Instead, Johnson split his force and rode north to stave off Foster's approach to Madisonville while Martin and Woodward continued toward Dover and Fort Donelson with the balance of the regiment. The supplies in Madisonville were too valuable to leave unguarded. Johnson rode north to Madisonville where he had about 200 men to defend against Foster's 600. In Dover, the remainder of the 71st Ohio under the command of Maj. James H. Hart awaited them in the newly constructed, and smaller, fortification there.[25]

22 Johnson, *Partisan Rangers*, 113-114, 355.

23 Ibid., 115, 303, 353-355; Timothy B. Smith, *Shiloh: Conquer or Perish* (Lawrence, KS, 2014), 181; *Houston Tri-Weekly Telegraph*, Nov. 26, 1862; Ordnance Returns for the 71st Ohio, 4th Quarter of 1862, M-1281, Roll 4, National Archives.

24 Johnson, *Partisan Rangers*, 116; John W. Foster to Oliver Morton, Aug. 2, 1862, Morton Telegraphs.

25 Johnson, *Partisan Rangers*, 116; Martin, "Service by Kentucky Cavalry," 114.

Chapter 7

"It seemed a pity to down such fine fellows"

If Martin and Woodward were hoping for another easy victory over the men of the 71st Ohio, Major Hart and his companies defending the small fortification would soon dash their hopes. News of Clarksville's fall had reached the Federals in Dover, Tennessee, who were determined not to dishonor themselves. Johnson's tactical instincts would be missing, and Martin and Woodward would prove that they were not up to the task.

The fort that Woodward and Martin looked to capture was not the imposing Fort Donelson that had surrendered earlier that February. Instead, a smaller one, more easily defended by a garrison force such as the four companies comprising the 71st Ohio, was erected in a cemetery outside of Dover. The works sat west of town and faced south, with a perpendicular set of works that looked to the east, close by Main Street. Inside the fort, an assortment of non-combatants, including chaplains, sutlers, and clerks, joined the 155 men of the regiment. The Federals also placed two artillery pieces, former Confederate guns surrendered during the Battle of Fort Donelson in February. Both guns, a six-pounder and an old howitzer, needed modifications by the Buckeye soldiers. The Chaplain of the 71st Ohio wrote, "our boys had [the six-pounder] and the howitzer . . . hauled a mile and a half. They hollowed a log, put the six-pounder into it, fastened it there, mounted it on trucks and placed it in position. . . . [They] manufactured ammunition for both out of musket cartridges, except a few canister shots, minus the powder for the small gun, which the boys picked up. This was our artillery." Normally, an artillery piece required several men to operate. However, the Ohioans may have produced their own artillery drill much like they produced their own ammunition.

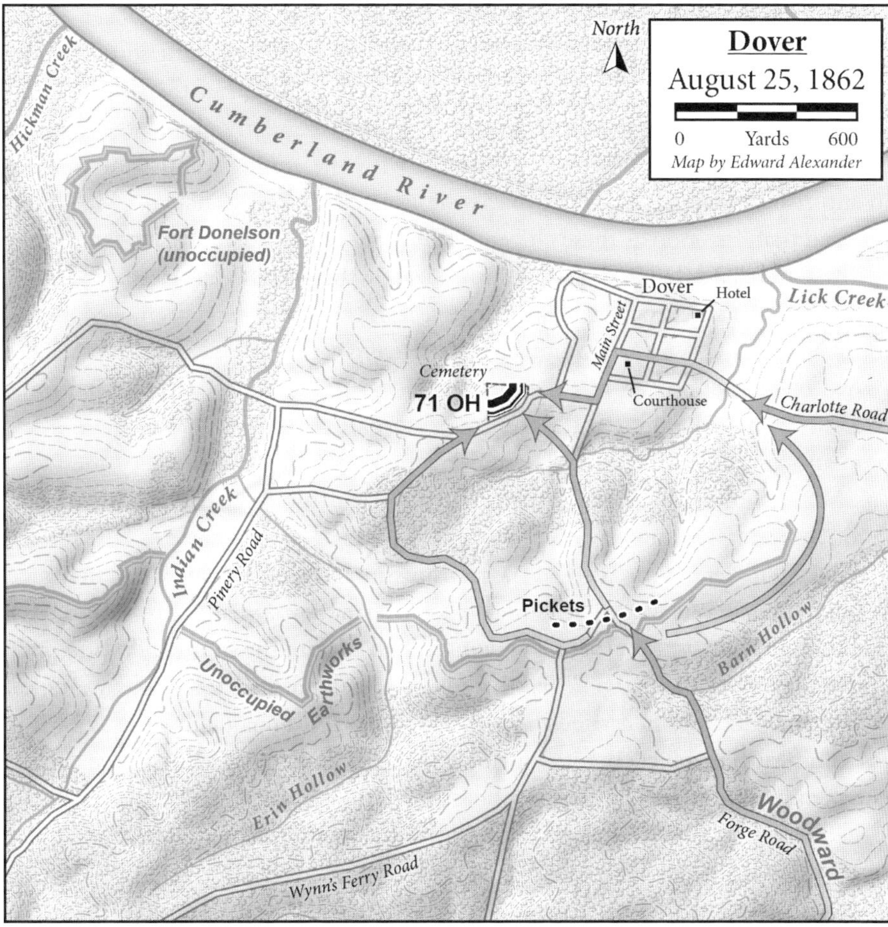

Major Hart had serious misgivings about his situation. His closest support was the 5th Iowa Cavalry posted at Fort Henry and Fort Heiman, about 12 miles to the west. Rumors reached him of large numbers of guerrillas organizing in the region, and he knew of Mason's surrender at Clarksville. Realizing that his four companies offered another alluring prize, he wired General Grant:

> You are doubtless aware of the surrender at Clarksville to the forces of Colonel Woodward on Monday. . . . It leaves me here at this post with the four remaining companies of the Seventy-first, numbering less than 200 men, with limited rations, no artillery or cavalry, threatened by Woodward and Others. Will you allow me to suggest the importance of re-enforcements as early as possible? Whether re-enforced or not I will hold the place until forced to yield. Can I have re-enforcements?[1]

1 Frank Moore, *Rebellion Record*, vol. 5, 591; *OR* 17:2, 183; Stewart, *Redemption*, 103.

On August 25th, Woodward and Martin advanced toward Dover where carnage had raged six months before during the Battle of Fort Donelson. The 71st Ohio had plenty of pickets thrown out to prevent surprise, but the Confederates took advantage of their lack of uniforms. Civilians regularly passed through the Union lines to enter Dover or do business with the soldiers, and so it came as no surprise to have civilians approach the isolated pickets. Chaplain McKinney recorded that, "as soon as these citizens were near enough to our pickets they drew their revolvers and demanded their surrender. By this means they captured eight." With the pickets neutralized in an entire sector, the Confederates enjoyed a clear line of approach toward the Union works free from early alarms. "The first warning we had of their approach was their appearance in force not to exceed a half-mile from our camp. The 'long roll' soon sounded, and the men were in line in a few moments," recalled McKinney. As soon as the threat was known, Hart messaged Col. W. W. Lowe of the 5th Iowa Cavalry to send reinforcements immediately. Union defenders had no way of knowing if the message ever arrived at Fort Henry, or if the Confederates intercepted the transmission. The Southerners had managed to cut the telegraph wire that connected Dover to Fort Henry, Smithland, and other Union posts, so Pvt. J. L. Davis volunteered to "run the gauntlet . . . and carry a dispatch to Colonel Lowe." Davis, though nursing a sprained ankle, mounted a horse and successfully carried the message to the Iowa colonel, who was already marching to their relief. Before cutting the line completely, one of the partisans sent a confident message. The Rebel boasted, "Confeds are now whipping hell out of the Yankees in Fort Donelson and will be down your way soon and catch you." Time would tell if the boaster was correct.[2]

Woodward and Martin hoped to repeat the surrender of Clarksville at Dover, but they did not possess Johnson's natural military mind. For this operation, Martin later wrote that he made a mistake in ceding control of the force to Woodward. He lamented, "Then it was I made a fatal mistake by sending for Col. Woodward, who had more experience than I. When he rode up I told him I would waive rank, and asked him to take command and make the fight." Woodward's plan nearly mirrored the plan for Clarksville. Martin again carried the white flag and demanded the surrender of the defending officers, who requested thirty minutes to make a decision and craft a reply. Major Hart and the Ohio officers unanimously agreed that the answer should be "no." Martin, undoubtedly surprised at the answer in the face of a superior force, delivered the refusal to Woodward. Though a reckless man, Woodward recognized the benefits of avoiding an attack upon the prepared works. He again sent the flag of truce and this time accompanied Martin, whom

2 Moore, *Rebellion Record*, vol. 5, 591, 593; *OR* 17:1, 37-38.

Hart complimented "as a gentleman." McKinney recorded that Woodward offered "the most honorable terms, and protest[ed] his reluctance to hurt us." According to McKinney, the Kentuckian claimed to marshal 450 infantry and 325 cavalry, plus the small gun. Like Clarksville, Hart asked to verify Woodward's statements of numerical superiority. Hoping that a quick tour of his lines would compel the major to surrender, Woodward agreed.[3]

The man tasked with the twenty-minute reconnaissance was Capt. Henry K. McConnell of Company B. McConnell was one of the many officers to defend Mason's conduct at Shiloh, but now found himself nearly surrounded. McConnell, like his colleagues at Clarksville, viewed as much of the Confederate force as he could in the allotted time. When he returned to Union lines, he reported that Woodward and Martin "did not number over four hundred, or possibly five hundred, and one small cannon (which was captured from our boys at Clarksville) and that we could whip them." To change Hart's mind, Woodward mentioned that he had more horsemen posted to the south but would not allow him to view these men as the agreed upon twenty minutes had elapsed.[4]

Before the attack commenced, the Ohioans tied their flag to the wheel of their antiquated howitzer and "resolved not to strike it without a desperate struggle." The Confederate colors, presumably the new flag recently gifted to them at Clarksville, was likewise unfurled and planted in full view of the Union defenders. At 3:00 p.m., the rebel yell echoed in the hollows and woods around the town. The battle for the control of Dover commenced.[5]

The four companies of the 71st Ohio blazed away with their Enfield muskets from behind their breastworks as the gray clad horsemen stormed forward. Chaplain McKinney recounted that the rebels "charged in fine style down the hill, lying east of our intrenchments, into the ravine." The large targets presented by the horses and riders made work easy for the Ohioans. Clearly, sending the men through the rough terrain of the ravines toward the entrenched enemy is not something Martin originally planned.[6]

At some point during the day, the soldiers of the 71st, under orders from Hart, intentionally burned several buildings in Dover, including the courthouse, to create a clear field of fire and to prevent the Confederates from enjoying cover. In his report Hart felt justified: "Of the prudence of this course I have no doubt."

3 Martin, *Kentucky Cavalry*, 115; Moore, *Rebellion Record*, vol. 5, 591; *OR* 17:1, 37-38.

4 Moore, *Rebellion Record*, vol. 5, 591; Mason, *Rodney Mason Testimony to Abraham Lincoln*, 8-11; *OR* 17:1, 37-38.

5 Moore, *Rebellion Record*, vol. 5, 591.

6 Martin, *Kentucky Cavalry*, 115; Moore, *Rebellion Record*, vol. 5, 591; *OR* 17:1, 37-38.

McKinney later recalled, "Just as the attack was made a number of buildings were fired. . . . In the height of the engagement thick volumes of smoke were ascending from the houses and the red tongues of flame were leaping from the windows and darting through the roofs. The sharp crack of the rifled muskets, the heavy booming of our nine-inch howitzer and six-pounder, the wild shouts of the combatants, and the roar of the consuming flames, made a scene of terrific sublimity." The fire turned a large portion of Dover into rubble.[7]

Flames and burning buildings notwithstanding, Woodward pushed the combined force onward. The horsemen attempted to fire their weapons at the entrenched enemy but with hardly any effect, except the occasional *zip* to cause a soldier here or there to duck for the safety of the earthwork. Fire from the cannons and well-placed volleys stymied the Confederate onslaught. As the Confederates thundered down the road toward the line of works in column formation, they presented themselves as easy prey to the Federal cannon. Though outdated, and situated on a makeshift carriage, a shot of improvised canister killed eight of the attackers and repulsed the initial attack. The Union rifles also found several targets as men and horses once again bloodied the former battleground. Even Woodward was not immune to the fire. As he led the men forward, his horse received three bullet wounds and crashed into the dust just feet away from the Federal defenses. The situation forced the short-statured Kentuckian to abandon the dying animal along with his personal side arms. An amused Chaplain McKinney reported that "[t]he chivalrous Colonel did some fine crawling for about twenty feet to escape the shots directed toward him. A bullet broke the skin slightly on the side of his head."[8]

While Woodward searched for another horse, a second wave of partisans descended on the Union works. McConnell's Ohioans carefully fired their rifles and "poured into them such a galling fire that they were again repulsed and scattered in the wildest confusion. I saw more than a score of riderless horses careering over the hills and through the ravines." Hart reported that the smoking buildings in Dover "contributed greatly to the confusion of the enemy's cavalry."[9]

Major Hart wrote that after about 30 minutes of intense fire by his soldiers, and ill-advised charges on the part of the Rebels, the fighting ended. He also reported that the partisans suffered "5 to 10 men, killed and wounded, and 4

7 Moore, *Rebellion Record*, vol. 5, 592; *OR* 17:2, 183.

8 Moore, *Rebellion Record*, vol. 5, 592; *OR* 17:1, 37-38; Martin, "Service by Kentucky Cavalry," 115; Cooling, *Fort Donelson's Legacy*, 102; Thomas Woodward US, Compiled Service Records of Confederate Soldiers Who Served in Organizations from the State of Kentucky, 1861-1865, M319, Roll 0018, National Archives. In 1864, Woodward put in a claim to the Confederate government for the loss of the horse at Dover. He stated that the horse was a four-year-old bay mare worth $600.

9 Moore, *Rebellion Record*, vol. 5, 592; *OR* 17:1, 37-38; *OR* 17:2, 183.

Modern view from the position held by the 71st Ohio in Dover.

Author

horses killed." These numbers appear to be extremely light for the nature of the Confederate attacks and the length of the fight and contradict some of the other sources. McKinney stated that the number of Rebel dead and wounded was "constantly coming in," and that the number of their casualties "will not fall short of thirty killed and wounded." Both Hart and McKinney reported that the 71st Ohio suffered zero casualties. The defense of Dover seemed to be a fine way to redeem the regiment's muddled reputation.[10]

Robert Martin, who regretted handing command over to Woodward, admitted that the action was an embarrassing defeat. He lamented, "We were badly whipped. . . . He had reversed my whole plan of attack." The failed attack on the Federal defenses at Dover may have caused Martin to realize the futility of charging a prepared Union defense. In September, when Martin was again in command of the regiment, the failure at Dover may have continued to weigh heavily on his mind as he confronted Union soldiers at Owensboro, Kentucky.[11]

The Confederate force retreated without opposition. As infantry, the 71st Ohio was incapable of pursuit, and they could not leave the fort unguarded. The gray horsemen fell back toward Clarksville with the clouds of defeat hanging over their

10 Moore, *Rebellion Record*, vol. 5, 592; *OR* 17:1, 37-38; Cooling, *Fort Donelson's Legacy*, 102.

11 Martin, "Service by Kentucky Cavalry," 115.

heads. Just days before they had experienced the thrill of victory, and now they rode away from the enemy "badly whipped." The Confederates pushed eastward along the River Road and made camp at midnight, thoroughly exhausted but not entirely demoralized.

Unfortunately for Martin and Woodward, Federal cavalry pushed hard from Fort Henry to give the partisans a new threat.[12] As soon as the message arrived at Fort Henry detailing the events at Dover, Col. William Lowe and his 5th Iowa Cavalry immediately rode to the relief of the 71st Ohio with six companies and one piece of artillery. Private Davis, who had earlier escaped the Rebel trap, met Lowe riding at the head of the column only three miles out of Fort Henry. Undoubtedly, Davis provided Lowe with more solid information. Lowe's cavalrymen rode hard and reached Dover at sundown, well after the Confederate withdrawal. In a later report, Lowe alluded to an "interview" he had with Woodward. Whether he was describing a literal conversation with the ranger commander or referring to something else is not entirely clear. One historian maintains that Lowe did indeed speak with Woodward and flatly told him that he had "fifteen minutes to get beyond Union picket lines."[13]

Before the pursuit of Woodward and Martin, the men of Lowe's command had spent most of their service in western Tennessee and the southwest part of Kentucky. There they chased guerrillas, scouted, engaged Confederate cavalry, and even guarded court proceedings in Murray, Kentucky. Not willing to ride into a nighttime ambush, Lowe waited for first light on August 26th before beginning his pursuit. His 120 troopers caught up to the partisans approximately ten miles from Dover after a grueling ride. Woodward and Martin put together a defensive line at the burned-out Cumberland Ironworks to contest the Federal advance. According to Lowe, the raiders were in a "strong position."[14]

During the ensuing skirmish, it is unclear if Woodward or Martin commanded the Confederates at the ironworks. Whoever it was, he dismounted most of the Rebels and immediately set them in line along a valley or ravine "along a cornfield-fence and behind houses," with skirmishers thrown forward. Martin never again mentioned Woodward after the Dover fiasco and it is unclear whether the two forces had split by the time they reached the ironworks. Martin commented that "the valley at that point was quite narrow, and at a glance I saw we had a fine

12 *OR* 17:2, 183; Cooling, *Fort Donelson's Legacy*, 102; Martin, "Service by Kentucky Cavalry," 115.

13 Cooling, *Fort Donelson's Legacy*, 101; Moore, *Rebellion Record*, vol. 5, 592; *OR* 17:1, 37; Kurt D. Bergemann, *Brackett's Battalion: Minnesota Cavalry in the Civil War and Dakota War* (Nepean, Ontario, 2004), 43.

14 *OR* 17:1, 39.

position. The ironworks, having been burned, left a stone foundation just the height for breastworks." A muddy creek also separated the two contested lines and left little room for mounted movements. The Rebels took up positions along the trees and ruined foundation, while one out of every four men removed the horses to the rear.

Colonel Lowe advanced his companies B and D as dismounted skirmishers, and quickly engaged the Confederates in a sharp fight, "driving them in fine style." The original plan for the pursuit called for infantry and a ten-pound cannon to follow Lowe. However, due to miscommunication, this support did not leave Dover until two hours after Lowe's companies departed. Some of the partisans reportedly threw down their weapons and fled, closely followed by the Iowans until they came within 75 yards of the main Confederate line. Here, the defenders began a steady fire with the "muskets recently captured at Clarksville."[15]

The incoming raider fire forced the Federals to move rapidly against their enemy. In his report, Lowe states that some points of the lines were only 10-20 yards apart. Martin directed the recently captured artillery piece to fire on the advancing cavalry, albeit with only makeshift canister. Though the troopers took little damage from the gun, Lowe considered it "somewhat annoying" and ordered it silenced. The task fell to Lt. Milton Summers and Lt. Erastus McNeely. As the two officers remounted their troopers, Company B surged forward. Summers discovered a bridge that spanned the muddy creek offering a direct avenue of advance toward the raider gun. He "immediately gave the order to charge" as he led the men, eight abreast, across the bridge. Martin remembered the charge well, and that the horses' hooves roared "like distant thunder" as they approached his position with sabers drawn. As the Union cavalry galloped toward his line, Martin stopped at the bridge to provoke the Yankee horsemen. He began "to wave them on; but there was no special need for that, for here they came." Martin then rode back and ordered Clarksville native W. B. Allbright to "send his men and caisson to one side, as they would be crushed by the horses if exposed, and to save his fire until he could see the whites of their eyes." Allbright responded that he "would do his duty."[16]

Allbright's cannon, loaded with a sack of Minie balls, prepared to receive the onslaught. He watched the charging cavalry in a scene that he described as

15 Martin, "Service by Kentucky Cavalry," 115; *OR* 17:1, 37; Moore, *Rebellion Record*, vol. 5, 592; Iowa Adjutant General's Office, Roster and record of Iowa soldiers in the war of the rebellion, together with historical sketches of volunteer organizations, 1861-1866 (Des Moines, IA, 1908), 850; Report of the Adjutant General of the State of Iowa, 988-989; Bergemann, *Brackett's Battalion*, 43.

16 Martin, "Service by Kentucky Cavalry," 115; *OR* 17:1, 39; *Report of the Adjutant General of the State of Iowa*, 988-989.

"magnificent . . . it is vivid with me still." He ordered his squad to safety while he alone remained with the piece. Since the Rebels lacked friction primers, all he had to fire the cannon was a small torch. He later recalled the tension of the moment: "There I stood waving my firebrand to keep it alive, and at the same time keeping an eye on my gun and the enemy. It seemed an age for them to cover that short distance leading up from the bridge. I was eager to have it over."[17]

Lieutenants Summers and McNeely led their men across the bridge and down the road toward the gun. Allbright wrote that the drawn sabers of the Iowans flashed in the morning light and spurred their horses to gallop faster. He hesitated to fire on such men. Martin recalled upon watching the charge that "it seemed a pity to down such fine fellows." Finally, the moment came. The Tennessean checked the flame on his torch and lowered it to the vent of the cannon. The gun discharged the Minie balls just as Summers and McNeely reached the gun. The smoke so enshrouded the area that Allbright struggled to see the damage of the shot. He wrote that the combination of powder smoke and the dust of the horses' hooves made the scene "dark as Egypt." Though blinded by the smoke, he eventually discerned the carnage as the road "seemed to be piled full" of horses and men. Allbright himself had been thrown next to a large tree, the gun several feet in the opposite direction and upside down. Despite the carnage caused by the gun, Summers and McNeeley managed to reach it and dismantle it. Lowe commented that the charge had "rendered [the gun] perfectly useless." Lieutenant Summers' own actions helped paralyze the gun when he reportedly grabbed the wheel when he neared the piece.[18]

Lieutenants Summers and McNeely continued past the damaged cannon as they tried to exploit their success. Lowe advanced Companies A and L in support, but the additional manpower did little to help. Martin, or possibly his men on their own, recognized the danger of the gap in the line and rushed to fill the opening. The dismounted Confederates, most likely from Capt. Lorenzo Fisher's company, moved on the Union cavalry to repel their sudden breakthrough. The raiders quickly captured a severely wounded McNeely, while Summers continued to advance. The lieutenant became a target for the hidden Southerners in the burned-out cellars and several musket balls removed him from his horse. The 5th Iowa's regimental historian later wrote that Summers tried to regain his footing, but enemy troops surrounded him. "Although unable to rise to his feet, he cut at his assailants with his sabre, and split one of them from the shoulder to the centre

17 *Roster and record of Iowa soldiers*, 850; Martin, "Service by Kentucky Cavalry," 115; *OR* 17:1, 39.

18 *Roster and record of Iowa soldiers*, 850; Martin, "Service by Kentucky Cavalry," 115; *OR* 17:1, 39; Cooling, *Fort Donelson's Legacy*, 102.

Modern view of the area near the old Cumberland Ironworks.

Author

of his body, and cut the hand of another nearly off. He fought with the sabre till it became so bent as to be useless, and then shot five times with his revolver, when the crowd of rebels, pressing on him from all sides, wrenched the pistol from his grasp, and made him a prisoner." Within a day, Summers's wounds proved fatal and he died near the ironworks. His father eventually retrieved his remains and returned them to his hometown in South Pekin, Illinois.[19]

Lowe, with less than 120 men, realized the futility of further offensive action against the strongly posted Confederates, who still numbered several hundred. The colonel ordered the remnants of his companies to an open space some distance from the Confederate line, ready to receive a possible counterattack. After an hour of waiting, Lowe retreated to Fort Donelson, his men and horses "suffering much from fatigue and want of food." Lowe reported Union losses as four killed, 14 wounded, and 11 captured. In a follow-up report, he noted that "reliable information" placed enemy losses at 35 killed and wounded. There has yet to be any source detailing the number of Confederate casualties at the skirmish.

19 Addison A. Stuart, *Iowa Colonels and Regiments: Being a history of Iowa regiments in the war of the rebellion* (Des Moines, IA, 1865), 624; *Report of the Adjutant General of the State of Iowa*, 987-988.

Martin regrouped his command, repaired the cannon, and moved north to join Johnson in Kentucky.[20]

Martin tried to fill Johnson's void at Dover and the ironworks, but the 22-year-old was naturally more of a scout and fighter than a tactical thinker. Johnson, while facing off with fewer men against Col. John W. Foster's larger force, would at least be able to claim a favorable result in the subsequent action north of Madisonville. The setback at Dover did not reverse the success of Clarksville, but a trend had started. Without Johnson leading the regiment, success did not come so easily. In September, Martin would have another chance to extend the string of victories, but he would fail then as well. At the same time, Federal bureaucratic inefficiency and piecemeal strategy would slowly give way to a more concerted anti-partisan effort. Lessons were being learned that would soon bring Union efforts to terrifying efficacy.

20 *OR* 17:1, 39; Bergemann, *Brackett's Battalion*, 44.

Chapter 8

"The enemy did as they generally do—'skedaddled'"

While Woodward blundered at Fort Donelson, and Martin escaped with the rest of the command, Johnson made for Madisonville. He arrived in the city well before Foster and his force of cavalry, infantry, and artillery. Foster's column, intending to destroy Johnson's supplies, moved slowly, even though just days later Foster stated that his men did not bring any camp equipage and lived off the county. Though in command of a much smaller force, Johnson would continue to foil Foster's plans.[1]

The news of Clarksville's fall had greatly alarmed Foster back in Henderson. Rumors ran wild about a possible incursion by famed Confederate raider John H. Morgan, and Henderson's political situation seemed tenuous. The mayor had already disappeared to join Johnson and the city council had all resigned. Foster's 65th Indiana had only arrived in Henderson on August 20th, and the 4th Indiana Cavalry still lacked proper training and armaments. Foster wired Governor Morton: "Morgan in force will soon be in this region and overrun that part [of] KY and threaten the border[.] My latest information from the . . . affairs at Clarksville confirm this. I will march into [the] interior as soon as cavalry is ready with 800 infantry, 200 cavalry, and two pieces of artillery." He readied himself to disrupt Johnson's plans in Tennessee.[2]

1 Morton Telegraphs, Morton telegram book, no. 7, 297, https://www.ulib.iupui.edu/digitalcollections/Telegraph, (hereafter "Morton Telegraphs"); Reid, *4th Indiana Cavalry*, 9-10.

2 Morton Telegraphs, Morton telegram book, no. 7, 263.

Captain Richard Miller, 65th Indiana
LOC

But the force Foster expected to bring with him did not materialize as he had hoped. Too many of the soldiers were still not ready for the field. With only 600 men, Foster moved south in two sections on the morning of August 24th. His advance into the interior consisted of companies of the brand-new 4th Indiana Cavalry, companies of the 8th Kentucky Cavalry, and some artillery. These units proceeded overland from Henderson to Madisonville, a movement of about 40 miles. Two companies of the 65th Indiana provided infantry support, and they took a steamer up the Green River and disembarked at Ashbyburg. Then they marched southwest to join the cavalry and artillery north of Madisonville.[3]

The day would be extremely eventful for Maj. John Platter's 4th Indiana. On August 24th, the men arrived in Evansville and finally received their horses and some of the necessary equipment. A mounted battalion drill still had not taken place. The ferries began taking them downriver to Henderson where they joined Foster's column for the march to Madisonville. The 4th had their horses for less than 48 hours when the time came for them to meet the enemy.[4]

On August 25th, Johnson deployed two companies north of Madisonville, commanded by Captains Sam Taylor and Al Fowler, to slow the Union advance and ambush the column. However, the two sides collided before a proper ambuscade was established. Fowler immediately attacked, and then slowly fell back. Foster does not mention Southern numbers, only the particulars of the action. In a telegram to Gov. Morton, he related the events of the march to Madisonville. "At ninehalf oclock this morning cavalry was fired upon by the guerrillas two miles from here in ambush[.] After falling back cavalry dismounted and drove them back a mile through the thick brush and hills where they waited for infantry." Johnson

3 *Evansville Daily Journal*, Sep. 2, 1862, 1; Morton Telegraphs, Morton telegram book, no. 7, 263.

4 Reid, *4th Indiana Cavalry*, 9.

called Foster's advance "cautions, dilatory, even timid," and that he had "little to fear from this Yankee colonel." Obviously, the cavalry's lack of long arms hindered their pursuit and ability to deal Johnson a decisive blow. Once the infantry arrived, Johnson simply fell back out of range.[5]

A soldier-correspondent with the *Evansville Daily Journal* filed a lengthy story while marching with Foster's command. His report details the blistering heat and lack of water that slowed the infantry during the regiment's first march, and how the column constantly stopped to rest. "The day was terribly hot, and our men were very tired, some of them gave out entirely, and dropped off all along the road," the Hoosier wrote. While the infantry slogged on toward Madisonville, the cavalry had already began skirmishing with Johnson's blocking force.[6]

The two companies of the 65th finally arrived on the scene sometime in the afternoon. The infantry deployed on the road with one company advancing on the right side and the correspondent's company moving forward on the left. After marching in line of battle through wooded terrain, they finally saw their enemy. One soldier in the 65th related, "We came to the edge of a tobacco field when we saw them on a little hill just beyond, about 100 yards distant. Our officers then ordered us to *fire!* which we did with a will. The enemy did as they generally do—'skedaddled.' We did not get a man hurt, for they only fired a few shots in return." Foster reported to Morton: "[T]wo companies were deployed and drove them back after a sharp engagement when the rebels fled. Five rebels killed, wounded unknown. Seventeen prisoners." The fight did not go as Foster intended, as Johnson did not have any reason to offer anything more than the delaying action they executed. The Federals lost just one man killed and only a handful of wounded.[7]

The thirsty, hungry, tired, and frustrated Hoosiers marched into Madisonville with colors flying. Union citizens came out to provide provisions while the "secesh citizens shut up their stores, and run away." Many of the men helped themselves to anything they wanted. "We broke upon their business[,] houses and took bacon, coffee, beans, sugar, salt, cigars, &c," wrote the soldier-correspondent. They also played jokes on the terrified prisoners by shouting things like "hang them" and "shoot them." The men laughed but never intended to carry out the threats. The exhausted soldiers then camped for the night on the courthouse lawn.[8]

Johnson had found a way to escape from Foster once again. He removed his supplies before the Federals entered the town, much to the chagrin of the

5 Morton Telegraphs, Morton telegram book, no. 7, 297.

6 *Evansville Daily Journal*, Sep. 6, 1862, 1.

7 Ibid.; Morton Telegraphs, Morton telegram book, no. 7, 297.

8 *Evansville Daily Journal*, Sep. 6, 1862, 1.

A typical view of Union soldiers on the march. This particular image shows the 134th Illinois outside Columbus, Kentucky, in 1864. *LOC*

soldiers hoping to have a thorough fight with the elusive Rebels. Without camp equipage slowing his advance, Foster should have been able to beat Johnson to Madisonville. He had the numbers to brush aside Johnson's two companies. But the heat, coupled with the lack of sufficient drill, hampered his efforts. With 20 more miles to travel, Johnson still managed to deploy his thin force and remove the supplies. Granted, Foster could never have had any idea of the size of the force Johnson commanded, and the papers tended to always overestimate the size of the Partisan Rangers.[9]

Foster did relay some positive outcomes from his anti-climactic adventure. "We captured a number of horses and arms," Foster assured Governor Morton, along with a few prisoners and some Rebel casualties. It appears that Foster implied to Morton that he meant to sit at Madisonville and wait for Johnson to return. He wrote that he expected Confederate reinforcements to be moving his way from Clarksville. Foster did not ask for reinforcements or make any indications of a forthcoming march to Henderson. Evidently, he believed he had sufficient men available to repel any attack by Johnson and fight the deciding battle of the partisan war in western Kentucky.[10]

Even though the advance forced Johnson to move his supplies, he had again eluded capture. Johnson sent for Martin to reunite the rest of the regiment and plan their next conquest. The deciding battle that Foster hoped to fight and

9 *Johnson, Partisan Rangers*, 116-117; Morton Telegraphs, Morton telegram book, no. 7, 297.

10 Morton Telegraphs, Morton telegram book, no. 7, 297.

win would not take place at Madisonville. The past several days and weeks had been a whirlwind for both sides in the region. Johnson had captured two towns, taken hundreds of prisoners, gained hundreds of recruits, acquired much-needed weapons, seized one cannon, and pilfered valuable supplies. He also continued to frustrate Foster. However, the Union men would eventually have their day.[11]

11 Johnson, *Partisan Rangers*, 117.

Chapter 9

"The Union men of that section will rally with enthusiasm to the starry flag"

As Johnson remained elusive, inefficiency, misplaced priorities, and recruitment difficulties continued to undermine a more effective Federal response. Union authorities raised more regiments and sent them to the region. One was destined to be an emergency backfill to hold important points along the Ohio River for only a few weeks, while another, raised for the long term, offered more mobility for a variety of situations. However, these regiments faced the same challenges as those under Foster's command in Henderson. Bureaucracy and regulations hampered the efforts of commanders on the ground to capture Johnson, and the rushing of untrained men into the breach undermined morale and sapped manpower.

In the late summer of 1862, nearly 300 men of the 78th Indiana, under the command of Lt. Col. William Farrow, encamped in Uniontown in response to Johnson's Newburgh raid several weeks before. The 78th's mission differed from typical Federal regiments, even those serving behind the lines. One of the emergency 60-day regiments, the men of the 78th could hardly expect to see any real fighting. Union commanders hurriedly formed these regiments in the aftermath of Newburgh and sent them to guard strategic places along the Ohio River. The 78th contained "very nice people indeed. They were farmers, preachers, lawyers and doctors, and made a very civil soldiery in the main, although there were some rough characters among them."[1]

1 Terrell, *Report of the Adjutant General of the State of Indiana*, vol. 3, 21-22; Foster, *War Stories*, 96.

Before commanding the 78th, Farrow had served as the lieutenant colonel of the 43rd Indiana. He returned to Indiana in July 1862, at the time of the raid on Newburgh. The *Evansville Daily Journal* had high expectations for Farrow and his regiment. The paper reported:

> [t]hat Lieut. Col. Farrow of the 43rd Indiana, has been sent to Kentucky with a battalion of men to assist in ridding that State from the prowling bands of thieves who are robbing and plundering her loyal citizens. Col. Farrow is the right man for the duty. His experiences amid the canebrakes of Arkansas, has taught him important lessons in guerrilla warfare which will be of unspeakable advantage to him in his present field of labor. To the gallant Gavin and the dashing and heroic Netter, Col. Farrow will be invaluable. His men are as noble a specimen of gallant sons of Indiana as ever marched to the field. We shall follow their movements with the greatest confidence and hope.[2]

In just a few weeks, the *Journal* would sing a very different tune.

The 78th was a true emergency regiment. On July 31st, they mustered into service at Indianapolis and immediately hurried south to face the threat of the "guerrillas" and protect Indiana from another Rebel incursion. Due to events unfolding at the Ohio River and the necessity of their presence on the border, the regimental officers never found adequate time to complete the regiment's muster-in rolls. Proper drill and instruction for the regiment's raw soldiers also evidently fell by the wayside in the haste to move south.[3]

Some of the officers of the green 78th enjoyed limited experience. Captain Tilghman A. Howard, of Company C, had served in the 14th Indiana as a lieutenant for nearly a year, and saw action in Virginia and West Virginia. While in West Virginia, the 14th participated in battles at Cheat Mountain and Greenbrier. In March 1862, they engaged in one of the several battles for Winchester. For the first year of the war, Howard made it through unscathed and the young officer had the experience the 78th desperately needed.[4]

Though a few of the officers, such as Howard, enjoyed combat experience, most of the men in the ranks were first time soldiers, such as Ransom Hawley, who doubted they would see any action in their short time of service. Hawley was typical

2 Indiana Adjutant Generals Office, *Report of the Adjutant General of the State of Indiana*, vol. 2 (Indianapolis, 1865), 421, 429; *Evansville Daily Journal*, Aug. 2, 1862, 3.

3 Tilghman Howard (Captain, 78th Indiana Inf.), widow's pension application materials, 1866, Civil War and Later Pension Files, Department of Veterans Affairs, National Archives; Hawley to Family, July 29, 1862, VCPL.

4 Indiana Adjutant Generals Office, *Report of the Adjutant General of the State of Indiana*, vol. 2, 113-114, 120-121; Pension application for Captain Tilghman Howard; *Evansville Daily Journal*, Aug. 2, 1862, 3.

of most teenage boys during the war years. A yearning for the supposed excitement and adventure that service in the Union army could offer was quite normal. Some felt it their duty to fight, and others enlisted, driven by the thought that fellows like them were dying and sacrificing while they enjoyed the comforts of home. A few, such as Ransom Hawley, struggled to win parental approval to enlist.[5]

At the outbreak of hostilities, 17-year-old Hawley attended Wabash College where he watched several friends and acquaintances go off to fight, including his older brother. Up to this point, his parents forbade him to enlist because they thought that one son serving was enough. However, Hawley persisted. He reminded his parents of their older family members who had served the country, and that his patriotic duty demanded that he serve. Yet even when he argued as to why he should fight, he still asked his parents for permission. "Can't I go? Can't I go?" he always begged. Hawley did not go in 1861, or in the spring of 1862. In many of his early letters of 1862 to his family, he mentions his serving friends, acquaintances, and the happenings of local regiments, as if to convince them of his desire to fight as well. In one letter he explained:

> And now I want to go, and it is strange when the flag of our country has been torn down and a traitor's flag planted instead? When nearly every student has gone to the war, or is going there, or going home, but when 4 or 5 go to recitation, and such tremendous excitement is going on constantly, is it strange that a boy whose Grandfathers both did their country's service, is it strange that he . . . would not want to go too?[6]

In his June 4, 1862, letter, Hawley referenced previous correspondence where he must have informed his parents of his intentions to enlist. He explained to them:

> You ask where I will go? I will go wherever I am needed and wherever I am commanded whether to guard prisoners, supplies, or bridges or to fight. . . . But I do not believe the three months troops will be placed in the advance in preference of the well disciplined troops. . . . I can say now I [feel] more and more determined to serve my Savior. We had a good prayer meeting this evening. I have not spoken to Prof Hadley about going, but of course he will oppose as he would for any of the boys going.[7]

5 Ransom Hawley to Family, n.d. 1861, Ransom E. Hawley Letters, VCPL.

6 Sean A. Scott, *A Visitation of God: Northern Civilians Interpret the Civil War* (Oxford, 2012), 140-141; Hawley to Family, Feb. 15 and 24, 1862, VCPL; Hawley to Emmeline Hawley, Apr. 7, 1862, VCPL; James J. Barnes and Patience P. Barnes, eds., *500 Strong: Wabash College Students in the Civil War* (Carmel, IN, 2013), 181-182.

7 Hawley to Family, June 4, 1862, VCPL.

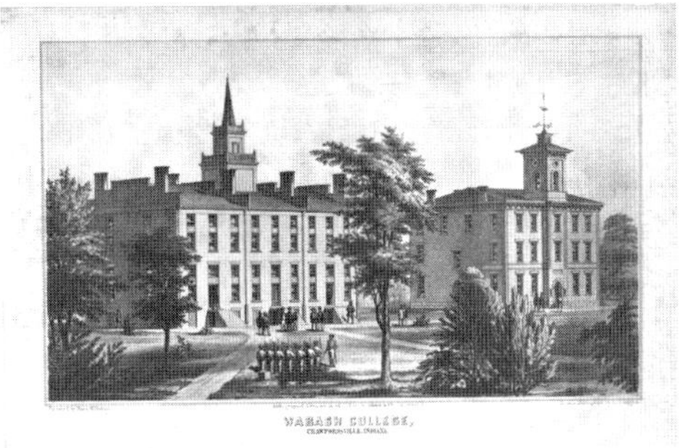

1858 Lithograph of Center Hall and South Hall on the campus of Wabash College in Crawfordsville, Indiana. *Robert T. Ramsay Jr. Archival Center, Wabash College, Crawfordsville, Indiana*

Hawley finally decided to act on his inclinations and enlisted in the 78th Indiana at Indianapolis, and there awaited his new regiment's orders. "The guess is we are going to Kaintuck to guard the ballot box. We expect to leave to day. Col Farrow is our Commander in chief I suppose, I am beginning to get acquainted a little. . . . I am not anxious. . . . Well I had to quit again [writing the letter] to be sworn in. 'Its did now' I am in for 'sartin [sic]'," he informed his family. Hawley was "in for certain" and very quickly he would see the action he doubted he would ever experience. The war and the 10th Kentucky Partisan Rangers would give Hawley a rude awakening from his romantic illusions.[8]

Another new regiment, a Kentucky mounted regiment, commanded by newly promoted Lt. Col. Gabriel Netter, also began to take shape. Netter may have been one of the least likely persons to recruit a regiment in 1862 Kentucky. Not a natural-born Kentuckian, or American for that matter, Netter had emigrated from France and had only lived in the United States for a few years when the Civil War began. Not only that, but Netter was Jewish. Netter's foreignness would prove the least of his troubles raising a regiment in a region thick with deeply divided loyalties.[9]

Gabriel Netter was born in Bergheim in Alsace, France in 1836, a member of a large Jewish family with 11 siblings. About 1855, Netter, possibly a younger brother, and his younger sister, immigrated to the United States. Netter eventually settled in Ohio County, Kentucky, while his sister, Pauline Fournier, and her hat-making husband, John, settled in Evansville, Indiana. By all accounts, Netter became a well-liked businessman and merchant who passionately loved his adopted homeland. He offered his service to its preservation in 1861.[10]

8 Hawley to Family, July 29, 1862, VCPL.

9 Stanley Chyet, "Ohio Valley Jewry During the Civil War," *Bulletin of the Historical and Philosophical Society of Ohio*, Volume 21, No. 3 (1963): 182; Lee Shai Weissbach, "Kentucky Jewry During the Civil War," *The Register of the Kentucky Historical Society* 110, no. 2 (2012): 165-84.

10 Isaac W. Bernheim, *History of the Settlement of Jews in Paducah and the Ohio Valley* (Paducah, KY, 1912), 37, 41; 1860 U.S. Census, Vanderburgh County, Indiana, population schedule, Evansville,

During the winter of 1861-1862, Netter excelled as a company commander in the 26th Kentucky. In his first taste of action, he pushed far ahead of the main Union body during an attack on a Confederate cavalry camp in Woodbury, Kentucky. He led a successful raid behind Confederate lines that resulted in the burning of the Whippoorwill Bridge, an important part of the rail link between Confederate controlled Bowling Green, Kentucky, and Clarksville. At Shiloh, he received praise from superiors for his leadership on the second day of fighting. During the advance on Corinth, Mississippi, in May 1862, Netter's commanding officer, Col. Stephen Burbridge, brought charges against Netter. He stood accused of behavior that was "insubordinate" and using "mutinous language to a superior officer." The second charge was "disobedience of orders." Netter had a verbal disagreement, in front of the enlisted men, with a higher-ranking company commander whom he felt unqualified, a perfect example of his independence of mind.[11]

As recruiting for his new regiment began, Netter's reputation preceded him. One of his future recruits later wrote, "I had formed an opinion, from what I had heard of him, that he was a reckless dare-devil, and hesitated somewhat to enroll myself under his standard." Though Netter carried a reputation for impulsiveness, his men also described him as "courteous and affable in his manner and as polite as the proverbial French dancing master. Gentle as a lamb, he was as brave as a lion." Such a reputation proved to be significant in the campaign against the 10th Kentucky Partisan Rangers later that fall.[12]

Netter traveled back home to Hartford, Kentucky, to recruit his new regiment. Unfortunately, he had some competition, and it did not come from the Confederate army. Quintis Shanks was recruiting the 12th Kentucky Cavalry in nearby Cloverport, James Shackelford sought men for the 8th Kentucky Cavalry in Henderson, and Judge George Yeaman was actively building a regiment in Owensboro for the 34th Kentucky. The adjutant general of Kentucky ordered Yeaman to cease his recruiting efforts for the 34th because the 8th, 12th, and Netter all recruited men in and about the same region. An advertisement placed

---

p. 29, dwelling 151, family 156, John, Pauline, and Clandine Fourneir, digital image, http://fold3.com, accessed Apr. 18, 2018.

11 U.S., Compiled Service Records of Volunteer Union Soldiers Who Served in Organizations from the State of Kentucky, 1861-1865, M397, Roll 0380, National Archives. Charges against Netter were prepared by Colonel S. G. Burbridge, 26th Kentucky Infantry, May 15, 1862. See *OR* 4:1, 220-221; *OR* 7:1, 485; *OR* 10:1, 368-370; Ed Porter Thompson, *History of the Orphan Brigade* (Louisville, KY, 1898), 54-55; *Evansville Daily Journal*, Dec. 10, 1861, 2; Don Wilson, *The Boys from Calhoun: The Story of Camp Calhoun and its Contribution to the Civil War* (Calhoun, KY, 2008), 9; Gabriel Netter Compiled Service Records of Volunteer Union Soldiers Who Served in Organizations from the State of Kentucky, 1861-1865, M397, Roll 0380, National Archives.

12 Bernheim, *Settlement of Jews*, 41.

for Shanks's regiment in the *Owensboro Monitor* on August 20th proclaimed, "All persons who desire to enter the service under these gallant officers must report at Hartford by next Friday night." Recruiting in the Hartford area appeared to be getting rather crowded.[13]

Competition aside, others, like the *Evansville Daily Journal,* beamed at the prospect of having Netter commanding troops so near, especially after the Newburgh fiasco. The *Journal* wrote:

> Our citizens will remember the gallant, dashing Capt. Netter—the terror of guerrillas and the admiration of loyal Kentuckians. They remember how he galloped to and fro through that State at the head of his company of cavalry, smiting the Philistines hip and thigh, cutting off their communications and rendering their situation at Bowling Green uncomfortable. Well Capt. Netter is with us again, this time as a Major, and yesterday we had the pleasure of shaking him by the hand. . . . He is also authorized to organize battalion or regiment of cavalry as he may deem proper. The gallant Major designs entering upon the duties of his new position at once, and with his accustomed energy. We predict a warm time for the guerrillas who have been infesting that section of country. . . . Major Netter is so well known throughout the Green river country, and his skill and daring as a soldier is so highly appreciated, that the Union men of that section will rally with enthusiasm to the starry flag when it is unfurled by him. . . . [H]undreds of them will rally under their old flag, and such will hail with joy the advent of such a gallant and experienced leader as Major Netter, who knows every foot of the country in which he has to operate, and the character of the rebels with whom he has to deal. We need hardly add that the rebels know him, and what mercy they may expect at his hands if they continue in arms.[14]

By late July, Netter received his official commission as lieutenant colonel of United States volunteers. The promotion made the task of raising his regiment no less easy. As in many aspects of life, politics and jealousy actively injured the cause of the Union in the area between the Ohio and Green Rivers. Netter believed he was to raise a regiment of cavalry, the 15th Kentucky, for 12 months' service. Instead, he received word that his regiment would be mounted infantry, the 38th Kentucky. This might not seem a consequential distinction to modern-day readers, but unlike cavalry, mounted infantry only rode for transportation. Otherwise, mounted infantry fought just like regular infantry, complete with the same types of weapons and equipment. One historian described mounted infantry as a force that "produced a mixture of fire and maneuver" and that it "was expensive in horseflesh and horse-holders, but it achieved the result more

13 *Owensboro Monitor*, Aug. 20, 1862, 3.

14 *Evansville Daily Journal*, July 29, 1862, 2.

convincingly." Cavalry, on the other hand, had a completely different purpose, and therefore attracted recruits in a way that mounted infantry could not, especially with the new emphasis on raiding and scouting. It is important to note that if a mounted infantry regiment did not receive mounts, then it would convert to regular infantry. This confusion, and Federal bureaucratic interference, frustrated Netter and his recruiting efforts. He had amassed more than 300 men at Hartford, but upon learning their enlistments would be for three years instead of one, he released the recruits from their obligation. On August 14th, Netter wrote to his friend in Frankfort, "After liberating them—I called upon them to remain—for the sake of their State—cause—& people—for their honor's sake—Two hundred of them remained by my side."[15]

In a letter to George D. Prentice seething with indignation, Netter desperately sought answers to the organizational confusion. Prentice, a friend and editor of the *Louisville Journal*, forwarded Netter's letter to Governor Robinson. In the letter, Netter complained about the local recruiting competition:

> H. D. McHenry—who will never forgive me—to have done with 20 men, that which his brother the Col. refused to do with 150—has been at work in Frankfort- ever since his arrival & there—doing all the mischief to my interest that he possibly can—I have been changed from the 1, to the 3, years service—Mr. Mc,Hy. wrote home, to his wife a letter which promenaded the streets here—with much show—that I would be ordered away from here & that such an order was made out before he McHy. reached Frankfort . . . Shanks is prominating [sic] and the letter of McHenry's to-day—stating that I will be changed from cavalry to infantry—or cannot be accepted.[16]

Adding to Netter's frustration was that 100 of his men had already been uniformed and armed as cavalry. On July 25th, he had also been told by Gen.

15 John W. Finnell to Nathaniel Gaither, Jr., 25 July 1862, Office of the Governor, Beriah Magoffin, Governor's Official Correspondence File, Military Appointments, 1859-1862, MG7-9, Kentucky Department for Libraries and Archives, Frankfort, KY. Accessed via the *Civil War Governors of Kentucky Digital Documentary Edition*, discovery.civilwargovernors.org/document/KYR-0001-018-0391 (accessed July 27, 2018); Gabriel Netter to George D. Prentice, 21 Aug. 1862, Office of the Governor, James F. Robinson, Governor's Official Correspondence File, Military Correspondence, 1862-1863, R2-22 to R2-23, Kentucky Department for Libraries and Archives, Frankfort, KY. Accessed via the *Civil War Governors of Kentucky Digital Documentary Edition*, discovery.civilwargovernors.org/document/KYR-0001-027-0015 (accessed Mar. 11, 2018); Paddy Griffith, *Battle Tactics of the Civil War* (New Haven, CT, 1987), 184.

16 Gabriel Netter to George D. Prentice, Aug. 21, 1862, Office of the Governor, James F. Robinson: Governor's Official Correspondence File, Military Correspondence, 1862-1863, R2-22 to R2-23, Kentucky Department for Libraries and Archives, Frankfort, KY. Accessed via the *Civil War Governors of Kentucky Digital Documentary Edition*, discovery.civilwargovernors.org/document/KYR-0001-027-0015, (accessed Oct. 1, 2018). Apparently some animosity existed between the two officers after the Woodbury skirmish.

John Finnell, the adjutant general of Kentucky volunteers, that his men would all be mounted as soon as permission was received by the War Department. All of that seemed to be coming apart. In the same letter, Netter blasted the apparent favoritism received by some officers and organizations. Netter claimed that Shanks "who does not know how to drill a squad," and with only 73 men, had already been accepted into the service, while he, with over 300 men, was left in limbo. Governor Robinson echoed Netter's sentiments in a message to Secretary of War Edwin Stanton when he mentioned the absurdity of not arming and equipping new regiments until a mustering officer properly mustered them into service. Robinson decried the situation and explained, "This will be disastrous to my efforts in Kentucky. Our recruiting camps are in the midst of an enemy. The presence of Government recruits is an invitation to attack. It is cruel to expose the brave fellows to attack and slaughter without any means of defense." Thousands of men had joined new Kentucky cavalry regiments that summer, and acquiring cavalry arms remained a major issue. Finnell wrote to Stanton that "A week since we were advised that cavalry arms (Ripley) had been forwarded to Kentucky. We have had no further intelligence of them. We have 5,000 cavalry ready for arming and mounting and have no arms."[17]

Raising mounted regiments—whether cavalry or mounted infantry—to combat the irregular Confederate forces in the state became paramount. Gen. Horatio Wright, commander of the Department of the Ohio, explained to Stanton, "I am much in want of cavalry to capture or break up rebel bands forming through the State, and detachments from some of the not fully organized regiments are now employed in that way and doing good service. . . . The rebels are getting recruits rapidly throughout the State and it can be stopped by cavalry parties only."[18]

As dismal as the situation appeared, it did not dampen Netter's fighting spirit. Netter wrote General Boyle on August 28th: "Before I can do some good I must be armed and mounted." He also continued to inquire about weapons for his men. He had requisitioned 200 revolvers, but only 66 showed up. Netter also went so far as to request Colt repeating rifles and pistols. He boasted to Boyle that he might expect anything from his men if they could procure these types of arms, and he was eager to take the field as soon as he received proper arms and mounts. So eager was he to begin service, in fact, that Netter seems to have accepted the

17 Gabriel Netter to George D. Prentice, Aug. 21, 1862, Office of the Governor, James F. Robinson: Governor's Official Correspondence File, Military Correspondence, 1862-1863, R2-22 to R2-23, Kentucky Department for Libraries and Archives, Frankfort, KY. Accessed via the *Civil War Governors of Kentucky Digital Documentary Edition*, discovery.civilwargovernors.org/document/KYR-0001-027-0015, (accessed Oct. 1, 2018); *OR* series III, vol. 2, 404, 464.

18 *OR* series III, vol. 2, 404, 465.

branch change without protest and mentioned in his letter that his men would be mounted infantry; he signed his letter to Boyle as commander of the "38th."[19]

By August 29th, Netter transferred his command from Hartford to Owensboro and encamped on the fairgrounds west of town near the Ohio River. The move to the Ohio River most likely had something to do with increased Confederate activity, as his camp in Hartford appeared vulnerable. In a message to President Lincoln, Governor Robinson remarked that several of his new regiments faced trouble as the "territory assigned to them [is] threatened by rebels and occupied by guerrillas, so as to retard recruiting and to prevent the filling up of the regiments." Stanton's reply was rather cold and merely suggested that "[i]f the rendezvous are exposed to danger, the place must be changed." Perhaps Stanton, in Washington, was not fully appraised of the situation in western Kentucky, or the bureaucratic and command troubles that plagued the Federal effort in the region. Otherwise, he might not have adhered so rigidly to regulations nor been so worried about government property being double-issued to Kentucky troops. General Wright concurred with Robinson that not equipping or arming the Kentucky regiments until their muster was quite foolhardy. "We risk the loss of many recruits from Kentucky regiments. They are being formed in districts liable to raids, and they can't defend themselves without arms, even if fully organized. I am sensible to the evils to which you refer, but in the condition in which the state of Kentucky now is I am sure they are the lesser," Wright argued.[20]

Once in Owensboro, the situation improved. In September, the 38th finally began to receive horses, and the *Louisville Journal* reported that Netter's ranks swelled to 500 men. Over the next few weeks and into September, Netter and his recruits drilled and prepared for war. The *Evansville Daily Journal* reported:

> Col. Netter's regiment arrived from Hartford Friday evening, and are now encamped at the Fair Grounds. We learn that it is to be one of the best equipped regiments in the service.
>
> We hope it will be equipped at once and put into the field. Col. Netter is the very man for the work. He is well acquainted with the various localities infested by the guerrillas. He is brave, intrepid and resolute. He believes in making war, and he owes the rebels not good will. We hope to hear soon that the lion-hearted Netter and his gallant regiment are in

19 Gabriel Netter to George D. Prentice, Aug. 21, 1862, Office of the Governor, James F. Robinson: Governor's Official Correspondence File, Military Correspondence, 1862-1863, R2-22 to R2-23, Kentucky Department for Libraries and Archives, Frankfort, KY. Accessed via the *Civil War Governors of Kentucky Digital Documentary Edition*, discovery.civilwargovernors.org/document/KYR-0001-027-0015, (accessed Oct. 1, 2018); U.S., Compiled Service Records of Volunteer Union Soldiers Who Served in Organizations from the State of Kentucky, 1861-1865, M397, Roll 0380, National Archives.

20 *OR* series III, vol. 2, 404, 464.

> the field. We know we should hear a good account of them. When he takes the field, the rebels will seek their holes.[21]

Obstacles notwithstanding, Netter continued to gain recruits and arms for his regiment. Until this time, Johnson had mostly operated west of the Green River, but continued supply needs would push his regiment to operate on the east side. Though Netter's regiment eventually began to coalesce, the Partisan Rangers would test its readiness and the pluck of its commander.

21 *Evansville Daily Journal*, Sep. 6, 1862, 1; *Louisville Journal*, Sep. 15, 1862, 3; *OR* series III, vol. 2, 417, 479.

Chapter 10

"I frankly acknowledge I was scared"

While Gabriel Netter moved his Federal recruits to Owensboro, Johnson and Martin set their sights on another target, Uniontown, Kentucky, roughly 30 miles west of Henderson. Located on the Ohio River, near the point where the Wabash River converges, Uniontown sat directly across from Northern territory at the southwest point of Indiana. Not a large place, but like the other key towns in this part of the country, Uniontown benefited from the traffic on the Ohio. Union authorities considered the town and its location important enough for river security that the 30-day 78th Indiana received orders to move there and occupy the area.[1]

Uniontown possessed weapons, ammunition, and supplies that Johnson still desperately needed. To Johnson, the town appeared easy pickings, with the 300 inexperienced men of the 78th guarding it. He planned to use similar tactics as before: rush, surprise, and overwhelm enemy forces with superior numbers before they could properly react, surround them if possible, and force their surrender. It had worked at Hopkinsville and Clarksville, and it would work at Uniontown as well, though with less surprise and more fighting.[2]

The Indiana men had been in Uniontown for some time before Johnson's attack. They encamped in an open wood, with an open field between them and denser woods, which held the picket posts. On September 1, 1862, the 78th's new

1 Johnson, *Partisan Rangers*, 117, 346; *Evansville Daily Journal*, Aug. 2, 1862, 3; William H. H. Terrell, *Report of the Adjutant General of the State of Indiana*, vol. 3, 1866, 21-22.

2 Johnson, *Partisan Rangers*, 346.

A typical view of Union soldiers on picket duty. This image depicts men of the 134th Illinois on picket duty outside Columbus, Kentucky, in 1864. *LOC*

picket detail of only six men marched to its posts on the Morganfield Road, roughly one-half mile from town. As the unsuspecting relief took their new positions, the forward scouts of the Breckinridge Guards opened fire. The exchange of gunfire lasted only a few brief moments, but it was enough to send the Southern scouts back to the main force and for Farrow to learn of the impending attack.[3]

The Indiana men were not the only combat novices on the field. Sergeant Benjamin Field's Company E was at the head of the Southern column moving toward the sounds of the skirmish. He remembered:

> The first thing to greet my eyes was a magnificent horse shot in the breast which came out his flank and then through the thick part of his leg. That convinced me a man stood a poor show if one of those minne balls should strike him. . . . Lieut White was in command of our Company to-day. He was at the battle of Shilo and had heard balls whistle before. A few stray balls was heard and he told us to protect ourselves behind trees for if one of those spent balls should hit us they would hurt. I had seen that horse and was thoroughly convinced he was right.[4]

3 *History of Union County, Kentucky*, 518; *Indianapolis Star*, Sep. 4, 1862, 3; Field, *Memoir*, 32.

4 Field, *Memoir*, 33.

Johnson's main force now advanced toward the enemy, not yet knowing if they would stand and fight. Johnson later wrote that his regiment found the Union forces in line of battle, ready to meet him and his men. Johnson deployed his rangers in response and placed the captured gun from Clarksville—the "Clarksville Belle"—on the right of the main line. His instructions were to keep the gun trained upon the Federal front. Johnson then sent Martin to flank on the right while he himself advanced with the center.[5]

The 78th drew itself up in a line of battle in a cornfield and faced the oncoming Confederates with a small force of their skirmishers. The cornfield bordered a large, wooded thicket, which concealed much of the Confederate movements until they entered the field opposite the 78th. With a severe drought in the area, the cornfield would not have hidden the Federal defenders from the attacking raiders.[6]

Within the cornfield, Capt. Tilghman Howard led Company C and the 60 enlisted men under his command. At approximately 2:00 p.m., the first shots from the Confederate muskets and shotguns began hissing in his direction. Before the Union soldiers could do anything to stymie the Confederate onslaught, a musket ball struck the 22-year-old captain. The wound proved to be mortal, and he died several hours later, the only Federal soldier designated "killed" at Uniontown.[7]

The Confederates must not have had a clear line of site of the cornfield where Pvt. Ransom Hawley and the 78th were in line. "We could not see 50 yards in front of us for the foliage on the trees but before we reached the foot of that hill and I could see what was going on my fear left me," Ranger Benjamin Field explained. The dismounted horsemen were ordered to hold their fire unless they had a clear shot at the enemy. For such raw and untrained soldiers, the Confederates, somewhat surprisingly, obeyed this order. On many other occasions, green troops fired their weapons out of fear even if there was no readily available target. Obviously, the order itself owed to the regiment's ongoing ammunition shortage. This problem constantly drove Johnson's strategy and resulted in the unending need to raid the supplies and weapons of these scattered and isolated Union regiments.[8]

Hawley volunteered for the skirmish line meeting Johnson's advance. Here he could see the entire assault unfolding. He watched "some 700 men and boys on foot armed with shot guns or anything they could pick up" form up on the

5 Johnson, *Partisan Rangers*, 117.

6 Ransom Hawley hand-written notes found in *Partisan Rangers*, no date, VCPL; *Evansville Daily Journal*, Sep. 3, 1862, 2.

7 Captain Tilghman Howard, Widow Pension Application, Case Files of Approved Pension Applications of Widows and Other Veterans of the Army and Navy Who Served Mainly in the Civil War and the War With Spain, compiled 1861–1934, National Archives.

8 Field, *Memoir*, 34.

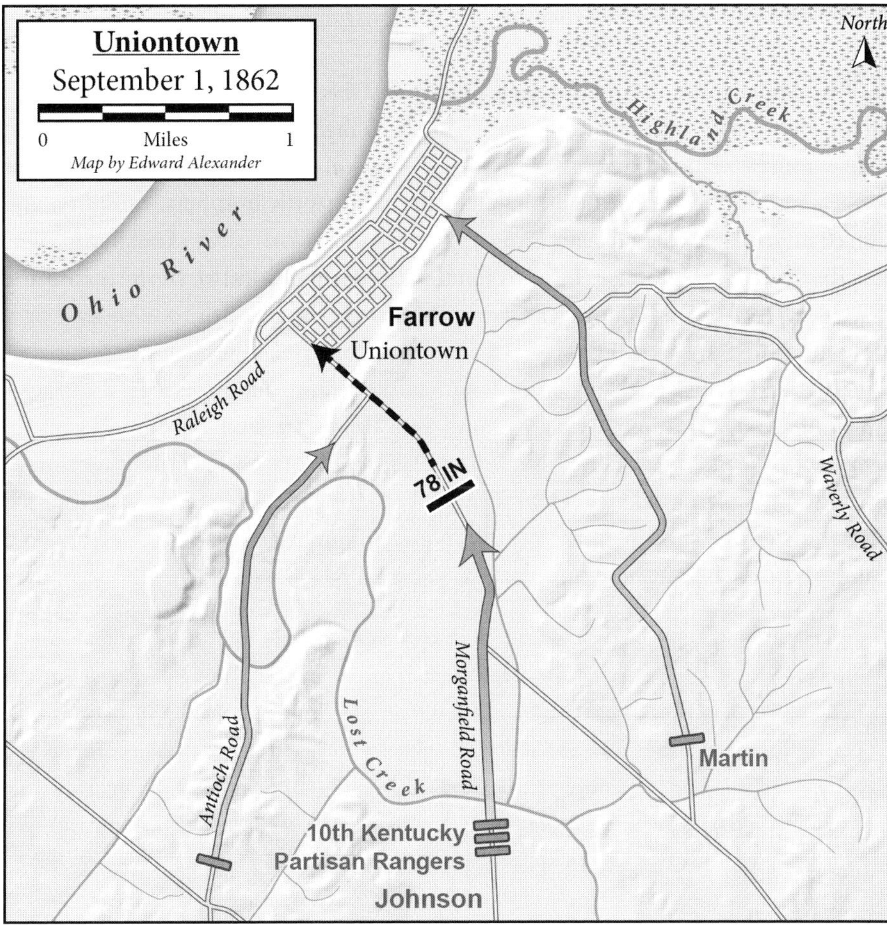

regiment's right and front. Hawley added that, "Johnson's infantry stretched from the Morganfield Road running north to the river road running east." The "infantry" that Hawley describes must have been Johnson's men moving forward in a dismounted manner.[9]

Benjamin Field experienced a roller coaster of emotions while entering his first fight, similar to what green soldiers such as Hawley felt on the other side of the battlefield. "Well orders came to *forward march* double quick. I frankly acknowledge I was scared and would of [sic] been glad if the order had been to go the other way. Lieut White gave the order and we started but not a double quick,"

9 Hawley notes in *Partisan Rangers*, no date, VCPL.

he remembered. Soon, Field encountered the terrifying *zip* and *buzz* of the Federal Enfield bullets.[10]

The fight in the cornfield lasted only a few minutes, though Hawley would later say that the 78th "gave him a good sharp fight." The regiment's adjutant, T. C. Grooms, claimed the fight lasted nearly two hours, but this is doubtful. The Rangers' ammunition shortage suggests otherwise. With numbers, mobility, and a piece of artillery, the Partisan Rangers made quick work of the Indiana soldiers outside of town. Field says he only had two opportunities to shoot before the retreat commenced. It is not clear if an officer ordered the 78th to withdraw or if the soldiers fled on their own.[11]

As the 78th fell back to Uniontown, soldiers continued to trade shots with the Confederates through Water, Second, and Third Streets. The Federals kept up this fire until some men gained the house of a Mr. Williams with the intention of making some sort of defense. Field says the Federals took refuge in an old tobacco factory. After one shot from the Southern gun, the men in the house surrendered along with the rest of the Union force. Field recalled:

> Our artillery was brought up and made noise enough to scare old regulars to death much less raw recruits as they were. Our ordinance for our cannon was blasting powder and a shot bag of minnie balls so whenever it was turned loose hardly a plank on that factory escaped receiving a ball. We soon dislodged them and they attempted to escape up the river. I saw one man in a garden of high weeds and from the direction he was going I saw he would soon be in a clear place in front of a window as he darkined [sic] the window I fired. Subsequently I saw a man as a prisoner and he related the incident and said he was not hit but he thought every pane of glass in that window was shattered.[12]

Union Pvt. William H. Allen wrote to the *Evansville Daily Journal*, "Our little command of 146 men . . . was attacked by 800 mounted guerrillas under Col. Johnson. . . . [W]e were surrounded and forced to surrender." Of course, Allen's numbers do not agree with other sources such as Johnson's, or other eyewitness accounts. A contributor from Uniontown, who also happened to be a Confederate sympathizer, wrote of the numbers at Uniontown:

> I understood from federal soldiers that their whole number at this place, including the sick, was 280. As near as I could learn, Johnson had with him here about 400 men; about

10 Field, *Memoir*, 33.

11 Hawley notes in *Partisan Rangers*, no date, VCPL; *Evansville Daily Journal*, Sep. 4, 1862, 1; Field, *Memoir*, 34; Johnson, *Partisan Rangers*, 117.

12 Field, *Memoirs*, 35-36.

> 250 of these were engaged in the fight. . . . Johnson's whole force was not with him; a part having been sent to Henderson county to intercept another party of Federal soldiers on their way to re-inforce Col. Shackelford's command. This I learn from one of his men. I do not know of my own knowledge whether it is true or not, but believe it to be so from the character of the information.

No other source mentions anything about Johnson splitting his forces to intercept an attack by Foster and Shackelford from Henderson. Not even from Johnson. Whether this actually happened is unknown.[13]

Before the fighting subsided, some men of the 78th managed to slip the closing Confederate noose. Field gives an intriguing story on what happened as he and some other Confederates tried to stop the Union soldiers from escaping. He wrote in his memoirs:

> About this time Col Johnson ordered us to cut off their retreat up the river. At this time I was on the extreme right with only three men between me and the end of our line. Immediately in front was a pond but a little to our right was a road with 2 gum trees on either side. The first man ran to the first tree the second followed. First one went to the second tree just as the 3rd man reached the road and immediately in my front a ball pierced his breast and with a groan he was dead. We three ran right toward the enemy before we could go in the direction we wanted. The ladies perfectly oblivious to danger were out in their yards cheering us on.
>
> We finally after running about two squares up intersepted [sic] them and as they would attempt to crass the street we would shoot and hollow [sic]. We succeeded in cutting one fellow down and whenever he would gather himself up and leap we would shoot and hollow. The Colonel had to come to us and tell us they had surrendered.[14]

Johnson relates that he found Col. Farrow in his headquarters "much excited, as he had been told that he need expect no quarter, for the rebels were only a band of guerrillas intent upon butchery." In looking at earlier similar situations, Johnson tended to label surrendering officers as "excited" or otherwise very nervous, and terrified of him and his men. According to Johnson, Farrow had told his men they might expect no mercy if they fell into the hands of the Breckinridge Guards. Others claim they never witnessed Farrow present during the fight, and that no soldier saw him until he surrendered to Johnson. After the surrender had taken place, another man reported that Farrow was "sitting in his tent flanked by a demijohn of whisky and a Rebel friend." The mystery Rebel citizen of Uniontown

13 *Evansville Daily Journal*, Sep. 3, 1862, 2.

14 Field, *Memoirs*, 37.

put it bluntly: "Colonel Farrow at the time of the attack was at his headquarters, some three hundred yards from camp, and all I can learn did not reach the field of battle during the fight. His men charge him with cowardice."[15]

An uneasy pattern had seemed to develop in this part of the war with cowardly officers unwilling to fight. The *Evansville Daily Journal* eviscerated Farrow for his alleged timidity. The paper did not hide its disappointment, especially since the editors had just recently lavished Farrow with high praise. Only days had passed since the perceived cowardly surrender at Clarksville by Colonel Mason, and now more of the same at Uniontown. The paper seethed, "We hope the government will investigate the conduct of . . . Colonel Farrow . . . and if they have acted as pusillanimously as is represented, that they will be severely dealt with."[16]

Others defended Farrow's conduct, which the *Daily Journal* printed. One defender wrote:

> Mr. Cowgill says, also, that after he was wounded, Colonel Farrow said to him not to leave the field if possible, and that if he could not stand, to sit down and fire away. It should be noted that Col. Farrow *could not* be seen by all his men through all the engagement. Few commanders can—especially in a fight that is sprung by a clandestine attack. . . . It is intimated that Mr. Farrow was drinking. Mr. Farrow may occasionally drink, but he is not known as a drinking man; and though I have known him for years, I have never heard of his being drunk. . . . I am not to apologize for even my friend if he has been grossly recreant of important trusts confided to him; when it appears that he did his duty fully, promptly and gallantly, then I feel it to be my duty to place his conduct in a just, and proper light, that the gallant and brave may not go unrequited of the honor due and really to be accorded by all patriotic citizens.[17]

The paper took pains to make sure their readers knew their stance on Farrow. They did not think of him as a coward and still held that belief. They did question his preparedness for such an attack and wondered why the regiment carelessly guarded Uniontown, however.[18]

The reputation of the Partisan Rangers as bloodthirsty marauders proved false, and the Federal prisoners were paroled and released to passing steamers en route to Evansville. Hawley says that the Rebels did not capture all the Federals at Uniontown. In one letter, he mentioned that Johnson "did not have enough

15 Johnson, *Partisan Rangers*, 117-118; *Evansville Daily Journal*, Sep. 8, 1862, 1.

16 *Evansville Daily Journal*, Sept. 3, 1862, 2.

17 *Evansville Daily Journal*, Sep. 6, 1862, 2.

18 Ibid., Sep.10, 1862, 2; Hawley notes in *Partisan Rangers*, no date, VCPL.

cavalry men to intercept our men who escaped up the river and were picked up next day by a steamboat." In another letter, "Two strong squads escaped up above the town; and were picked up by the steam boat next day."[19]

The Confederates loaded wagons full of weapons and equipment and moved to Geiger's Lake. They had captured at least 150 stands of "fine arms." Hawley indicated in his letters that his regiment fought at Uniontown with the British-made Enfield rifled muskets. Understandably, some of Johnson's men may have helped themselves to these new arms and thrown away their old shotguns. Benjamin Field recorded that they took 350 stands of arms but he likely over-estimated.[20]

One civilian witness gave an account of the Federal casualties as he heard them related by Johnson. He claims that he heard the Hoosiers had suffered one killed and 20 wounded. Barter added that the Confederates did not give an account of their casualties to him. Field says his side lost "1 killed and 3 wounded." The *History of Union County, Kentucky* states that two more men of the 78th died en route to Evansville and that the Confederates lost seven wounded and one man, Brown, killed. A Uniontown citizen recalled, "The Federals had six missing. Some of these were supposed to be dead, but none have been found up to this time. Several swam the river, one of which was reported drowned." The official roles of the 78th Indiana list no other man killed except Captain Howard.

The wounds suffered by the 78th give ample evidence of Johnson's need for better weapons. Several of the wounded Federals treated in Uniontown suffered from head and facial buckshot wounds that did not penetrate the skull. Hawley, one of the Union wounded, received a slight wound to the leg. While laid up on a cot he recalled a "Texas Ranger" placing the butt of his shotgun on the bed and bragging about the daring victories of the previous weeks. After he read Johnson's book more than 50 years later, Hawley wrote to a friend, "Johnson left that night he says he had sixty a number of men sick; posibly [sic] some of them had lead poison from our Enfield rifles. The citizens told us the next day Johnson hauled his dead and wounded away by wagon loads. He says nothing about his causalities."[21]

The unnamed Uniontown Rebel sympathizer recalled:

> After the surrender, the Federal troops were treated like brothers and especially the wounded were treated with brotherly attention both by the soldiers and citizens. The Confederate surgeons and the physicians of the town did all in their power for the

19 *Evansville Daily Journal*, Sep. 3, 1862, 2; Hawley notes in *Partisan Rangers*, no date, VCPL; Hawley to Miss Crawford, no date, VCPL.

20 Hawley to Miss Crawford, no date, VCPL; Field, *Memoirs*, 37.

21 *Evansville Daily Journal*, Sep. 4, 1862, 2; Field, *Memoirs*, 137; Hawley notes in *Partisan Rangers*, no date, VCPL; *History of Union County*, 518-519.

> wounded without regard to their politics. Many of the wounded were carried to private houses—both Federals and Confederate wounded were taken to the same house—and both received all the attention that could be given for their comfort and welfare, and as all the provisions were taken from the prisoners the houses were thrown open to them and they were supplied with food as long as they stayed in town; many of them were high toned gentlemen and deserved to be treated as such.[22]

The Federal forces across the Ohio in Illinois were not entirely unaware or unconcerned with the action at Uniontown. Colonel John Crebs of the newly organized 87th Illinois Infantry based at Shawneetown, Illinois, received word of Rebel movements on the Kentucky side of the Ohio. Initially, all information pointed to the Confederates attacking Caseyville, several miles downriver. Crebs mobilized a force to proceed on steamers to Caseyville. Upon arriving they learned that the town remained unoccupied, but that Uniontown had fallen. Crebs ordered his Illinoisans back to the boats to return to Shawneetown for reinforcements and artillery. Officers of the 87th later reported that the plan was to set off from Shawneetown in the early morning hours of September 2nd. After some difficulty in loading the guns, the steamers finally set course well after daybreak. Reports indicate that Crebs requested the boat captains to land his men right at Uniontown's riverbank in order to take the Confederates by surprise, but the captains flatly refused. Instead, they disembarked three miles downriver, where the 87th posted a strong picket line and dispatched scouts toward Uniontown. Reports came back to Crebs that Johnson's men had left the town, so the Union soldiers boarded the steamers for Uniontown. The officers reported:

> The *Sallie List* with the same companies as before . . . being in front, and three companies on each of the other boats, with orders to all stop if fired on from the town, that the artillery should reply, and all the boats be run ashore as soon as possible and charge into the town. We reached the wharf, however no shot was fired—what few rebel soldiers were there quickly got away, and we quietly took possession of the town.

Crebs and the 87th Illinois fanned out several miles into the interior around Uniontown, and finding none of Johnson's men, returned to the river town. Here the Illinois soldiers helped embark more of Farrow's paroled men to Evansville. In the initial report of Crebs's actions after Uniontown, printed in the *Evansville Daily Journal,* the boat captains claimed they urged Crebs into action. They maintained that they, not Crebs, proposed moving directly on Uniontown with the boats. This

22 *Evansville Daily Journal,* Sep. 8, 1862, 1.

report elicited the response of seven captains and thirteen lieutenants a week later. The Federal response to Johnson's success remained lackluster.[23]

Major General John Love, commander of the Indiana Legion, wired Governor Morton, who was in Louisville, of the disaster at Uniontown. Love relayed information "that Johnson captured three hundred at Uniontown killing Capt Howard only one hundred and seventy at Henderson. Johnson marching on Henderson tonight and expected to attack it tonight." Morton assented to the idea of sending the 91st Indiana, not yet fully organized, to defend Henderson.[24]

Of course, Johnson was not foolish enough to attack such a strong force. He admitted that many of his horses were in no shape to continue an active campaign to capture Henderson, which he ultimately wanted. Further, he realized that the news of Uniontown's capture would quickly spread to Henderson, which Foster's infantry, and Colonel Shackelford, and Major Platter's cavalry, used as their base of operations. Johnson rightly feared that those combined forces would capture his tired men. He suspected the Federals were already on the move toward Uniontown.[25]

The *Evansville Daily Journal* voiced its desire for Union forces to defeat Johnson: "Our people are getting aroused, and have determined to meet the traitors and guerrillas on the border, and mete out to them such punishment as their cowardly outrages deserve," the *Journal* blustered. "Our city presented a war like appearance yesterday, and the streets gleamed with bayonets." Other papers ran stories that 1,100 Rebels had sacked Uniontown and in so doing massacred a handful of citizens and Union soldiers. They erroneously reported that John H. Morgan led the attack. Over the course of the next few days, the paper would get more of the details and correct their initial reports. It likewise called for action against guerrillas, as they still had not been defeated in the region since the Newburgh raid in July.[26]

So ready to see Johnson defeated, the Evansville newspaper printed a dare and taunt to Johnson and his men on September 3rd:

> Johnson, we believe, prides himself on his chivalry, but he is always careful not to make an attack when there is a force any ways near equal to his to meet him. Robbing hospitals or disabled steamers is his forte. Johnson sent his compliments to the editors of the Evansville Journal and the Cincinnati Commercial, and says he is now in command of the post at Uniontown, and expects to remain there until the U.S. send a force there sufficient to

23 *Evansville Daily Journal*, Sep. 3, 1862, 2; Sep. 13, 1862, 2.

24 Morton Telegraphs, Morton telegram book, no. 7, 374.

25 Johnson, *Partisan Rangers*, 118.

26 *Richmond Weekly Platinum*, Sep. 12, 1862, 2; *Evansville Daily Journal*, Sep. 3, 1862, 2.

> drive him way. Why don't you bring us the word yourself, Adam! We promise you a warm reception and a gay time of it if you will visit Evansville. Why don't you hunt up Col's Foster and Shackelford? You ain't afraid are you? We fear Johnson is a humbug and a cheat, as he had scarce made the promise to stay at Uniontown when he skedaddled.[27]

Johnson made the decision to do what partisans often did—disappear into and blend in with the population. He ordered his regiment temporarily disbanded. Such an audacious order served two purposes. One, it allowed his men to disappear over an expanse of territory the Union army could not control. This should not have been too difficult for his men as "Johnson and his surgeon were the only men who wore anything like uniforms," and "[n]one of his men were uniformed," according to Hawley.[28] Second, each man became a recruiting agent for the regiment. News of Johnson's exploits, spread by those who witnessed and participated in the events, was the greatest recruiting tool at his disposal.

In the meantime, Johnson moved most of the newly captured supplies to Geiger's Lake, just south of Uniontown, where he and some of his officers and men would camp while the rest of the command scattered throughout the region. The regiment would rendezvous later. Benjamin Field traveled with a squad of 19 men with orders to report back to the regiment at White Sulphur Springs on September 5th.[29]

Meanwhile, the charges of cowardly Federal efforts continued to rile the population. Though the *Evansville Daily Journal* tepidly defended Farrow, its editors demanded bolder action. "There have been too many of these parties gobbled up by the guerrillas through the pusillanimity of their commanding officers. It is time they should end," demanded the paper. Little did the *Daily Journal* editors know their wish would come true in less than three weeks' time.[30]

27 *Evansville Daily Journal*, Sep. 3, 1862, 2.

28 Hawley, notes in *Partisan Rangers*, no date, VCPL; John Will Dyer, *Reminiscences, or, Four years in the Confederate Army: A history of the experiences of the private soldier in camp, hospital, prison, on the march, and on the battlefield, 1861 to 1865* (Evansville, IN, 1898), 60.

29 Field, *Memoirs*, 37; Johnson, *Partisan Rangers*, 118.

30 *Evansville Daily Journal*, Sep. 3, 1862, 2.

Chapter 11

"We needed not his assurance to know the Yankees were upon us and following in the retreat"

Geiger's Lake

As the command dispersed into small squads throughout the countryside, Johnson, Martin, and a few others encamped at Geiger's Lake, southwest of Uniontown in Union County. A short distance from the Ohio River where it bends southward as it flows toward the Mississippi, the camp's location seemed like an easy place to fall into Federal hands. Why Johnson chose Geiger's Lake for his sanctuary is unknown. Johnson later contended that he kept about 60 men with him while other sources say nearly 100. Reports indicate that several of those men suffered from exhaustion and sickness. In camp, he also kept much of the recently captured supplies and equipment from Uniontown. Here, the Confederates believed themselves to be safe from the Federal forces hunting them. Johnson could not have been more wrong.[1]

By uncharacteristically opting for defense rather than staying on the offensive, Johnson missed an opportunity to attack Henderson and its valuable stores: Foster and Shackelford were not even in Henderson as Johnson had believed, and only a meager force of 170 men defended the town.[2]

It was in fact a double blunder. Not only did Johnson miss a chance to mount a successful raid on Henderson, his retreat exposed him to greater danger. Shackelford, it turned out, was not only not at Henderson; he and three companies

1 *History of Union County*, 519; Johnson, *Partisan Rangers*, 118.

2 Morton Telegraphs, Morton telegram book, no. 7, 374.

Colonel James Shackelford, pictured later in the war after his promotion to brigadier general. *Schlamp-Meyer Family Collection, University of Southern Indiana*

of his 8th Kentucky Cavalry were on the move directly south of Geiger's Lake at Caseyville, on the Ohio River. He and some of his men had left Henderson on a "guerrilla hunt," even while the 8th Kentucky was still being recruited. Shackelford and Foster marched out from Henderson but split their forces near Morganfield in the days prior. Foster took his column southeast towards Slaughters, where many of Johnson's dispersed squads would surely be taking refuge. Shackelford moved southwest to Caseyville on the Ohio River. Johnson did not expect anyone to come from that direction, much less Shackelford's cavalry.[3]

On September 3, 1862, the small, ailing party of rangers had only been encamped for a few hours when word reached them that Shackelford's column was approaching. Johnson knew the numbers favored the enemy, but for once he had more than enough weapons. He still had several of the stands of Enfields from Uniontown, plus the small artillery piece. He also had Bob Martin.[4]

Johnson placed Martin with more than 50 men on the main road to the camp to ambush the Federals, while Johnson stayed with a small squad of less than 20, mostly incapacitated, in the camp. Unfortunately for Johnson, Shackelford advanced by another road and the ominous shot of a lonely picket was all that gave warning to Johnson and his invalids. They quickly mounted, carrying every new weapon they could manage, and rode around to the opposite side of the lake where they "left their camp and took to the brush."[5]

Shackelford and his men rode into the empty bivouac where they found some of the recently captured equipment and weapons. Believing the guerrillas had completely abandoned the camp, the men began to take stock of their prizes

3 *Evansville Daily Journal*, Sep. 8, 1862, 2; James R. Bently, "Memoirs of Thomas Speed," 237-238.

4 Johnson, *Partisan Rangers*, 118.

5 Ibid., 118; *Evansville Daily Journal*, Sep. 8, 1862, 2.

and "found in the camp a large pile of guns, and considerable other stores." A Federal officer with Shackelford reported that they burned the camp shortly after capturing it. While Shackelford pondered what could have happened to the Rebels and where they might have fled, Johnson and his small squad opened fire from the other side of the lake with "a heavy volley . . . poured upon them from the brush, killing one man and wounding ten or eleven others." The Union cavalry quickly retreated and regrouped while Shackelford ordered his men to dismount and return fire.[6]

Martin heard the shooting at camp and immediately rode back to his comrades. The former scout in Martin evidently had not left him; along the way he observed the number and location of the enemy. He hid his men in some tall weeds with the cannon and advanced alone into a field. He hoped to draw the attention and fire of the Federals to relieve some of the pressure on Johnson. Johnson later wrote that Martin "boldly took his way down this roadway as if he were out on a pleasure ride instead of for the purpose of attracting toward himself the fire of the Federal guns." His plan worked. A body of Union cavalry moved his way and Martin galloped toward them as if leading a hundred men. In his brave and imprudent ride, Martin had his hat shot off and suffered several new holes in his clothing. His horse even received a wound. Despite the punishment, as later sources recounted, Martin somehow managed to laugh and shake his fist at the enemy as he rode back into the weeds where the rest of his men awaited his return.[7]

As the enemy advanced, Martin ordered his men to open fire at about 100 yards, including with the "Clarksville Belle." The firing at this close distance forced Shackelford's Kentuckians back. During the next attack, a young recruit rode one of the two mules that pulled the Confederate gun. The animals became agitated at the noise of the skirmish. The mules pulled the limber box out into the field in full view of both sides and back into the weeds again at a different location. This occurred several times more to the point where the Union troopers believed Martin to have numerous pieces of artillery and a much larger force than they anticipated. The Kentuckians' morale began to evaporate and the attack dissipated. Another ruse, even if unintended, had again saved Johnson.[8]

Shackelford had taken a piece of shot from the Confederate cannon in his foot during this part of the fighting. It could have been from one of the sacks of minie balls the Rebels fired or one of the cut bars of lead they used as improvised artillery

6 *History of Union County*, 158-159; *Evansville Daily Journal*, Sep. 8, 1862, 2; Johnson, *Partisan Rangers*, 119.

7 Johnson, *Partisan Rangers*, 119-120.

8 Ibid., 120; *Evansville Daily Journal*, Sep. 8, 1862, 2.

ammunition. This same shot killed his horse as well. With a painful wound, dead horse, dwindling ammunition, and enemy fire coming from two sides, Shackelford ordered the retreat of his cavalry back to Caseyville. It was another victory for the Partisan Rangers, but this time by the skin of Johnson's teeth.[9] In fact, so narrow was the victory that one of Johnson's men, who had found himself isolated from both groups, had begun throwing some of the raiders' weapons into the lake lest they fall into Federal hands. Luckily, Martin returned with his squad and put a stop to the panic.[10]

This small but important skirmish resulted in few casualties. Shackelford's wound, though not life-threatening, kept him—and his aggressive nature—out of the saddle for weeks. The Rebel citizen from Uniontown seems to have erroneously reported that the Federals lost nearly "thirty killed and wounded, and were still bringing them in." The Federals appear to have only lost one man killed and several wounded, with Johnson losing about the same.[11] But if not a decisive strategic encounter, there were positive consequences for Northern morale. The Northern press seemed desperate for anything resembling a victory in western Kentucky. Even in faraway Michigan, the *Detroit Free Press* released a sensational headline, "REBELS ROUTED IN KENTUCKY." The paper reported, "On Sunday last Col. Shackelford met a force of rebels at Morganfield, and surprised them, killing some and taking several prisoners. Shackelford then divided his force, sending Lieutenant Colonel Foster, with two companies of cavalry, in the direction of Slaughtersville. Foster overtook a part of the enemy, killed two, took twenty-three prisoners and forty horses."[12]

The summer campaign of the Partisan Rangers could have ended that day had it not been for a little bit of luck and some daring on the part of Robert Martin. Obviously, Geiger's Lake was no longer a safe haven after Shackelford's attack. The 8th Kentucky moved back into Henderson where Shackelford took some time to recuperate. With the 8th Kentucky Cavalry spread over various locations across western and southern Kentucky, Maj. James Holloway took over temporary command of the Henderson battalion of the regiment.[13]

At Morganfield, Foster sent a message to Governor Morton in which he describes Shackelford "scattering" Johnson's men after pursuing them "night and day." However, "It was impossible to reach them before they took Uniontown

9 Johnson, *Partisan Rangers*, 120; *Evansville Daily Journal*, Sep. 8, 1862, 1, 2.

10 *History of Union County*, 158-159.

11 *Evansville Daily Journal*, Sep. 8, 1862, 1.

12 *Detroit Free Press*, Sep. 7, 1862, 1.

13 Bently, "Memoirs of Thomas Speed," 238.

An unidentified Union soldier thought to be from a Kentucky cavalry regiment.
LOC

their movement was swift and very rapid." He ended with a plea, "our cavalry force is insufficient cant [sic] you send more[?]" Foster correctly believed that if they had more cavalry, or at least fully equipped cavalry, unlike the 4th Indiana, Johnson's outfit could have been bagged and their swift maneuvers countered.[14]

In the days following Geiger's Lake, the Partisan Rangers planned to rendezvous and concentrate again in western Kentucky. The summer campaign had so far been nearly flawless, minus the setbacks at Dover and Geiger's Lake. Numerous towns and garrisons had fallen into their hands, often without a shot fired. Johnson's men suffered only the lightest of casualties, and the ranks continued to swell with young Southern men eager to fight. Union counter-offensives remained halting and ineffective, threatening Northern morale. With events transpiring in such a positive manner, Johnson decided that the time had come for him to travel to Richmond. There he could obtain commissions for his officers, turn in his muster rolls, and legitimize his regiment, which he believed was important not only for his recruitment efforts, but also to guarantee proper treatment should any of his raiders fall prisoner to the Federals. With Johnson traveling to Richmond, the 22-year-old Robert Martin took command of the regiment. He would not enjoy the same success.

* * *

After the victory at Uniontown, Sgt. Benjamin Field and a small squad of 19 men scattered throughout the countryside. Having narrowly escaped Geiger's Lake, Johnson established a new sanctuary in western Kentucky, in Union County. This position afforded him ready targets on the Ohio, Green, Cumberland, and Tennessee Rivers. It was sanctuaries like this on which the Partisan Rangers relied for food and refuge, provided by supportive civilians. Though in friendly territory,

14 John W. Foster to Governor Oliver Morton, Sep. 3, 1862, Morton Telegraphs.

Johnson had ordered his men not to quarter themselves in houses as it was too easy to be captured. Field's squad did not entirely heed this order, and other squads acting in a similar manner allowed the struggling Union forces an opportunity to strike back.[15]

On September 5th, Col. John W. Foster messaged Governor Morton from Madisonville: "I left Morganfield on the second with two companies of cavalry in pursuit of 200 guerrillas fleeing towards Webster County—after several hours march I found their trail and followed it through the thick woods and swampy by ways for thirty miles. We came upon the . . . company yesterday in the hills of Webster County and attacked them . . . taking twenty two prisoners . . . [and] all their arms including a part taken at Uniontown and all their company papers." As he had on the 3rd, Foster again pleaded for more cavalry: "[I]f we had more cavalry we could prevent further concentrations in this region." One 65th Indiana soldier, Thomas Henderson, wrote in a letter describing the constant search for the guerrillas: "[S]ince my last to you I have been knocked around in so many different places that I have had little time to write to anyone. . . . Day before yesterday our company started on a scout and captured 8 prisoners, 2 wagons, 20 horses and 12 mules and returned late last night. I am very tired as you may guess," he wrote on September 7th.[16]

Wherever Foster concentrated forces, he threw out pickets to prevent surprise attacks by Johnson. These pickets were attacked on a near-nightly basis, so Foster sent out patrols to capture anyone suspected of committing these attacks. Field and the men with him were probably not the ones committing the attacks but to the Union troops that rode up that morning, it did not matter.

Field's 19 men stayed at a Mr. Stull's home where they had previously bunked. Federal troops still lurked in the area, even after Uniontown, although Field's group seemed to be unaware of the fact. Field recorded that the men felt so secure that they did not post a single picket. "Some of the boys had brought in some peaches and we were lounging around in the shade eating peaches and haveing [sic] a good time generally," Field recalled later, "never dreaming the enemy was in 50 miles of us, did not have a picket out even feeling so secure we had vanquished every enemy in that part of the state."[17]

15 Field, *Memoirs*, 38; Richard P. Gildrie, "Guerrilla Warfare in the Lower Cumberland River Valley, 1862-1865," *Tennessee Historical Quarterly* 49 no. 3 (1990): 166-167.

16 John W. Foster to Governor Oliver Morton, Sep. 5, 1862, Morton Telegraphs; *Chicago Tribune*, Sep. 8, 1862, 2; Letter of Private Thomas D. Henderson to Jeff, Sep. 7, 1862, BHL.

17 Foster, *War Stories*, 100; Field, *Memoirs*, 38.

The Federal troops surrounded the unsuspecting Rebels who promptly surrendered without fighting. "It looked to me they wanted to kill everyone of us," Field remembered. Field had the idea of shooting an unsuspecting Yankee but thought better of it and surrendered. Two others tried to escape capture but were killed in the process. The Kentuckian recalled, "Two of our boys who went just in front of me into the same garden and jumped over the fence right in the midst of the enemy and were mercilessly shot down would not heed their entreaties to surrender. These poor unfortunate boys was John Cottrell . . . and Tom Robberson [Robertson]." Field knew both men well.[18]

The *Owensboro Monitor* reported that Federal cavalry surrounded local "guerrillas" in an orchard. One of the Rebels shot a Union soldier after being told to surrender, but then "he fell pierced by a dozen bullets. Thomas Robinson [Robertson] was also killed. The rest were taken prisoners."[19]

The Union troopers brought Field and the other captives to Madisonville where a schoolhouse became their prison. Other prisoners, captured earlier, also populated the building, identified by Field as political prisoners. The men entertained themselves as best they could with dancing and singing. Citizens brought food from the hotel, and the men fashioned the school desks into a type of dinner table.[20]

The next day Foster arrived and "very pompously informed us that nearly every night his men on picket were fired on and just the night before [he] had a man killed and he would not put up with it any longer and hereafter if one of his men was hurt he would retaliate on us." He was responsible for restoring order in the area and ridding it of guerrillas, yet his men remained targets for night raiders. His frustrations grew. In his message on September 5th, Foster informed Morton, "For each one murdered a captured guerrilla shall be shot."[21]

Field remarked that what Foster said was true and that the Confederates were supplied stationary to write to their commanders and inform them of the threat. They did not get the reply they hoped for as some Confederate officers sent a reply that "two would play at that game." Johnson's sense of urgency to travel to Richmond and turn in the regiment's roles, which would allow them to be treated as prisoners of war instead of guerrillas, continued to mount.

18 Field, *Memoirs*, 38-39.

19 *Owensboro Monitor*, Sep. 10, 1862, 3.

20 Field, *Memoirs*, 40-41, 43.

21 Field, *Memoirs*, 41; Foster, *War Stories*, 100; John W. Foster to Governor Oliver Morton, Sep. 5, 1862, Morton Telegraphs.

On September 7th, Field and some other prisoners were placed in wagons, ten men and a guard in each. A column of several hundred cavalry and infantry escorted them north. Field insisted that Foster expected to be attacked during the march. If that happened, then the prisoners were to be shot first. The column marched to Ashbyburg on the Green River to await a steamboat, but other guerrillas had gotten there first and sunk the boat. Without boats, they marched to Henderson.

Field remembered, "We were placed in an old storehouse for the night which was as filthy as a hog pen. We never got a mouthful to eat the whole day or night. The next morning I was given about 3 mouthfulls of corn bread and again took our places in the wagons." Rations for prisoners were very meager at this point. Some of the men cast aside the bad blood caused by war, if only for a moment. The driver of Field's wagon dug up some sweet potatoes, filled his hat with the vegetables, and gave them to his enemy. That night in Henderson, Union soldiers placed the prisoners on barges and sent them upriver to Evansville.[22]

The Confederates arrived in the Northern city on September 9th. Ever since Johnson's raid on neighboring Newburgh in July, the entire region was on high alert, fueled by a general antipathy for guerrilla types. The *Evansville Daily Journal* reported, "Col. Foster was in town yesterday in fine health. He brought up some thirty four prisoners captured in his late expedition, whom he forwarded to Indianapolis. We will give their names tomorrow."[23]

The men were marched through the streets amid crowds of jeering onlookers. "After marching on the principal streets as a curiosity and allowing every possibly indignity heaped upon us to that extent I do really believe if it had not been for the guards we would of [sic] suffered violence at their hands. Finally we were marched to the depot and placed on the cars and taken to Tarrehaut where we changed car for Indianapolis," Field remembered. He and the other prisoners traveled to Camp Morton in Indianapolis and then to Johnson's Island in Ohio as prisoners of war. Nearly three months passed before he was exchanged and returned to the Partisan Rangers.[24]

Skirmishes continued to be played out in the press. The *Evansville Daily Journal* made good on its promise by printing the names of several partisans the next day:

> The following are the names of the guerrilla prisoners captured by Col. Foster's command, and sent to Indianapolis on Tuesday.
>
> *Captain S. B. Taylor's Company—*

22 Field, *Memoirs*, 43-45.

23 *Evansville Daily Journal*, Sep. 10, 1862, 2.

24 Field, *Memoirs*, 45-46, 53.

Confederate prisoners at Camp Morton in Indianapolis, Indiana.

LOC

Theodore White, 1st Lieutenant; J. Handley, 2nd Lieutenant; M. V. Proe, 2nd Lieutenant; John M. Green, 3rd Lieutenant; H. S. Jones, William Fisher, R. B. Head, James Hobbs, Benjamin Fields, J. W. Hewitt, Benjamin W. Taylor, William Eaves, R. W. Taylor, J. T. Sutton, Francis M. Wright, Luther C. Ellis.[25]

Fighting Back Against Ambushes

In the early weeks of September, Johnson's detached companies continued to skirmish with Federal forces between Madisonville and Henderson. On September 12th, Lt. Col. Thomas Johnson of the 65th Indiana commanded a Federal column marching from Madisonville back to Henderson. This force included cavalry from both Maj. James H. Holloway's 8th Kentucky and Maj. John Platter's 4th Indiana. Munday and some of the Partisan Rangers unexpectedly collided with this column on the Madisonville Road south of Henderson. A brief fight ensued which saw the Confederates flee after just a few shots. "We heard the firing in front and saw Capt. Fisher with his cap shot off and rushing down the hill on foot and saw his men wheeling in retreat. We needed not his assurance to know the Yankees were upon us and following in the retreat," remembered Munday.[26]

25 *Evansville Daily Journal*, Sep. 11, 1862, 2.

26 Munday, *Diary*, 4.

Foster reported that "the guerrillas concentrated in all their force and made continual attempted attacks to cut them off and destroy the train. They repeatedly attempted to ambush our forces but were always driven off by our skirmishers on the first fire. They never awaited our attack always running as we approach." Though this force was not as large as Foster believed, Munday's account corroborates Foster's telegraph message. Munday recorded that "as soon as the enemies fire was poured upon us and indeed there was few of us that remained long enough to receive it and these fortunately escaped with but a mark or two and the loss of one horse. On reaching the safe side of the field," he continued "we formed in the woods to receive them. Apparently satisfied with their 'moral victory' they did not pursue."[27]

Munday's group collided with the same column the next day. This time the Federals advanced in force. The Confederates repeated their strategy from the day before, not willing to allow the Union cavalry to close with their lines by continuously falling back. The continued pressure forced the lines to buckle, however. The partisans delivered a quick fire and hurried back through the thickets away from the Union cavalrymen. One Confederate was wounded and left at a nearby house, while the rest fled. "The enemy's cannon was leveled, but not in time to harm us," Munday wrote after the fight.[28]

Foster went on to relay, "The march was conducted in good order and with military precision. Great credit is due to Major Holloway and Major Platter and their commands." He also reported that the Union column suffered two killed and several wounded while inflicting casualties on the Southerners, killing at least five and wounding a number more. Foster erroneously believed that Johnson's entire force under Martin had assembled to attack Lt. Col. Thomas Johnson, Holloway, and Platter, when in reality the Confederate force amounted to only a few dozen. The constant firing and retreating may have made their small number appear greater than it really was.[29]

Foster was determined to build up a force that could handle anything the Confederates threw at him. Again, Foster repeated his earlier plea and reminded Morton, "As soon as the cavalry is mustered and the infantry fully equipped I will be ready to take the field much more efficiently." On September 13th he wired Morton, "F. M. Thayer of Evansville desires authority to raise a company for light artillery pieces, four pounders on light carriages. They could be made very effective against the guerillas, the defense of the border, and any department. I earnestly urge that authority be given him for the purpose the company can be

27 Munday, *Diary*, 4; Morton Telegraphs, Morton telegram book, no. 8, 184-186.

28 Munday, *Diary*, 4-5.

29 Morton Telegraphs, Morton telegram book, no. 8, 184-186.

raised immediately." He sent another message on the 16th requesting a different type of artillery. Foster seemed adamant about bolstering his firepower any way he could. "I understand there are a number of light Dahlgren guns at Cairo in naval wharf boat not being used. I have fitted up a little steamer for service on Green River and this part of the Ohio. Can't you have two light guns sent me from there immediately? I will have the locks repaired in two days," he assured Morton. Foster also pleaded for more infantry:

> I telegraphed two days ago the importance of more troops in order to make my force effective. You were absent at the time I refer you to my dispatch. Ninety First (91st Indiana Infantry) at Evansville has five companies ready to muster. Can they not be mustered and sent to Henderson in charge of a major or Lieut Col.? I could use them here as a garrison till the rest of the Regt. is full and go into the country with any present force. I would like as much cavalry as you can send me and if any carbines can be had, arm with them by all means. . . . With a proper force I think I can be [sic] effective work. Can I have the ninety first at this place?

Unfortunately for Foster, none of his requests were provided. Nevertheless, the Federals were beginning to show signs of life in their fight against Johnson. They were finally taking the fight to him. As the Union cavalry discovered in the recent skirmishes, Johnson's men did not relish the idea of a protracted stand-up fight against a pressing enemy. Under pressure, the Confederates were likely to flee.[30]

When Federal troops offered stiff resistance, they began to see results. While Johnson's regiment spread out in the region, small groups of Rebels had moved east of the Green River. They appear to have been on the lookout for Union soldiers on furlough, picket duty, or in small, isolated detachments that they could easily destroy. The *Owensboro Monitor* printed a story of an attack on a detachment of three Union soldiers searching for small groups of Rebels in Daviess County. The Federals, armed with Henry rifles, unexpectedly met a force of Rebels who ordered them to halt. The Unionists hid themselves in the weeds and "poured a continual fire" into the Southerners, forcing a hasty retreat. More Confederates arrived and charged down the lane, but the heavy fire of the Henry rifles repulsed them again, allowing the three Union men to escape. The defenders reported that they inflicted three casualties on the Rebels, along with the killing of five horses.[31]

Another event magnifies the unwillingness of small portions of Johnson's command to fight when faced with superior firepower. On September 13th, Lieutenant Colonel Netter ordered a squad of his new recruits to scout the area

30 Morton Telegraphs, Morton telegram book, no. 8, 182.

31 *Owensboro Monitor*, Sep. 17, 1862, 3.

south of Owensboro. About 40 of Johnson's men ambushed the Union scouts, but quickly fled after they believed they had attacked a much larger force and that they would no longer be able to surprise the main Union body in Owensboro. During the fight, one of Netter's men "finding himself hard press [sic], treed behind a stump, and opened on his pursuers, discharging his sixteen shots in rapid succession. His comrades then took up fire in turn from behind the fence; thus they kept up a continuous fire for some two rounds apiece, when the guerrillas, thinking they had stirred up the entire regiment, broke and fled."[32]

The Union Navy

The Union Navy actively worked to suppress further Rebel activity on the Ohio once Johnson's band grew into a regiment. After Johnson dispersed his command into smaller squads, some of these groups continued guerrilla operations along the river near Caseyville, several miles south of Uniontown and Geiger's Lake. Steamers reported groups of 50–60 guerrillas around the small village as they sometimes attempted to lure the steamers to shore, while others simply fired upon the vessels. To quell these irritations, U.S. Navy Lieutenant LeRoy Fitch ordered punitive measures taken against guerrillas and those harboring them in the Caseyville area. The urgency of the situation required Fitch to arm a "small steamer" and run it north up the Ohio. In an order to the commander of the *Cordelia Ann,* Second Master George Groves, Fitch wrote, "In approaching Caseyville, be particular to keep your men hid from observation, and use every precaution to disguise the true character of the boat and expedition. Should you be fired into at Caseyville, or any resistance offered, destroy the place at once." Fitch also authorized the boat's commander to arrest anyone suspected of aiding the guerrillas. As for the guerrillas themselves, Fitch ordered Groves to avoid taking them prisoners.[33]

In his own steamer, the *Fairplay,* Fitch continued upriver and reached the vicinity of Shawneetown, Illinois. Fitch armed the former Confederate steamer with four 12-pound brass guns. While cruising the river, Fitch noticed the presence of several dozen Rebels on the Kentucky side of the river and tried to land his soldiers and sailors to destroy whatever Confederate encampment they could find. He realized his landing party would not be able to land quickly enough, so he ordered the guns onboard to fire several shells toward the shore. When his men made it

32 Munday, *Diary*, 4; *Evansville Daily Journal*, Sep. 13, 1862, 2.

33 *ORN* 1, vol. 23, 310, 322.

U.S. Gunboat *Fairplay* commanded by LeRoy Fitch.

Naval History and Heritage Command

to the Kentucky side, they advanced three miles inland and chased away a small group of guerrillas encamped near Cypress Lake. The Union needed more speed.[34]

The Indiana Legion

Across the Ohio River in Spencer County, Indiana, state militia forces drilled and patrolled along the river. Their sudden increased activity that summer was in response to Johnson's raid on Newburgh in July and his subsequent actions in the region. As he and his Partisan Rangers roamed western Kentucky, the Indiana Legion of Spencer County prepared to meet him. When they did, they would take the fight to the Confederates.

After Fort Sumter, and Governor Morton's call for the raising and arming of a state militia force for the defense of the state, Col. John W. Crooks took command of the 4th Indiana Legion Regiment, which also came to be known as the Spencer County Legion. He had the necessary experience gained from the war with Mexico and was a trusted leader of the community.[35]

Multiple companies from all over the county made up the Spencer Legion. Not all Indiana Legion companies and regiments around the state were equal. Some

34 *Evansville Daily Journal*, Sep. 18, 1862, 2; *ORN*, 1, vol. 23, 310.

35 Etter, *Indiana Legion*, 86.

wore dashing uniforms, carried decent weapons, and enjoyed proper drill. Others had none of these. The Spencer Legion lacked uniforms but many of the companies were at least partly well-armed. The French Island Guards, from the western part of the county on the Ohio River, carried both Belgian smoothbore muskets and Mississippi rifles. The Love Guards were in possession of Belgian muskets. The Rough and Readies had 39 .69 caliber smoothbore muskets and 20 Belgian muskets in .54 caliber. To the Morton Home Guards the Legion issued "Old Harper's Ferry rifled muskets" that had been converted from flintlock to percussion. The Ebenezer Guards, Anderson Tigers, and McClellan Guards were lucky enough to have the Austrian Lorenz rifled musket, the third most used weapon of the war behind Springfields and Enfields. The most well-armed company was the Graf Township Home Guards with the Springfield rifled musket. The Enterprise Home Guards shouldered Springfields, but the older .69 caliber smoothbores fired buck and ball ammunition. Other companies, such as the Benjaminites, Home Cadets, and the Clary Guards, reported having just "muskets" or "rifles," "common muskets," or even "altered muskets." Other companies picked up a handful of British Enfields.[36]

The age range of the men of the Legion varied. Many Legion commanders complained that the constant calls for volunteers to United States service thinned their ranks of fighting-age men. Some companies dissolved, while others saw the need to consolidate. Though many of the fighting-age males were no longer available for Legion service, the Spencer County Legion endured. There were still soldiers as old as 60 and as young as 15.[37]

For the most part, the companies of Crooks's regiment could perform the basic battlefield movements and drill expected of a home guard unit. Most companies in Indiana were rather lax in their drill; being so far from the action, the need did not seem important. The Newburgh raid shook the Legion in the southern counties of Indiana out of its slumber. Drilling in the 4th Legion was frequent, and the men became so proficient at the task that they would later be compared to veterans. When not on active duty, the companies drilled independently once a month. While they were on active service, the drilling occurred more frequently and sometimes daily. Minerva Thomas of Rockport wrote, "our whole country Is In a state of confusion all the Business houses are closed at 2 o clock every day for the purpose of Drilling they have been getting anew [sic] supply of Arms & are still looking for more." The Spencer Legion may not have been a regular army

36 Company Muster Rolls of the 4th Indiana Legion Regiment, Box 25 and 26, Indiana Legion Papers, Indiana State Archives; Etter, *Indiana Legion*, 14-24.

37 Etter, *Indiana Legion*, 29-34; Company Muster Rolls of the 4th Indiana Legion Regiment, Box 25 and 26, Indiana Legion Papers, Indiana State Archives.

regiment, but they would surprise many, including the Partisan Rangers, with what they could accomplish in a fight.[38]

Johnson's command had enjoyed considerable success since he began operations in June 1862. That success would end after the Union forces in the region began to take the fight to his ranger regiment. Foster in Henderson, and the Indiana Legion across the Ohio River, waited for their opportunities to strike back.

38 Minerva Thomas to George Thomas, Sep. 20, 1862, Thomas Family Letters, University of Notre Dame Rare Books and Special Collections, https://rarebooks.nd.edu/digital/civil_war/letters/thomas/5014-21.shtml, accessed Dec. 11, 2017.

Chapter 12

"Secession flags were waved in our faces by females, and we were insulted on all occasions"

The citizens of Owensboro, Kentucky, and Rockport, Indiana—two communities on the Ohio River—shared many of the fears and concerns as other Americans. Both communities had to face the realities of a costly Civil War, whether that was in human lives or the effects on the river commerce that they relied on so heavily. Though they differed in their politics and their on-the-ground experiences in the war, the two towns were deeply connected throughout 1861-1865.

Owensboro, the county seat of Daviess County, was deeply divided, the city and county providing scores of men to both armies, sometimes from the same family. The town was Union in sentiment, but Southern in culture. Its newspaper, the *Owensboro Monitor*, edited by Henry Woodruff, reflected a strong Unionism but at times sympathized with Southern sentiments. The *Monitor* rejected secession as much as it did abolitionism. In 1862, Owensboro had, so far, escaped the more brutal aspects of the war. Its political ambivalence and the presence of a Union army camp meant it would eventually become a target for Johnson's Partisan Rangers.[1]

In 1860 the county held a population of 12,035 not counting those enslaved, larger than that of neighboring Henderson by nearly 3,500. The peculiar institution heavily influenced Daviess County. From 1850-1860 the number of slave owners grew by 12.5%, from 585 to 689, roughly 5.5% of the population owning enslaved persons. In that same decade, the slave population grew by 17%

1 *Owensboro Monitor*, Sep. 6, 1862, 1.

from 2,883 slaves to 3,489. Of its neighboring counties, only Henderson possessed more slave owners and slaves, with nearly 1,000 slave owners and 5,800 slaves.[2]

Daviess County relied on agriculture, like most of the Kentucky counties in the 1860s. The most heavily cultivated crops in Daviess were tobacco, corn, wheat, and hay, with the tobacco crop reaching a harvest of over 5 million pounds in 1866. Famed local industries, such as bourbon and wagon making, had not yet established themselves, so the county relied on agriculture and the Ohio River traffic to transport those goods.[3]

Owensboro was a rapidly growing community, and with that growth came commerce. The town itself saw an increase in businesses and shops in the late 1850s including a photography studio, jewelry store, and millinery for local women. Advertisements for G. A. Peters and Co. informed readers in the *Owensboro Monitor* that they sold "a fine assortment of staple and fancy dry-goods." The new courthouse erected in the middle of town became the center of gatherings and meetings, but to some it would come to symbolize the power and authority of the Federal government. Owensboro was a town on the move, and in the direction of what some would consider progress.[4]

Like the rest of 1860s Kentucky, Daviess County and Owensboro are difficult to understand in political terms. In the 1850s the county took a swing from favoring the Whig party to the Democrats, but favored neither Democratic candidate in the 1860 election. The county instead sympathized with Tennessean and former Whig, John Bell, the presidential candidate of the Constitutional Union Party. Many Kentuckians, urged on by John J. Crittenden, saw Bell as a good compromise between the anti-slavery Republicans and the secessionist Southern Democrats. Bell was a large slave owner yet came out against the Kansas-Nebraska Act. Though viewed as a man that could keep the peace between the two splintering sides of the country, Bell ran on a platform that was decidedly pro-Southern rights: essentially a desire for Union, but one that protected slavery. His was a candidacy of reconciling the irreconcilables, which is undoubtedly the reason that Daviess County supported him. When the inevitable splintering

2 Daviess County Slaves, Free Blacks, and Free Mulattoes, 1850-1870, *Notable Kentucky African American Database*, http://nkaa.ukky.edu/nkaa/items.show/2325, accessed Aug. 26, 2018; Henderson County Slaves, Free Blacks, and Free Mulattoes, 1850-1870, *Notable Kentucky African American Database*, http://nkaa.ukky.edu/nkaa/items.show/23267, accessed Aug. 26, 2018.

3 *History of Daviess County, Kentucky: Together with Sketches of Its Cities, Villages, and Townships, Educational, Religious, Civil, Military, and Political History, Portraits of Prominent Persons, Biographies of Representative Citizens, and an Outline History of Kentucky* (Chicago, 1883), 181.

4 Aloma Williams Dew, "Little Ado About Much—Life on the Homefront in Civil War Owensboro," *Daviess County Historical Quarterly*, Apr. 1984, Volume II, Number 2, 38; *Owensboro Monitor*, Aug. 13, 1862, 1.

came, it would have devastating effects on regions such as Daviess County that had attempted to compromise with the coming storm. After counting the ballots, 1,074 votes went to Bell, while Breckinridge and Douglas received 654 and 530 votes respectively. Abraham Lincoln, who grew up just across the Ohio River in Spencer County, Indiana, received a meager seven votes. The voters of Daviess County had spoken, and they did not relish the idea of having to pick a side in the coming crisis.[5]

On April 12, 1861, the news of the bombardment and surrender of Fort Sumter reached the city. The anonymous author of a county history published years after the war stated, "It is to be taken for granted, however, that whatever public course any man chose to pursue in the terrible ordeal, his motives were patriotic. He either stood up for the party he honestly thought was originally right, or for what seemed to be the quickest way to end the fratricidal war." By the late summer, and despite Kentucky's proclaimed neutrality, companies for both armies organized in the city. In September, men that would form the nucleus of Company F, 4th Kentucky Infantry, moved to Tennessee to join the Kentucky Confederate forces concentrating along the border. Also in September hundreds of men under Daviess County resident and attorney John McHenry moved into Owensboro from Ohio County to form the 17th Kentucky Infantry and fight for the Union cause.[6]

Days after McHenry's arrival, rumors circulated that a large Southern force threatened Owensboro and that the town might willingly capitulate and its citizens cooperate with the Confederates. One soldier reported to *Leslie's Illustrated Weekly Newspaper*, "It is rumored that the enemy were in force at Owensboro, where we arrived the following Wednesday morning about daylight, only to find the town in possession of Union men, the Home Guard of Evansville. Secession flags were waved in our faces by females, and we were insulted on all occasions." Indiana Governor Oliver Morton telegraphed President Lincoln and suggested that a Federal gunboat anchor at Owensboro in order to deter any Rebel activity. Union Navy Captain Andrew Foote arrived on September 25th and found the city safe. He wrote, "We reached Owensboro, found no batteries. I sent for the authorities of the place and directed them to prevent the display of secession flags. A strong disunion sentiment is manifest in the place," Foote reported, "but no disrespect was offered me, although I have been much among the people." The 17th, along

5 Kenneth H. Williams and James Russell Harris, "Kentucky in 1860: A Statistical Overview," *The Register of the Kentucky Historical Society* Vol. 103, No. 4 (Autumn 2005): 743-764; Finck, *Divided Loyalties*, 26-30.

6 *History of Daviess County*, 158.

with the recruits of the 11th Kentucky, feared they would not be able to hold in the event of an attack.[7]

Eventually these regiments, and others that made Owensboro a temporary stop, moved to Calhoun on the Green River to begin the formation of Gen. Thomas L. Crittenden's division. It appeared that the war had moved on from Owensboro and the banks of the Ohio. Occasionally the Provost Guard arrested citizens for disloyalty, aiding guerrillas, helping Union Army deserters, or other similar charges. A passing steamer to Louisville picked up the suspected Rebels where they would be kept for a short time and then released after taking the oath of allegiance to the United States.[8]

Though Owensboro was not the seat of war, the conflict already yielded its pernicious effects on the city's commerce and agriculture. The embargo on goods from south of the Ohio River severely hampered the trade on which many Daviess County citizens relied, especially with their Indiana neighbor, Rockport. River traffic was always at risk. Guerrillas often fired at steamers on the Ohio from the southern bank, or traffic completely shut down for fear of Confederate invasion of Indiana. Though most of the inconveniences were commercial, this was about to change.[9]

Union forces occupying the city seemed to have incipient secessionism well in hand. Local home guard companies frequently formed and disbanded, and most citizens generally distrusted them. Sometimes local authorities asked the Indiana Legion from the southern counties of that state to protect the town, and sometimes provost soldiers from Louisville visited. But the fall of 1862 would witness a drastic increase in the Federal presence in Owensboro as new regiments began to organize. This heightened presence tended to exacerbate, rather than suppress, the area's latent secessionism. Though a slim majority of the population appeared to favor Unionism, many families and individuals remained ardent Southern sympathizers. Ella Johnson was a young child of one of these families and wrote of Union soldiers occupying her family's home. In her old age she remembered,

> Union troops were in possession of our house and had ordered my mother to prepare a meal for them. She appeared to obey, and took me and a negro woman to the outdoor kitchen and from there escaped through a window, and the three of us spent the night in hiding, in a turnip field. Now this is what I think I remember, lying in my mother's lap

7 *History of Daviess County*, 159; Aloma Williams Dew, "'Between the Hawk and the Buzzard': Owensboro During the Civil War," *The Register of the Kentucky Historical Society* 77, no. 1 (1979): 1-14; *OR* 23, 348.

8 *History of Daviess County*, 160-161.

9 *History of Daviess County*, 160.

> and looking up at the stars. Presently she put her hand over my eyes and said, "Go to sleep, Ella." I don't remember where we were, but I do remember the stars.

In another incident, soldiers arrested Ella's father and detained him at the house. "A line of blue coated soldiers picketed along our front fence. My father, in irons, was brought to the gate and my mother allowed to speak to him from the front steps; no nearer. I never knew why it occurred nor what it was all about, but Mimi carried me down and held me up while I put my head between the bayonets and kissed him. Being manacled, he couldn't raise his hands. He was later taken away as he had come, under guard." Some in Owensboro grew restless under the occupation of Federal troops.[10]

In its "Salutatory" column, the *Owensboro Monitor* clearly laid out the beliefs of the editors in its first issue on August 13, 1862. The paper attempted to untangle the Gordian Knot in which this pro-Union, pro-slavery community was caught. It stated a firm support for unionism and an ardent hatred for abolitionism. For the paper, secessionism and abolitionism caused the problems Owensboro now faced.[11]

Owensboro, like much of Kentucky, could be as independent-minded as any city in the North or South, but this independence did not prevent the war from paying a harsh visit. When the Partisan Rangers arrived, it forced the true loyalties of many to be revealed.

Rockport, Indiana

In 1861, Spencer County, and the county seat of Rockport, embraced the wave of patriotic fervor that swept the northern half of the country in the aftermath of Fort Sumter. Apparently the entire male population of the county was ready to fight for the preservation of the Union. Barbecues, parades, speeches, dinners, balls, and flag presentations dominated the spring and summer.[12]

Once the news of the surrender of the fort reached Spencer County, seemingly everyone left their farms and country homes to flock to the towns to hear the news. Groups of men of all trades and social standing talked and argued amongst themselves about how to deal with the South. Many were eager to lend their hand in putting down the rebellion.[13]

10 Ella H. Johnson, *Granny Remembers*, 12-14.

11 *Owensboro Monitor*, Aug. 13, 1862, 2.

12 *History of Warrick, Spencer, and Perry Counties, Indiana: From the earliest time to the present; together with interesting biographical sketches, reminiscences, notes, etc.* (Chicago, 1885), 375-376.

13 *History of Warrick, Spencer, and Perry Counties, Indiana*, 375-376.

However, most men were not able to march off to fight immediately. Of President Lincoln's call for 75,000 volunteers, Governor Morton offered the President more than 10,000. Indiana's quota was only six regiments, about 6,000 men, which left many eager Hoosiers out of the fight. Many simply waited for the next call for volunteers or began drilling in local militia companies. These militia companies eventually formed the core of the Indiana Legion, the home guard for the state.[14]

On July 4, 1861, there had so far been little bloodshed. Bull Run would come, but for the moment, Union arms seemed invincible. Independence Day festivities were well advertised throughout the county and excitement grew for a great celebration in Rockport. Ceremonies included floral drapings, a thirty-four-gun salute, banners bearing mottoes, and music. The local home guard companies paraded to the sound of martial music and a delegation of loyal Kentuckians from Daviess County appeared as special guests. Prominent citizens gave speeches and prayers for the Union as the Stars and Stripes flew above the town to the salute of guns and muskets. There was even a choir of young girls in white dresses that sang "The Star-Spangled Banner"—thirty-four girls for thirty-four states.

Patriotism seemed to be everywhere. A few days later, the first group of men who had volunteered for U.S. service left their homes for Evansville and the war. Before they left, the citizens of Rockport treated them to a dinner, two flags, and a sending-off by boat accompanied by a crowd of about 600 well-wishers. A few days later, another company of men left for Evansville and enjoyed a similar send-off as the men before them.

Over the course of the next few weeks, such scenes were common, as companies from the area left via Rockport to Evansville, or merely passed through. It seemed that Democrats and Republicans had put aside their political differences for the preservation of the Union.

For Spencer County, the election of 1860 was not quite like the election in Daviess County across the river. With four possible candidates to choose from, it appeared that Spencer County only slightly favored its former resident, Abraham Lincoln. Lincoln received 1,296 votes compared to 1,108 for Douglas and the Northern Democrats. The *Rockport Democrat* endorsed Douglas and his running mate and future Confederate vice president, Alexander Stephens. The other two candidates, Breckinridge of the Southern Democratic wing, and Bell of the

14 Etter, *Indiana Legion*, 13.

Constitutional Unionists, both received under 200 votes. The county split, almost evenly, between Democrats and Republicans.[15]

On December 8, 1860, when the secession of Southern states seemed imminent, a Union meeting occurred at the courthouse in Rockport. The group selected a five-man committee to draft a resolution expressing the general feeling and attitude of the county. In it, they "Resolved, That in the opinion of this meeting the election of any citizen of the United States to the office of President, according to the forms of the Constitution, is no just course for secession." By all accounts, this enthusiastic meeting had boldly proclaimed Spencer County's undaunted loyalty to the Union.[16]

Located in southern Indiana, Spencer County sat directly across the Ohio River from the border and slave state of Kentucky. For the people of Spencer County, trade was vital with the Kentucky counties across the river. Many personal ties grew between Hoosiers and Kentuckians from Spencer and Daviess Counties. Ferries between the two counties carried goods and travelers back and forth on a regular basis. When a Spencer County company left to join the 25th Indiana in Evansville, a delegation from Daviess County crossed the river to present a flag to the men with a motto of "No South, no North, but the Union Forever."

It was no secret that many Kentuckians wished to push the Commonwealth into the Confederacy. Many believed that the secessionists had friends and allies in Indiana. Would these disloyal Copperheads try to force Indiana to relinquish her place in the Union? Would they aid Confederates from Kentucky to invade their homeland?[17]

Spencer County had always been willing to fight and defend the Union from the outset, as had been evident by the number of eager volunteers. J. L. Tinsly, a resident of Grandview, wrote to Governor Morton in September 1861, requesting arms. "The citizens of this place viewing the danger they are placed in here on the border is paramount that you will send us a small cannon from 6-12 pounds for our protection," he begged. Tinsly wrote to Morton again a few weeks later in October. He reiterated his previous request:

> I can raise a company (artillery) in a short time . . . and they are waiting on me to see if I can succeed they are mostly Germans and Danger is staring us in the face they tell us that there is a company of 90 cecsh [secessionists] . . . now in camp within 4 miles of us

15 *History of Warrick, Spencer, and Perry Counties, Indiana*, 375-376; *Rockport Weekly Democrat*, Oct. 27, 1860, 2.

16 *History of Warrick, Spencer, and Perry Counties, Indiana*, 375-376.

17 Ibid., 378-379.

> . . . a recruiting and they threaten our place with fire[.] I would like to have authority to move them if you can lend us the arms. . . . [W]e will get organized and be redy for duty on the border where ever Danger threatens with the strongest beet [sic] we wish to . . . [defend ourselves].[18]

Spencer County, and Rockport especially, would be an important part of the lifeline for the Union early in the war by helping connect the Midwest states to the Ohio River. Gunboats heading south routinely stopped at its wharfs, which always brought large crowds of cheering citizens. The fairgrounds outside of Rockport temporarily transformed into Camp Reynolds in November 1861, for the purpose of recruiting, organizing, and training. Camp Reynolds during the winter became a small village itself, as 500 men built small winter quarters out of logs and other ready materials. The soldiers kept themselves comfortable in the cabins and with the aid of the citizens. By late winter, the 500 recruits became members of the 53rd Indiana. Prominent Spencer County citizen, George Thomas, became the regiment's quartermaster and served in that position for two years while his wife kept him up to date with the latest local news in her letters.[19]

As the war dragged into 1862 and the battles of the Western Theater began to produce their chilling rates of casualties and destruction, Spencer County began to feel the effects of the conflict. The county formed a committee that would visit the battlefields and hospitals to care for and comfort the soldiers of Spencer County. Volunteers would visit the scenes of battle and bring back the dead if possible. At places like Fort Donelson and Shiloh, Spencer County men died or received terrible wounds.[20]

George Thomas and the 53rd Indiana arrived at Pittsburg Landing on April 24th, two and half weeks after the Battle of Shiloh. Upon viewing the battlefield, Thomas remarked, "No persons could pass over that battle field without being convinced that there had been on that ground one of the most fearful conflicts that the world has witnessed[.]" Reaching for something of a poetic allusion, Thomas described "[p]ortions of the field [as] an open woods and I doant know whether there is a single tree for considerable distances at a time without its having been

18 J. L. Tinsly to Governor Oliver Morton, Sep. 1, 1861, and Oct. 2, 1861, Indiana Legion Box 25 and 26, Indiana State Archives.

19 *History of Warrick, Spencer, and Perry Counties, Indiana*, 381-382; George Thomas to Minerva Thomas, Apr. 27, 1862, Thomas Family Letters, University of Notre Dame Rare Books and Special Collections, https://rarebooks.nd.edu/digital/civil_war/letters/thomas/5014-09.shtml, accessed Dec. 11, 2017.

20 *History of Warrick, Spencer, and Perry Counties, Indiana*, 383.

perforated with a ball from Each side." Many of the bodies, exhumed from hastily dug graves, returned home for burial nearer kith and kin.[21]

As the spring of 1862 passed into summer, it seemed that little threatened the farms and towns of southern Indiana. Large Rebel field armies were far away. But the small and dangerous bands of guerrillas that roamed the Kentucky countryside shattered the belief of complete safety. One southern Indiana woman in neighboring Perry County wrote to her husband in the Union Army about her fear of the Confederate guerrillas. Her husband attempted to comfort her and wrote:

> On the subject of being afraid, up until now there hasn't been any danger in our immediate area, the *Guerillas* who are on the lower Ohio are too weak to cross the river, since they would all be captured, but a woman with children has nothing to fear anyway, since on both sides women and children are protected by officers and soldiers, the only thing to be perhaps afraid of are thieves and vagabonds, but we're at the mercy of those rascals even in peacetime. If one breaks in at night, shoot him to pieces. Make sure the rifles and pistols are well loaded, there's no place for fearfulness and timidity in these times. If my duty and circumstances permitted, I would have come home long ago, since there are perhaps only a few who love their family more than I do.[22]

The summer of 1862 saw increased activity and recruiting for these small bands of Confederate guerrillas and partisans. In July 1862, Adam Rankin Johnson pulled off one of the most daring feats of the entire war by using two "Quaker guns" to capture Newburgh. The capture of Newburgh was quite an embarrassment for the Indiana Legion, caught in a lackadaisical state. The event sent fear all along the southern Indiana counties, with many citizens wondering if their communities would be next. The 4th Regiment of Indiana Legion did its best to bring calm and a sense of security back to the Rockport area and Spencer County.

It was also during this summer that the United States passed the Conscription Act of July 17, 1862. Indiana, having nearly fulfilled her quota of men for the service, was not widely affected as some other states. It was not until the second Conscription Act, passed in 1863, that the war began to sour in the minds of some Hoosiers. However, Spencer County and all her townships had already met the required quotas and were safe from the draft.[23]

21 Ibid., 383; George Thomas to Minerva Thomas, Apr. 27, 1862, Thomas Family Letters, University of Notre Dame Rare Books and Special Collections, https://rarebooks.nd.edu/digital/civil_war/letters/thomas/5014-09.shtml, accessed Dec. 11, 2017.

22 Susan Carter Vogel, *Germans in the Civil War: The Letters They Wrote Home*, Walter D. Kamphoefner and Wolfgang Helbich, eds. (Chapel Hill, NC, 2006), 258.

23 Charles E. Canup, "Conscription and Draft in Indiana During the Civil War," *Indiana Magazine of History* 10, no. 2 (1914): 70-83.

Though at first the two communities would only feel the pains of war at a distance, that reality would soon be shattered. The arrival of the Partisan Rangers to Owensboro thrust Rockport's citizens into the maelstrom just across the river from their homes. The hard hand of war waited on the doorsteps of both Ohio River towns.

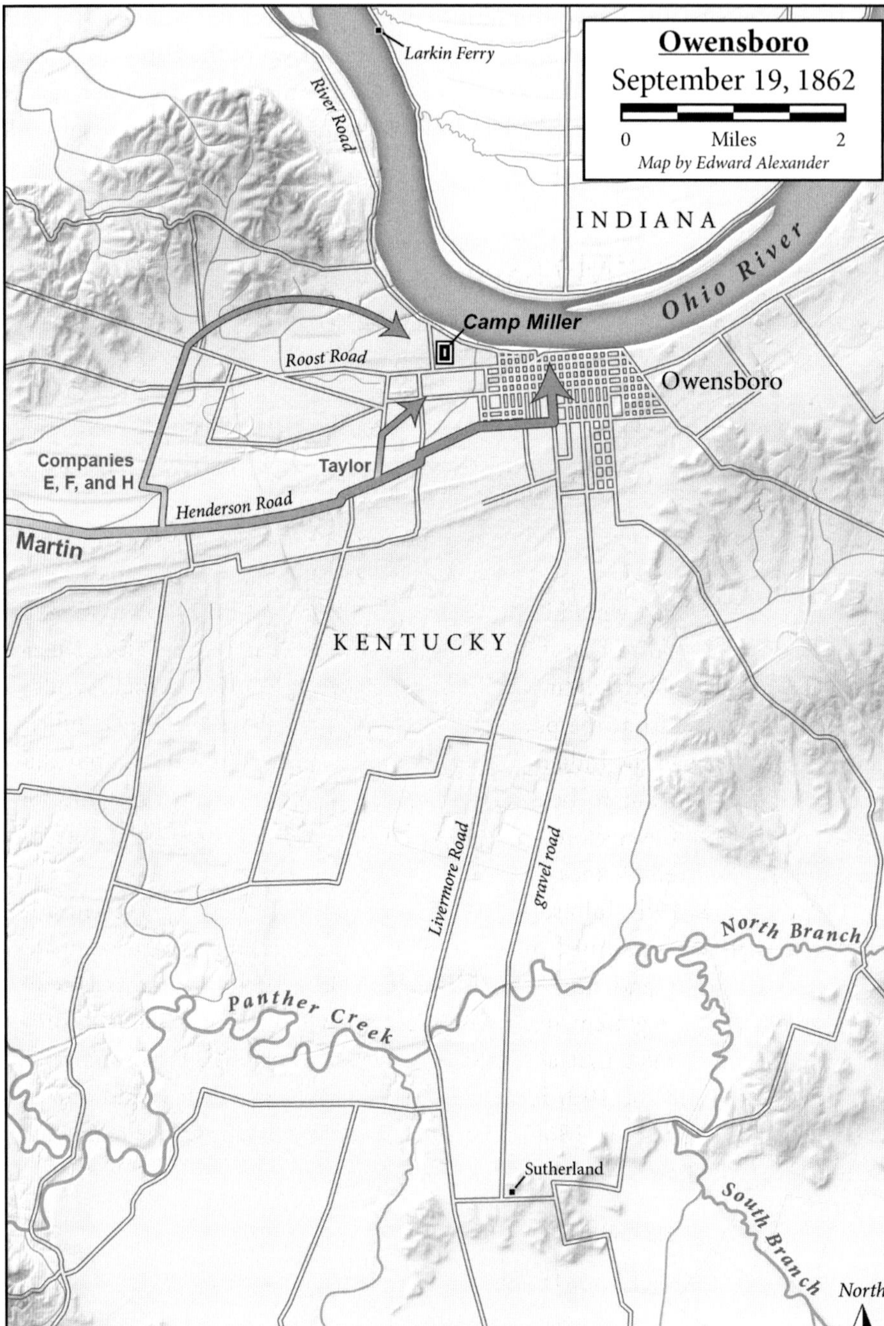
Owensboro
September 19, 1862
0 Miles 2
Map by Edward Alexander
Larkin Ferry
River Road
INDIANA
Ohio River
Camp Miller
Roost Road
Owensboro
Companies
E, F, and H
Taylor
Henderson Road
Martin
KENTUCKY
Livermore Road
gravel road
North Branch
Panther Creek
Sutherland
South Branch
North

Chapter 13

"My Savior has come"

September 19, 1862, would be remembered by the residents of Owensboro for years to come. Up to that date, the war had mostly spared the city of major violence, unlike the surrounding areas. Besides a few scares and small bands of armed men stealing from the populace, not much had happened. Local officials occasionally called on the Indiana Legion from across the river for help, but those pleas usually turned out to be over false alarms. This time, however, Johnson's partisans rode for Owensboro, and they intended to do more than just ride through. They wanted Netter's camp.

By September 19th, Johnson's command would have been considered a full regiment had it been attached to the regular army. It comprised ten companies with elected officers and non-commissioned officers, with a letter assigned to each company. The regiment just needed its papers turned in to the authorities in Richmond, and once that administrative burden was lifted Johnson's raiders would be designated the 10th Kentucky Partisan Rangers. They would officially attain that moniker later in 1862. Johnson and Martin organized the regiment in the following manner:

Company A - Captain Andrew W. Ray

Company B - Captain Lorenzo D. Fisher and Captain William M. Marr

Company C - Captain John E. Prow

Company D - Captain Thornton Mobley Hammock

Company E - Captain Samuel Burk Taylor

Company F - Captain John Strother Chapman

Company G - Captain James N. Taylor

Company H - Captain Henry Clary Merriwether

Company I - Captain Alvin Fowler

Company K - Captain William Currens Dimmitt[1]

James Munday, along with the rest of the regiment, broke camp early in the morning and began the final movements to capture Owensboro and the Federals encamped nearby. Men of companies E, F, and H, commanded by Captains S. B. Taylor, J. S. Chapman, and Clay Merriwether, began a circuitous approach toward the Ohio River, west of Owensboro and the camp. This detachment would attempt to capture Camp Miller should the Federals make a move toward the Confederates in town. The main body, divided into two columns, headed directly for Owensboro.[2]

One person in a very disadvantageous situation was Lt. Col. James Holmes, a Daviess County native on leave from the Federal 3rd Kentucky Cavalry for health reasons. His home was situated between the villages of Philpot and Knottsville, several miles east of Owensboro, where he was convalescing from a loss of vision caused by a severe fever earlier that spring. After Bragg moved into Kentucky, Holmes decided to make his way back to the 3rd rather than loiter any longer at home. Stopping in Owensboro, he heard that soldiers were heading that way, but no one seemed to know to which army they belonged.[3]

Holmes made his way to the house of a Mr. Dorsey, a local banker and close friend, whose home was only two blocks southeast of the Federal camp. Holmes was in full uniform, and dashed into Dorsey's front door as the unknown soldiers rode down Fourth Street. The soldiers carried a Southern flag, and Holmes feared the Confederates had already spotted him as he hid behind the door. The Partisan Rangers, however, had other quarry: the Federal camp toward the north. Instead of escaping the city, Holmes thought he could reach Netter's camp. He convinced Dorsey to venture into Owensboro to get a horse. Dorsey brought back one of Holmes's horses, before the raiders could procure the mount for themselves.[4]

1 Lynn, *Company K*, 91.

2 Munday, *Diary*, 6; Arthur C. Truman, *At War with Ourselves, 1861-1865: A Military History of the Daviess County, Kentucky Area* (Owensboro, KY, 1994), 20; *Owensboro Monitor*, Oct. 1, 1862, 3.

3 *Owensboro Messenger*, Dec. 14, 1902, 11.

4 Ibid., 11.

Holmes was not the only person caught by surprise that early morning. The Rangers dashed into town so suddenly that most of the citizens were stunned to see Confederate soldiers on every street corner. Confederate R. W. Burch later wrote that the Rangers made a rush into Owensboro precisely at daybreak, riding hard down Frederica Street, then fanning out through the town once they made it to Second Street, or Main Street. The soldiers scavenged for powder and ammunition and posted guards at all essential points of town. The Rebels seized weapons, ammunition, horse tack, food, and other "non-essentials"—watches were especially popular. Martin personally stopped Rangers from looting any further. Pillaging, after all, was bad for recruiting.[5]

The Confederates rounded up and arrested prominent Unionists, such as Judge George Yeaman. Yeaman had recently tried to recruit his own Union regiment in Owensboro but with Netter, Shanks, and Shackelford having already harvested most of the Federal wheat, orders arrived to cease recruitment. Afterward, General Boyle appointed Yeaman to command the local Union home guards and militia of Daviess County some weeks before the Partisan Rangers arrived. As the town's unofficial provost, Southern sympathizers accused Yeaman of unfairness by arresting those whom he merely suspected of Confederate sympathy. Yeaman had issued a proclamation in which he described his mission. He assured the population:

> Our object is the defense of the lives and property of the loyal and peaceable citizens of the county, and more especially against guerilla warfare. I am by the voice of those who will support me, intrusted [sic] with full power for that purpose. I will use it when necessary. The system of predatory warfare and robbery that is now scourging and wasting the counties south and west of us is the legitimate and necessary result of the enormous robberies and thefts committed upon the government at the incipiency of the secession movement. Its application to individuals and local communities is covertly authorized by the rebel government in the act for raising and equipping 'partisan rangers;' a very indicative name. It is a malignant and cowardly attempt to annoy and exhaust the border states into submission to rebel rule. We have resolved that end shall be soon.

The Rangers had no trouble identifying Yeaman as a threat.[6]

One account claims that Rebels led Yeaman out of town, a rope around his neck, with the intention of hanging him. Before the deed could be finished, a series of promises were "extracted" from Yeaman. He promised to end the arrests and alleged harassment of those citizens of Owensboro and Daviess County who

5 Tarnowieckyi, *Branded by the Lincolnites*, 668; *Owensboro Messenger*, July 11, 1909, 10; *The Twice-A-Week Messenger*, Jan. 27, 1903, 3.

6 *Owensboro Monitor*, Dec. 17, 1862, 2; *The Messenger*, June 10, 1900, 3.

This 1862 sketch depicts guerrillas "somewhere in the West." Though there is no evidence that the 10th Kentucky acted in this manner, a scene like this came to the mind of many when they learned of the Partisan Rangers taking a town. *LOC*

maintained Southern leanings. Rumors even spread that his captors forced him to take an oath of allegiance to the Confederacy, but this rumor was not widely believed. The *Owensboro Monitor* reported, "The Confederate officers treated him kindly, and whether from policy, or from other causes, exacted no harsh or humiliating terms." Fine compliments from a staunch Unionist paper.[7]

The Confederates threw Owensboro into chaos. The city had not yet witnessed the ugly hand of war, but now it was at the gates. Unionists feared for their lives and property as the Confederates appeared to be a conquering army with no intention of leaving anytime soon. Confederate supporters were overjoyed at the prospect of being "liberated" and "saved" from the Yankees; they brought baskets of food to the hungry and tired Southern soldiers. "Then there were days when a cluster of tents was pitched in a nearby field, and every one moved heaven and earth to take these gray-clad men all the food and clothing that could possibly be spared from our own scanty store, for these were 'our boys'; our own 'Johnny Rebs,' and we'd

7 *Owensboro Monitor*, Sep. 24, 1862, 2.

all gladly go hungry and cold to aid them," recalled Ella Johnson many years later. "We were ready to live and die for Dixie."[8]

The "liberation" of Owensboro by the Rangers led some grateful townspeople to religious ecstasy. One grateful woman hailed Maj. Joseph S. Scobee, a Methodist minister called "the Fighting Parson" by some, as her "savior." R. W. Burch remembered, "When near Fifth Street a lady ran out of a house and came towards us clapping her hands and shouting, 'Thank God, my Savior has come. Glory to God.' I had to rein my horse out of the ranks and up against the curbstone to keep from running over her. I would not have hurt a hair of her head for the whole town." An elderly Owensboro citizen instructed, "Fight 'em, Brother Scobee, Fight 'em," to which Scobee replied, "I will. I'll fight 'em till hell freezes." Others could be heard proclaiming, "Glory to God!" The *New Albany Ledger* reported that Martin, or Moreland as they erroneously called him, gave a speech to the citizens of the town. He proclaimed that they had come to "strike off the chains which now fettered Kentuckians, and make them free again, and a great amount of similar twaddle." Though many sympathizers agreed with the message, few wished to join the ranks.[9]

Some Unionists felt disgusted by the behavior of other professed "Union" men of Owensboro. They brought their wives to the occasion along with their own gifts of food and assistance, contrary to their earlier show of Union support. Even a few citizens seemed to think that liberation had arrived from the "Lincolnites," as if Kentucky was a permanent Confederate state. The *Owensboro Monitor* would later comment, "But alas! The morning that was so bright faded away into an evening of clouds, portending dangers and defeat where triumph had been so arrogantly and so confidently expected."[10]

The celebration would be short-lived, and Unionists made sure to watch who exactly was giving aid. "[M]en and families boldly and distinctly showed their hands on Friday. Who they are and what they are, what they said and what they did, who received information and made their preparations accordingly—all these, and far more, are no longer secrets. Murder will out," the *Monitor* fumed. Just as in Newburgh two months before, Unionists took names, but it was unknown as to what would happen once the excitement died down. War now threatened Owensboro at the personal level.[11]

8 Ibid., Oct. 1, 1862, 2; Johnson, *Granny Remembers*, 15.

9 *New Albany Daily Ledger*, Sep. 22, 1862, 2.

10 *Owensboro Monitor*, Sep. 24, 1862, 2; Oct. 1, 1862, 2.

11 Ibid., 2; Johnson, *Granny Remembers*, 15.

Capturing Owensboro was not Martin's primary goal. It held little strategic or symbolic value and he could not hold it for long. They did gain from it valuable powder and ammunition but the Yankee camp held much more. Muskets, a six-pound cannon, horses, valuable foodstuffs, and other supplies sat among the hundreds of Union recruits. Capturing the camp would materially improve the equipment and arms situation of nearly half his force. Clarksville and Uniontown brought large amounts of needed goods into the Confederate ranks, but Owensboro promised even more. How long could Unionists consider them a "guerrilla" band when his men were not only well mounted, but possessed things such as tents, a good supply of ammunition, feed and furnishings for the horses and mules, wagons, and did not have to rely on shotguns and squirrel rifles? A guerrilla band would not have Enfields and other military weapons. A guerrilla band would not have a section of artillery with multiple types of shot.

Martin detailed a squad under the command of W. B. Allbright to plant the "Clarksville Belle" on the small bridge that crossed a ravine west of town, pointed toward the camp. Without proper solid-shot and shell, it would not be very effective from that distance. Its purpose was not to assault the camp but to defend the town after luring Netter to attempt to retake Owensboro.[12] While the fog remained low, a man breathlessly ran into Camp Miller. A Unionist, he informed the soldiers that Rebels had taken over the town, hundreds of them, and that they must have ridden through the night to take them by surprise—a tactic used the previous month at Hopkinsville and Clarksville.

Netter immediately got his battalion of recruits up and ready for a fight. Almost immediately, a teenage African American boy who used to work for C. B. Mitchell made his way into camp. His information would stave off disaster for Netter. He had snuck out of the city as the Confederates took the town, but not before overhearing some Confederates talking about how they had divided their force. A portion did not go into Owensboro, instead positioning themselves in a woods and cornfield on the west side of the camp. They expected the Federals to make an advance toward the town, and having vacated their camp the detached raider group would then proceed to capture the undefended weapons and destroy the supplies they could not take. Such was their plan. Sergeant Mitchell took the young man to Netter where he relayed what he had overheard. After talking with the boy a little longer, Netter concluded that he was probably telling the truth. This development changed everything about how events proceeded over the next few days. Martin surely was unaware that intelligence about his plan had been

12 *The Twice-A-Week Messenger*, Jan. 27, 1903, 3.

leaked by an adolescent whose name has since been lost to history, but it soon become quite clear that Owensboro was not Clarksville.[13]

Camp Miller sat very near the Ohio River and about three quarters of a mile from the west side of town on the local fairgrounds. Union forces had roughly 350 men fit for a defense of the camp along with a near obsolete, brass six-pound artillery piece. A wooden fence surrounded the grounds, aiding the defenders. Netter had few options. There was no time to dig in and set up a stronger perimeter, and on top of that, he did not have the numbers to defend so large an area.

Netter decided to attempt an infantry-style breakout on foot, or at the very least, drive off one portion of the Rebels before turning his attention back to Owensboro. He left to guard the camp a company of at least 100 men and the gunners for the artillery piece under the command of Sergeant Major Freeman. Netter proceeded to march out of camp with the rest of his command, about 200 men. Even with a shrunken force protecting the camp, the Confederates would not have an easy time getting to it. The fence that surrounded the camp offered a difficult obstacle for cavalry on the attack.[14]

Quietly, the 200 recruits formed into column to march out of the camp. Before they could depart, an officer clad in gray and brown approached with a white flag. "W," who wrote to the *Owensboro Monitor*, described it as resembling more of a black-flag than a flag of truce, such was the accumulated dirt and grime on a device that had seen active and dirty service for a month. The pickets halted the rider and Netter attended to the matter. The colonel motioned for the pickets to let the man enter the camp a short distance. The rider—who some sources identify as Capt. Clay Merriwether, while others say Scobee—informed Netter of the situation. Owensboro was in their hands, and they had a force of about 800 men ready to attack the camp. This was their opportunity to hand it over without blood. Netter must surrender the camp, men, and all government property. The Frenchman politely asked the officer if he could address his men and the rider relented. "Boys, this officer comes with a flag of truce from Lieutenant Colonel Martin, who, with 800 guerillas, has possession of the town and demands of me a surrender of all my command and all of the government property in my possession. I want you to hear my answer," Netter announced. The soldiers anxiously awaited their commander's decision. Netter faced the Confederate messenger and with his hand, motioned to

13 Bernheim, *Settlement of Jews*, 42-43.

14 *Evansville Daily Journal*, Sep. 22, 1862, 2.

the ground and declared, "NEVER, till the last man of us is laid low in the dust." Turning back to his men he asked, "Boys, does my answer suit you?"[15]

Netter's green recruits swung their blue caps in the air and give three rousing "HURRAHS." The scene even deeply moved the Confederate messenger. As he turned his horse to deliver the message to Martin he remarked, "Colonel, I carry back with me the most profound respect for you and your brave men." The Confederate smartly saluted, spurred his horse, and galloped back toward the Southern positions near Owensboro. The stage was set and Netter's men resumed their march. Adjutant Ira Stout moved ahead of the Union body with a small squad and flankers protected both sides of the column from possible ambush.[16]

Meanwhile, Munday and his company dismounted near the Guthrie farm and moved into a cornfield and wood line near the ravine by the Ohio River. Here, to the west of the camp, they waited for the Yankees to march toward Owensboro so they could move in. They had no idea that the Yankee column was headed straight for them.[17]

The Federals trudged down Dublin Lane in the early daylight and turned west on the River Road. The only sound was the scuffle of the Union brogans. One of the mounted advance pickets discovered Rebel activity in the field just ahead of Netter and his men. He came galloping back with the report. Netter ordered his men to the double-quick until they came to the cornfield and the Confederate positions. The column formed into a line of battle and advanced into the corn. At that moment, a gunshot pierced the quiet of the morning and the fight was on.

Munday and his company immediately opened fire as the Yankees came into range. Several Union soldiers fell at the first volley. Netter's men returned fire. The Partisan Rangers answered with their shotguns, fowling pieces, and the few muskets they possessed. Such weapons had little effect. This had not been the plan anyway. They had thought the Federals would try to retake the town, not try to break out of the trap. They would have to pour in as much fire as possible and hope that the cornfield and trees could provide sufficient cover. The two forces were matched in numbers, but the Yankees had the better weapons. Stalks of corn shattered in front of the Confederates as the Union fire increased and became more deadly. Near Munday, a Federal ball killed recruit Dick Hayden. Others fell among the clipped corn stalks.[18]

15 *Owensboro Monitor*, Oct. 1, 1862, 3; Bernheim, *Settlement of Jews*, 44; Johnson, *Partisan Rangers*, 348.

16 Bernheim, *Settlement of Jews*, 45; *Owensboro Monitor*, Oct. 1, 1862, 3.

17 Munday, *Diary*, 6.

18 Ibid.; *Owensboro Monitor*, Oct. 1, 1862, 3; *History of Daviess County*, 166.

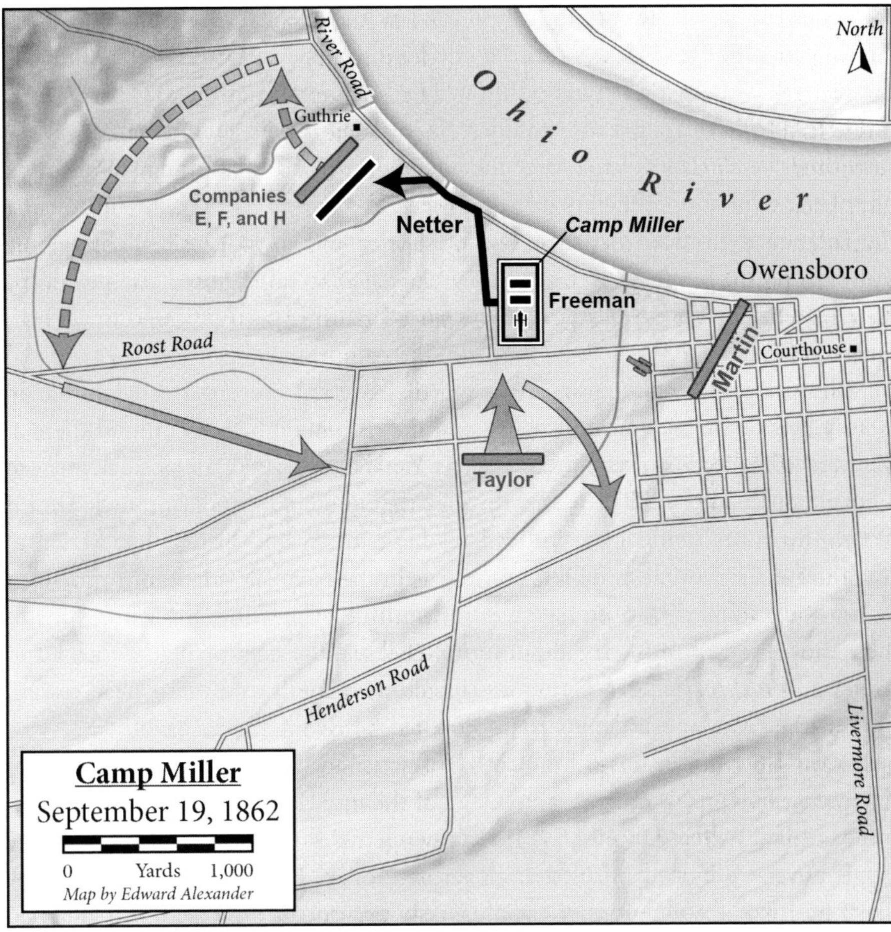

Smoke hung low over the field as the morning sun struggled to lift it away. The Union recruits fired volley after volley into the corn and trees where their enemy lay. Though lethal, the Union fire could not dislodge the Rangers. Netter needed to close the distance between them and make a push. He gave the order and the line moved forward. Netter advanced a few yards in front of his men, his arm extended with sword in hand. He looked back at his recruits with the command, "FORWARD!" His devoted soldiers followed in imperfect battle line formation.[19]

On the other side of the field, a dismounted partisan, Corp. Jim Hall, took up position next to a tree with his squirrel rifle. He had removed his hat and replaced it with a white handkerchief, probably wet to keep himself cool in the scorching heat. The line of blue slowly and menacingly made its way toward him and his

19 *Owensboro Monitor*, Oct. 1, 1862, 3; Munday, *Diary*, 6.

comrades. As usual, ammunition was low, so the men needed to choose their targets carefully. He would have seen the handsomely uniformed officer leading the Federal soldiers toward his position. His breathing intensified as he brought his weapon to rest against his shoulder. As in many battles, confident leaders can sometimes be all that holds a force together, and perhaps Hall understood this as he took careful and deliberate aim, at one of the brass Federal eagle buttons on the chest of the officer just then scaling a fence. When Hall pulled the trigger, the hammer on his piece slammed down on the cap and ignited the powder; a small lead ball exited the barrel and flew faster than the speed of sound toward the Union officer.[20]

The puffs of smoke from the trees to his front were perfectly visible to Netter. He and his men heard the hiss and wiz of musket balls fly around them as they moved forward toward the fence. As Netter negotiated the obstacle, he felt a burning pain as the bullet passed through his indigo coat and slammed into his chest. The bullet immediately robbed his lungs of air and his left hand tried to reach up to the wound as he fell to the ground. What little adrenaline remained in his body allowed him just enough strength to bring himself back up on his feet. The reports of musketry about him and across the field made orders hard to hear, but somehow Gabriel Netter mustered the strength to turn his head toward his men and yell above the roar and crash of battle: "Charge, bayon…!" As he attempted to finish the order, his breath left him and his heart's blood poured from the gaping hole in his chest. Gabriel Netter collapsed to the dusty ground, dead, just as he had predicted to the Confederate officer just minutes earlier.[21]

If not for the death of Netter, a more aggressive Federal attack would likely have continued throughout the rest of the day and possibly the next. Jim Hall had changed the course of the morning with a single shot.

Private W. C. J. Adams stood only feet away from his colonel. As Netter's orderly, he stayed as close as possible. He saw Netter climb the fence and encourage the rest of the boys to keep moving forward just as a bullet ripped into his chest. The puff of smoke directly across the field caught his attention at the same time. Adams raised his musket to his shoulder and immediately aimed toward where he had seen the smoke. He saw the white handkerchief. The 19-year-old aimed for that target and pulled the trigger. Hall was in the process of reloading as the

20 Munday, *Diary*, 6.

21 Bernheim, *Settlement of Jews*, 45; *History of Daviess County*, 162; *Owensboro Messenger*, July 11, 1909, 10.

Federal bullet entered the front of his head and exited out the back of his skull. Blood and brain matter darkened the tree behind him.[22]

The left of the Federal line began to crumble after Netter's fall. The recruits emptied their muskets toward the enemy but began to falter. In the center, undisciplined men disregarded the Rebels in their front and attempted to recover Netter's body, disrupting the formation of the line even more. It was as if a domino effect had hit the battalion, as the right also began to stutter and fall back. If it collapsed before the Rebels fell back, that would be the end. The men would lose the will to fight and the Confederates would take the camp and everything in it.[23]

Fearing a complete route of the force that was now his to lead, the adjutant, Maj. Ira Stout, instinctively took command of the men and the situation. He dressed the line, restored discipline, and ordered an immediate charge. The men were now wild with rage and anger, and those who had not emptied their muskets before the assault took careful aim and fired as they advanced, their gun barrels glistening and flashing in the sun.[24]

As the Federals neared the wood line, the Confederates began a general retreat. They mounted their horses and galloped away to safety, groups of them riding in different directions. Stout halted the battalion but some continued to shoot once they reached the woods. Eventually the firing ceased and the heaviest fighting of the day was over. Union sources put the Confederate casualties at 25-30 while Confederate accounts claim only a few.[25] Superior firepower and a resolute adjutant had, for the moment, overcome inexperience and the loss of Netter.

The skirmish had lasted no more than 30 minutes. The Confederates fled in a few directions, some toward the river and others to the west. Stout assessed the condition of his men. Lieutenant Thomas Cherry had a slight bullet wound. John London, A. W. Wallace, and another man who went by the name of Taylor also received slight wounds. Though they could claim victory in the skirmish, morale plummeted after Netter's death.[26]

The Federal recruits tended their wounded as best they could, and the wounded Confederate prisoners as well. They brought the casualties back to camp, except for a Rebel with a white bandana around his head, now soaked red. The Union

22 Munday, *Diary*, 7; *Owensboro Monitor*, Oct. 1, 1862, 3.

23 *Owensboro Monitor*, Oct. 1, 1862, 3; Bernheim, *Settlement of Jews*, 45; *History of Daviess County*, 162.

24 *History of Daviess County*, 163.

25 Ibid.; Munday, *Diary*, 7.

26 *Owensboro Monitor*, Oct. 1, 1862, 3; Etter, *Indiana Legion*, 87.

soldiers refused to move his body and he lay there for some time, unburied. That was the punishment for the man who killed their commander.[27]

Before accurate reports of the events left Owensboro, rumors and half-truths raced across the region. One such was in Bowling Green, Kentucky. Diarist Eldress Nancy recorded on September 21st that word reached her of some sort of action in Owensboro. She wrote, "We hear, Captain Woodward, a leader of Guerilla band of 800 men, surprised and surrounded Col. Netta with only 150 Federals, at Green River, and took the most of his men prisoners. Col. Netta was shot thro' the bowels. There is very little hope of his recovery. He made good his escape from capture by hiding under the cleft of rocks, so they did not find him." Six days later on the 27th she added,

> Samuel McGown was here to day, he confirms the report that Col Netta is killed. It is said that some guerillas had congregated at a home where there was some four of five women, and they made such a boisterous noise of cheering and hurrahing that Col Netta with some of his men went to ascertain the cause, when the Col. came in sight, the rebels shot him. This so enraged his men, they instantly shot the fellow, also three others of the guerilla band. They guarded these four rebel bodies and would not let them be buried, and threatened the life of any one who should attempt it; and that another party of Netta's men pursued the rest and killed 17 of them.

Such was the nature of rumor in 1862.[28]

Left behind to protect the gun, Mitchell and the rest of his company had heard the sharp fight only a short distance away. It was then that they noticed their adversaries nearly in range of the six-pounder. It appeared that about 200 Rebels tried to use the woods to conceal themselves for an attack upon the southern end of the camp. Due to poor communication, they may not have realized that Netter had attacked toward the west, instead of toward Owensboro, and began to move toward the camp as originally planned. The Union officer in charge ordered the cannon loaded with grapeshot. Once the Rebels were within 300 yards, he gave the order to fire.[29]

27 Minerva Thomas to George Thomas, Sep. 20, 1862, Thomas Family Letters, University of Notre Dame Rare Books and Special Collections, https://rarebooks.nd.edu/digital/civil_war/letters/thomas/5014-21.shtml, accessed Dec. 11, 2017; *Owensboro Monitor*, Sep. 24, 1862, 2. They also reported some horses as "lost" but it is unclear whether Confederate bullets killed them or if Rebel troopers took them. This could possibly mean that some of Netter's men fought mounted during the skirmish, but this is the only mention of the horses.

28 Eldress Nancy Moore, *The Journal of Eldress Nancy: Kept at South Union, Kentucky; Shaker Colony, August 15, 1861-September 4, 1864* (Nashville, 1963), 64, 66.

29 *Owensboro Monitor*, Sep. 24, 1862, 2.

Ranger Captain Taylor of Company E, who commanded the column approaching from the south, led his men toward the Federal camp. The Confederates attempted to move toward Camp Miller under the cover of woods, but the trees did not completely hide their advance and the Yankees spotted them. As soon as they were in range, the brass six-pounder came to life. The charges of grape and canister peppered the trees and hissed through the leaves and branches of the woods.[30]

The cannon stopped the Confederates on the southern end of the camp before their advance had even begun. They tried to move slowly forward again, but each shot of grape and canister stymied the attack. Some of the Federals fired their rifles, which seemed to dishearten the horsemen completely. They may have been outnumbered but they would cut down a considerable number of Southerners if they dared try to make another advance.[31]

If the Rangers were going to make an assault on the camp, they would pay dearly for it. Plus, they could now see that there were at least another 100 Yankees still there guarding the place, protected by the fence that surrounded the camp. Seeing the unfavorable situation, Taylor ordered his men to remount their horses and ride south out of range of the Federal gun.[32]

The partisans mounted their horses and fled south, the Belle clattering behind. The Federals also saw the Rebel companies which had previously engaged Netter's men move south from their former positions. Initially, the partisans rode in different directions but they began to gather again in small groups. An officer ordered Mitchell to lob shells toward the Confederates as they tried to consolidate. With each shot of the cannon, they scattered and retreated farther until they were out of range.[33]

Stout marched his somber, victorious men back to the camp where the rest of the battalion waited. His main concern was to protect the property there and try to hold off the Rebels as long as possible. Reinforcements would surely come. Though they had driven the enemy before them, the men understood that there were even more rangers in Owensboro, possibly heading their way. Martin, however, decided against any further attacks on the camp.[34]

During the retreat, James Munday had galloped in the direction of the Ohio River toward a large building where the Rangers had crossed a meadow to wait

30 Munday, *Diary*, 7; *History of Daviess County*, 163; *Owensboro Monitor*, Oct. 1, 1862, 3.

31 *Owensboro Monitor*, Oct. 1, 1862, 3.

32 Ibid., 3.

33 Ibid., Oct. 3, 1862, 3.

34 *History of Daviess County*, 163.

for developments. Had the camp surrendered? Rumor had it among the men that the Yankees and their own officers had agreed upon an unconditional surrender after Netter's death, but that was not the case. To make matters worse, something had gone wrong with his gun and since he could not fire, he stood watch on the road. The day was disappointing. They had hoped to get an easy victory so close to home but it seemed poorly planned in his opinion, too undisciplined, too ill-equipped. His company began a long ride around its former position to reform with the rest of the regiment south of town. All the while, Federal shells from the six-pounder crashed in the woods nearby. Munday was exhausted. He and his companions had been in the saddle for days on end and had not eaten since the day before. The further south they rode, the fainter the Yankee gun became. They were safe for now.[35]

In Owensboro, Martin received word of the skirmish west of town and that the Federals had driven off his companies. His men were now attempting to link back up with the main body somewhere south of Owensboro. Information also reached Martin that an unknown number of Yankee soldiers had somehow gotten themselves across the Ohio River and were now raising the alarm to the Indiana Legion and any other Federal units in the area. Owensboro would not be a good place to make a stand. If Federals attacked from the south, the Ohio River would be at his back. In addition, there were Federals to his east in Cloverport and to his west in Henderson. Colonel Foster commanded a strong force of infantry, artillery, and cavalry that could appear on the river in hours. Steamers would still be able to ferry men over from Indiana for a fight and gunboats would surely show up. Poorly trained cavalry would not stand a chance in a tactical environment such as that. A second attack on the camp did not seem like a prudent decision. The original plan to lure away the camp's defenders had failed. Now the position was too strong for an assault.[36]

They had already gotten out of Owensboro itself what they most desperately needed: ammunition. Now it was time to consolidate forces and relocate to a safer position. Martin's rangers quietly formed up and rode eight miles south down the Livermore Road toward Panther Creek and the Sutherland farm. The farm was about a mile and a half south of the creek. Munday thought the march to the farm was "miserable," and upon reaching the place they finally had a chance to rest. "We took the rest so inviting, so necessary to man and beast, and dropping the shade of the first trees that afforded protection from the still warm, but sinking sun we

35 Munday, *Diary*, 7.

36 Johnson, *Partisan Rangers*, 348-349.

forgot for a while in quiet ease our past hardship and the many dangers that still menaced," he recorded in his diary.[37]

The Rangers rested the remainder of the day, with a strong picket to the north. It was not until later in the evening that they had their first meal since noon the day before; their supper consisted of a small piece of bread and bacon. An Owensboro youth also made his appearance in the Confederate camp atop Sutherland's Hill. The way in which the Rebels consumed their food stunned him. He reported to the *Owensboro Monitor*, "I passed the guerrilla camp; it was supper time, and they seemed to be enjoying their breakfast, dinner, and supper, for the past two or three days in one meal, from the manner in which they snatched and fought over it."[38] After supper, the men positioned themselves as best they could to sleep away their exhaustion.

The Rangers had seen only success the entire summer, except for Dover, and had not experienced anything like their defeat at Owensboro. Why did Martin not make his entire force visible for Netter to see, like Clarksville? Why did they not use their numbers to their advantage and overwhelm the camp when Netter was engaged with Merriwether, like the attack at Uniontown? Why was communication among the several detachments so poor? The Rangers had used deception to their advantage before. Why did they not do so again? Why did they overestimate the threat from reinforcements, still many hours away? It seems the effort put forth by Martin and the Partisan Rangers was not up to the usual par. Martin's tactical decisions in this encounter had perhaps begun to reveal his lack of formal military training and experience commanding large formations. Was he overly concerned about the time it took to move supplies and parole prisoners? As daring and brave as Martin was on the battlefield while following orders, it appears he did not have the strategic mind of Johnson. The 22-year-old's lessons came at a high price, and that was only going to increase in the days to come.

The scene back at Camp Miller greatly disturbed Holmes. "The news of [Netter's] death had a most demoralizing effect on his men. I hastened to the camp and found the utmost confusion prevailing. Men were trying to get away in every direction and even to conceal their arms. I restored order as well as I could," he remembered.[39]

Word needed to get out or they faced possible annihilation. Union officers sought out Hugh Hales, a recruit of the regiment who happened to be from just across the river in Spencer County. With the river low from the drought, it was

37 Ibid., 349; Munday, *Diary*, 7.

38 Munday, *Diary*, 7; *Owensboro Monitor*, Dec. 17, 1862, 2.

39 *The Twice-A-Week Messenger*, Dec. 16, 1902, 12.

possible that a man could get across. Hales understood the gravity of the situation and agreed to go.

As the artillery piece boomed every few minutes, Hales snuck out of camp and made his way toward the river. He was out of range of the Confederates in town and he knew that they would have men watching the river in case the Indiana Legion attempted to cross. After some time of wading and swimming, he finally reached the Indiana shore.

Immediately, the soaked and tired Hales was met by members of the 4th Indiana Legion who had been picketing the Ohio River since the Newburgh raid. Hales told them the camp was in danger of being overrun or possibly surrendering and that Netter was dead. Word spread like lightning throughout Spencer County and the Rangers would soon discover what it was like to be on the receiving end of a determined attack.

While Martin's forces rode south out of Owensboro, Col. John W. Crooks spoke with Hales to verify the disturbances across the river. The message traveled across the region: Owensboro was in the hands of the Rebels. Crooks thought it magic how quickly word spread and with what alacrity his brave farmers and shopkeepers began to assemble. He admired their willingness to answer the call. One thing he worried about was the distance some of his men would have to travel to get to the Larkin Ferry on the Ohio River, in some cases more than 15 miles. Additionally, he was not sure what exactly awaited him on the other side. Would he find the camp surrendered? Would the Confederates be waiting for them to land and hit them on the shore of the river?

Crooks again spoke with Hales and instructed him, "I need you to tell your commander that he must hold out for a few hours. We will be on hand shortly once we have enough men to cross. Tell him to take possession of some portion of the south bank of the river where they can protect our crossing and landing. He needs to let me know where that point is, by you swimming the river again, or some other signal." Hales immediately made his way back to the river and crossed again. In time, he made the south bank and the Federal camp to relay the message to Stout and Holmes. Help would soon be on the way.[40]

By early afternoon, skiffs became available for the transport of the men of the Indiana Legion to the Kentucky side of the river. The steamers *Ben South* and *John T. McCombs* arrived to help ferry the Legion across at the designated location, downriver from the Union camp. Nearly 500 men bearing arms assembled at the Larkin Ferry on the Indiana side of the Ohio. All of this happened by 4:00

40 Etter, *Indiana Legion*, 86.

p.m., no small feat for a county militia to sound the alarm and bring together that many men.[41]

Spencer County was not the only place to hear that Johnson's regiment had struck again. Evansville hurriedly mobilized and word traveled along the telegraph wires to Governor Morton. The staunch Unionist and firm Republican was a decisive leader and wasted no time taking action. However, he received only half-true information. The first telegraph messages sent on September 19th and 20th stated that over 1,000 rebel cavalry had raided Owensboro and that Netter had been killed. Rumors also reached him that Adam Johnson was among the dead. General Love of the Indiana Legion promptly replied that Indianapolis was to stay notified and to inform Foster in Henderson of the developments in Owensboro. Perhaps he could aid in some way. Union authorities ordered the available steamers, especially the ones that could traverse the sandbars in the low waters of the river. In addition, the newly formed 91st Indiana remained on high alert as the regiment expected orders to move out of Evansville at a moment's notice. The 91st's role would be limited since it still lacked haversacks, canteens, and sufficient percussion caps to fire its muskets.[42]

Fortunately, for Crooks and the Legion, a steamer was moving upriver. The Hoosiers hailed the *John T. McCombs* to the Indiana shore and pressed it into service. As the boat transported the Spencer men across the Ohio, the remaining Union men on the Indiana shore traded shots with the Confederates that braved the riverbank at Owensboro. A veteran of the crossing remembered, "Our boys, not exactly understanding the situation, supposed the enemy were firing into the crowded mass on the boat; thereupon there was much ducking of heads and getting behind chimneys and the cabin of the boat."[43]

Under the cover of the Spencer County Artillery, Crooks and the first of his men landed down from Owensboro, a few miles on the west side of town, and moved toward the Union army camp. The Legion entered Camp Miller with its wide variety of weapons, uniforms, plain civilian clothes, and Federal colors ready to meet the Confederate enemy.[44]

There Crooks discovered Netter, whom he had aided several times over the past few weeks, dead. Crooks assumed that Netter's former battalion would be useless in an upcoming fight. These raw recruits had already lost most of their morale when Netter fell. His Legion men would have to make the fight without much

41 Ibid., 86-87; *Evansville Daily Journal*, Sep. 24, 1862, 2.

42 Morton Telegraphs, Morton telegraph book, no. 15, 272.

43 *Evansville Daily Journal*, Aug. 20, 1871, 2.

44 Indiana Adjutant General, *Indiana Legion Reports*, 36.

help. It was now late in the afternoon and it appeared there was no immediate Rebel threat to the camp. Holmes had already discovered that Martin and his men were only a few miles south and the two officers decided to come up with a plan.[45]

Some Confederate stragglers foolishly stayed behind in Owensboro to collect more plunder while others continued to arrest Union men and parole them. Crooks dispatched Major Towne and 100 Legion men to put a stop to it. Towne's men also occupied the Daviess County Courthouse, a more symbolic move than military, but it sent the message that the town was again in Union hands. Owensboro was finally secure.[46]

Crooks then began to assess his options. He expected Legion men from Warrick County to arrive by steamer later the next morning, along with additional men from Spencer County. Men of the 12th Kentucky Cavalry at Cloverport might also be riding toward Owensboro, but he had not communicated with Colonel Shanks. He knew that all of them would be much too late to affect the current situation. They had to act, and soon, or the Rebels would disappear into the Kentucky countryside, too far south for the Legion to be able to pursue on foot.[47]

Lieutenant Colonel William F. Wood of the 1st Indiana Cavalry happened to be in the southern Indiana area recruiting and arrived in town about 11:00 p.m. from Evansville. He assumed command of all Union forces in Owensboro, including the remnants of Netter's recruits and the Legion. Holmes yielded command to Wood due to the condition of his eyes. This was a positive development for the Union men, for as soon as Wood arrived he began "infusing confidence and restoring order." Crooks and Holmes, though no longer in overall command, continued to see to the concentration of the Legion, and a few of the Owensboro Home Guard as they arrived in town and at Camp Miller.[48] Like Major Scobee, one of his soon-to-be adversaries, Wood was also a minister, but of the Baptist faith. He was born in England in 1826 and eventually settled in Rockport, Indiana, and probably knew many of the men he now commanded. According to the 1860 census, Wood was a Baptist clergyman, and many advertisements spread the news of his preaching in Evansville and Rockport in the region's newspapers, even after he joined the service.[49]

Wood was no amateur when it came to fighting Confederates such as the Partisan Rangers. While an officer in the 1st Indiana Cavalry, Wood had initially

45 Etter, *Indiana Legion*, 86-87; *Owensboro Messenger*, Dec. 16, 1902, 12.

46 Etter, *Indiana Legion*, 86-87.

47 *Evansville Daily Journal*, Sep. 20, 1862, 2; Indiana Adjutant General, *Indiana Legion Reports*, 31.

48 *Evansville Daily Journal*, Sep. 21, 1862, 2; *Owensboro Messenger*, Sep. 24, 1862, 2.

49 *Evansville Daily Journal*, Nov. 23, 1861, 2; *Rockport Weekly Democrat*, Dec. 8, 1861, 2.

been posted in Missouri, in the Ironton and Farmington areas around Pilot Knob. This area was a hotbed for guerrilla and irregular warfare. Since Wood was a minister, he began his service as the 1st Indiana's chaplain but received promotion to major and then to lieutenant colonel and command of the regiment. Wood also served gallantly in other engagements such as the Cache River in Arkansas, also known as Bayou Cache. He received a slight wound in the thigh by enemy fire but his battalion won the day. By all accounts, Wood's men loved and adored him. One soldier correspondent to the *Rockport Democrat* remarked, "a kinder and better officer never lived. He is always at his post; and he treats [the] private with as much courtesy as an officer. In fact, since I've been in the regiment, I have found him to be a soldier's friend."[50]

By the autumn of 1862, Wood was in command of the 1st Indiana, as Colonel Baker moved up to command a brigade. But Wood continued to recruit in Indiana. No account explains why he personally left to recruit instead of sending another officer. By late August, advertisements for volunteers to join the 1st Indiana appeared in the *Evansville Daily Journal* with Wood's name attached as the officer to see. By August 28th, the paper reported that he had arrived in Evansville and was ready to accept recruits.[51]

In the late hours of the night of September 19th and 20th, Wood had to plan both an attack and a defense. This situation was different from his experiences in Missouri and Arkansas. There was an enemy in the countryside, with a reputation for lethal success, possibly waiting to attack him. Wood had hundreds of men at his disposal, including Netter's battalion, but most of the Kentuckians were unfit for an immediate fight. He possessed nearly 500 Legion infantry and one fossilized artillery piece. The Spencer County guns, and everything that was required for their use, could be ferried across the river, but Wood did not have time to wait. The one gun would have to do.[52]

Owensboro was not a peaceful place that night, even though it was under Union control again. Militia and civilians scurried about. The officers prepared their men for the fight that was sure to come the next day, and many citizens took advantage of the lull in fighting to flee to safe places known only to them. The Owensboro Home Guard, amounting to three small and undersized companies, finally assembled in town as well. Would the Rebels reappear in the morning and

50 *Rockport Democrat*, Mar. 1, 1861, 1; *OR* 13, 146-148; *Evansville Daily Journal*, July 22, 1862, 1.

51 *Evansville Daily Journal*, Aug. 28, 1862, 2.

52 Ibid., Sep. 27, 1862, 2.

attack the town again? For many civilians, the answer did not matter, and they did not wait around to find out.[53]

The Owensboro Home Guard's showing, or lack thereof, disappointed many of the Indiana soldiers. It appeared to them that many of the "Union" men suddenly had business to attend to elsewhere, went missing, or had some other excuse as to why they could not join the combined force. One Hoosier remembered, "the Union men of Owensboro did not, as we thought they ought, turn out and go with us to hunt up and whip the rebels." Some of the Indiana men began to wonder why they were defending those who refused to defend themselves.[54]

In defense of the Owensboro Home Guards, the area was ripe with divisions of loyalty. If a man were to leave his family, how could he know whether a guerrilla band prowling near his defenseless home might attack? What if his Southern-leaning neighbor was waiting for an opportunity to strike a Unionist's home while he was away with the Home Guards? It is a thought that was surely going through the minds of some men. The Confederates had disappeared from town, but they could always come back.

Soon, Wood received additional intelligence that the Confederates had removed themselves about eight miles south of town on the Livermore Road near Panther Creek. Wood conferred with the other officers present and decided to take the fight to the Confederates in the morning. They planned to attack the Confederates and rid the county of their presence. There was no time to wait for the arrival of the 12th Kentucky Cavalry nor the Warrick and Vanderburgh County militias. If they did not attack at sunrise, there was a good chance that the partisans would escape the area only to return and unleash mayhem once more. They needed to be destroyed or dealt such a severe blow that they would not be able to recover.[55]

Only 60 men from Netter's former battalion volunteered to go with the Legion; Major Towne would command them. Holmes later claimed he was the one in command of this force. Naturally, they would be the lead elements and scout the road as the rest of the force advanced safely behind. Holmes, retelling the story years later, remembered, "My plan was to attack the Confederates with my full force, but Wood at once changed this plan [and] ordered me to take the cavalry and 'play with the enemy.'" Objecting, Holmes "explained the newness of the horsemen, declared I could not 'play' with such troops and said I feared the

53 *History of Daviess County*, 163.

54 *Evansville Daily Journal*, Sep. 24, 1862, 2; *Owensboro Monitor*, Oct. 8, 1862, 3; Indiana Adjutant General, *Indiana Legion Reports*, 35.

55 *Owensboro Messenger*, Dec. 16, 1902, 12; Etter, *Indiana Legion*, 87.

first shots of the first field piece which I knew they had at the hill would scatter my men. This brought peremptory order that I obey and at once. This I did." Two experienced cavalry commanders disagreed about how to use green troops.[56]

The infantry marched behind the mounted men, which consisted of 350 Spencer County Legionnaires and a few locals commanded by Crooks. At least one man carried a Henry repeating rifle. Wood brought the old artillery piece from the camp and placed it under the command of Sgt. J. C. Finch.[57]

The remainder of the Owensboro Home Guard and Indiana Legion remained in Owensboro and the Federal camp in case things did not go according to plan. The Warrick County Legion would not arrive until well after daylight as their steamboats continued to chug up the river. To catch the Rebels off guard, they had to attack them at dawn. For once, a Union officer planned a serious move against the partisans.

56 *Owensboro Messenger*, Dec. 16, 1902, 12.

57 *Evansville Daily Journal*, Sep. 27, 1862, 2; Terrell, *Report of the Adjutant General of Indiana*, vol. 1, 292-293.

Chapter 14

"Right here we shall conquer or die"

Colonel John W. Crooks formed up his Spencer County Legion in Camp Miller, ready to follow the Union cavalry out of camp and south toward Panther Creek and Sutherland's Hill where the enemy slept. At 2:00 a.m., he reported to Lt. Col. William F. Wood that the column was in line and ready. They first moved east toward Owensboro where other Spencer Legion detachments joined the battalion. From there, they marched south. They had to keep up a pace of at least two miles an hour to arrive at the Confederate bivouac at first light. Crooks worried about the condition of his men, as some of them had walked upwards of 20 miles the day before to rendezvous with the rest of the regiment at the ferry. They still had several more miles to go before they expected to fight.[1]

The 60 cavalry troopers departed camp first, to reconnoiter and shield the infantry and artillery as they marched south. One would not be able to see because of the darkness, and the horses and marching men kicked up massive amounts of dust, covering clothing and weapons alike.[2]

The infantry column trudged southward, and at some junction the Union force turned east off the Livermore Road to a raised gravel road. They may have taken this road when they marched through Owensboro, but they could have also turned south on the Livermore Road just before the Courthouse and then moved to the eastern gravel road. Taking the gravel road would allow Wood to cross Panther Creek and march south in a way that allowed him to approach the

1 Etter, *Indiana Legion*, 87; Indiana Legion Collection, Indiana State Archives, Box 2.

2 Etter, *Indiana Legion*, 87; *Evansville Daily Journal*, Sep. 27, 1862, 2.

The remains of the "gravel road." After the war, it was turned into a railroad, but it has since been removed. *Author*

long part of Sutherland's Hill from a distance and then order an advance with Crooks's infantry. The densely wooded roadside provided the Union troops at least some concealment as they marched.[3]

If Wood continued down the Livermore Road, he risked appearing out of the trees less than 150 yards from the enemy position on the crest. Approaching down the gravel road gave Wood the option of appearing at the Confederate front at more than half a mile's distance. Then he could form his line, deploy the gun, and advance and engage the enemy. It still would not be easy, as reports indicated that the Confederates outnumbered his own force nearly 2:1, and they had the advantage of high ground. Wood detached a company of infantry under Capt. John Meeks to hold the attention of the Confederate left flank from the north. In his later report Wood stated, "Between daybreak and sunrise on Saturday morning, we encountered the rebels about eight miles south of Owensboro, posted in a strong position evidently waiting our attack. I immediately pushed on a small force of cavalry to engage the enemy's attention in front, while I threw out a company of infantry to out flank them on their left."[4]

As dawn broke, the cavalry approached to within two miles of Sutherland's Hill. This particular hill is the largest and first hill that is seen after crossing Panther Creek. It runs north to south, parallel to the Livermore Road, rises rather steeply, and lays about a mile and a half south of the creek. It was a fantastic position from which to observe an approaching enemy and make a defensive stand. Nevertheless,

3 *Messenger-Inquirer*, May 1, 1910, 9.

4 *Evansville Daily Journal*, Sep. 27, 1862, 2.

as good as the hill was for a solid defense, Martin missed a prime opportunity to check or delay the Union advance at the creek crossings with a solid skirmish line. Perhaps it was because the creek was abnormally shallow from the drought, or that the wooded areas near the bridges were too thick with underbrush to position the men.

As the Union column neared Panther Creek the sun began to rise. The cavalry recruits under Major Towne or Lieutenant Colonel Holmes made an unwise push toward the enemy. Wood intended for the cavalry to make a demonstration to hold the Rebels' attention, not to make an all-out attack. Instead, the 60 Union cavalrymen crossed the bridge across Panther Creek, drove in the enemy pickets, and continued to follow the Confederates. For a moment the Union cavalry pushed the Rebels back as if they were experienced veterans. The troopers drove the Confederates south for at least three-quarters of a mile and then charged into what they believed was a smaller force upon Sutherland's Hill. They were very wrong.[5]

The firing of the pickets woke James Munday and the Partisan Rangers from their slumbers. They hastened to form a line on the hill to check the Union advance. Soldiers shouted that the Yankees were coming, and the men rushed to find their horses and ready their weapons. It was clear that their enemy must have marched through the night. Munday hunted for his horse, as some of them seemed to have gotten loose and roamed away. The sudden attack left the men no time to prepare their mounts and many of the Confederates left their blankets, sabers, and other equipment on the ground.[6]

Merriwether's company formed on top of the hill on the lane, in front of the farmhouse, but Munday was not able to join them in time. Some had their horses but many did not. He could hear the heavy sound of horse hooves as the Yankee cavalry burst out from the gravel road shielded by thick trees and brush. They made a daring, if not reckless, charge, following the lane and the Confederate pickets up the hill.[7]

When the Federal horseman galloped up Sutherland's Hill, there were no visible enemy troops, as they were on the other side of the ridge. When the Federals advanced up the slope, the Confederates came charging over the hill to meet them. As Martin's men fired into the mass of 60 horsemen, the horses became confused and panicked. This intense concentration of fire and the boom of the cannon scattered the untrained men and horses in all directions. Of this sudden clash

5 Terrell, *Report of the Adjutant General of Indiana*, vol. 1, 292-293; *Owensboro Messenger*, Dec. 16, 1902, 12.

6 Munday, *Diary*, 7.

7 Ibid., 7.

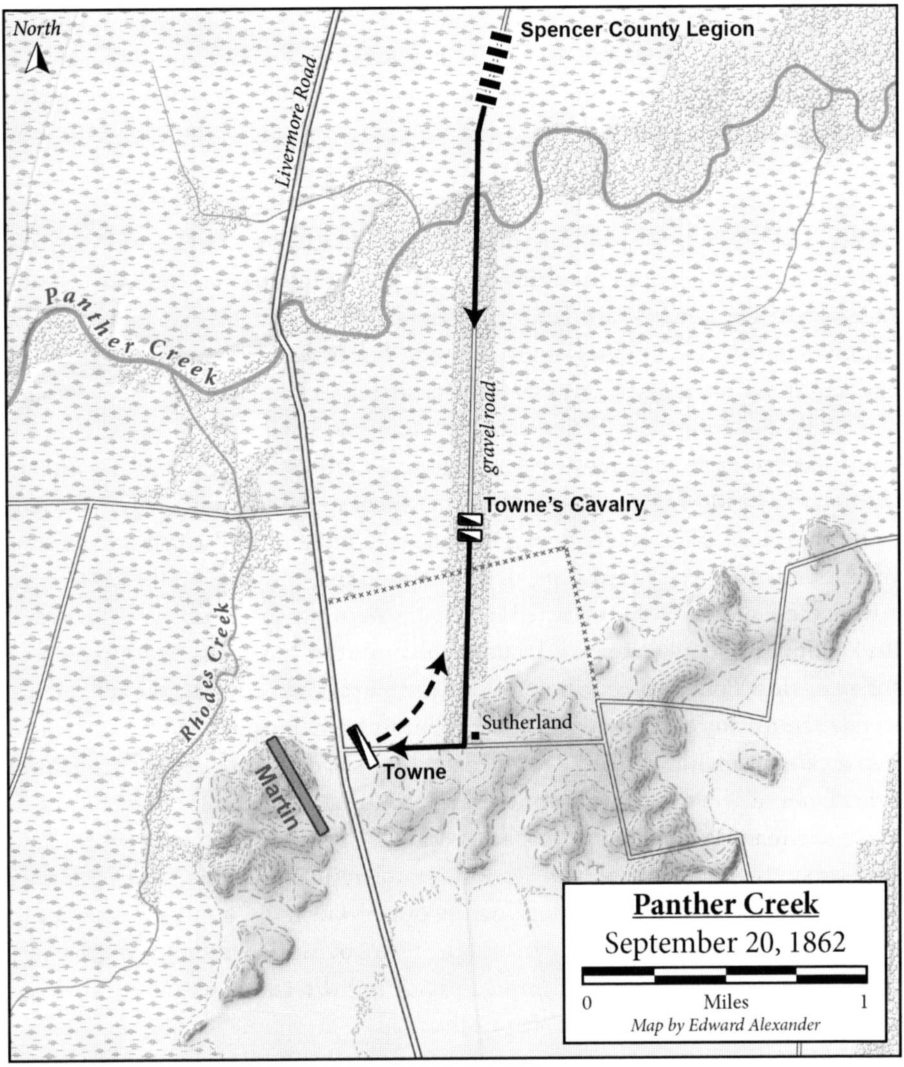

Holmes recalled, "They fired rapidly with muskets and rifles and a cannon and, just as I anticipated, my men were at once thrown into a panic. I had a strong voice then and I commanded them to turn about and face the enemy, but it was useless. They would only run, and directly away from the enemy. I even drew my saber and threatened to run it through the fleeing ones, but they paid no attention to me, to my voice or to my threats." R. W. Burch remembered that the Partisan Rangers were only able to get 65 men into proper formation. They positioned themselves in Sutherland's horse lot where they fired obliquely into the charging Union cavalry.[8]

8 *Owensboro Messenger*, Dec. 16, 1902, 12; Jan. 27, 1903, 3.

During this brief encounter, some of the Union cavalry were captured by the Rangers as their frightened horses galloped toward the enemy instead of away. At least nine men were taken captive and three wounded. Holmes, with no troops left to command willing to fight, joined with the infantry as a regular soldier.[9]

* * *

Too far away to support the mounted attack, Wood and Crooks, with the main Legion body, heard the firing erupt ahead: musketry and then two quick booms from the Confederate gun over a mile and a half away. Wood gave the order to double quick, and the Legion began a jog across the bridge spanning Panther Creek and down the gravel road with the artillery piece in front.[10]

When the militia crossed the bridge over Panther Creek, deep ditches on both sides flanked the roadway. One Legionnaire noted that beyond the ditches there was "an almost impenetrable thicket of briars and underbrush." These woods concealed the Legion on its march toward the Sutherland Farm until the unit emerged nearly 800 yards in front of the Confederate positions on the hill.[11]

As the Union column marched forward toward the sound of the fight ahead, the shooting suddenly stopped. In the light from the rising sun, the survivors of the foolhardy charge came galloping down the road, charging to the rear at full speed. The gallant charge toward the enemy just a few minutes before had turned into an ambush with which the raw Federal troopers could not cope. The flight to the rear was disgraceful to some of the Legion. "They turned their horses and fled down the road, compelling us to plunge into the briars or be run down by their riders and unmanageable horses. We were scattered in all directions on both sides of the road and in utter confusion," wrote one Hoosier. "Nor did they stop until they put the infantry between them and the forces of Scobee and Martin," Holmes admitted. After the friendly danger had passed to the rear, Crooks rallied the men to form a line in the ditch to the left of the road.[12]

Was Major Towne responsible for this debacle? It is difficult to tell, as the sources are mostly silent. In his reports written after the battle, Crooks does not mention Towne in a negative way, but he also does not praise him as he did other officers. Concerning Holmes's conduct, neither Wood, Crooks, nor the other anonymous member of the Indiana Legion mention him even once. The

9 Terrell, *Report of the Adjutant General of Indiana*, vol. 1, 292-293; *Owensboro Monitor*, Sep. 24, 1862, 2.

10 Terrell, *Report of the Adjutant General of Indiana*, vol. 1, 292-293.

11 *Evansville Daily Journal*, Sep. 24, 1862, 2.

12 Ibid.; *Owensboro Messenger*, Dec. 16, 1902, 16.

Modern view of Panther Creek near the location where the Indian Legion crossed.

Author

Owensboro Monitor, which reported on the engagement in the days and weeks that followed, failed to mark Holmes as even present until a week later. Then, the only reference he received was, "Col. Holmes was outranked by Col. Wood and hence had no command. Notwithstanding this and in delicate health, he was upon the battlefield with his gun. He is a true soldier."[13]

Whoever was in command of the cavalry, Holmes's argument was correct, as they were obviously not ready for such a "play" as he described earlier. As some had only been in the service for a little over a month, they had not yet had enough drill or experience. The horses, too, were not used to the booms and cracks of cannon and musket fire, so the cowardly retreat to the rear may have been out of the riders' control.

Colonel Wood allowed his men to rest for ten minutes, while fearing a possible counter-attack. He considered that the Confederates would attempt to follow up the rout of his cavalry and trap his infantry and artillery with their backs to the creek and the small bridge. Wood waited ten minutes, but no attack came. They still had about a mile and a half to march, so the rest was helpful for his footsore infantry. Wood gave the order to reform the men and resume the advance. As they proceeded south, with artillery in the front, potshots came from the west beyond the wooded thickets. The Legion ignored these nuisances and continued south.[14]

In viewing the action from the top of Sutherland's Hill, Martin watched the Federal cavalry charge up the hill in grand style only to face hundreds of his

13 *Owensboro Monitor*, Sep. 24, 1862, 2.

14 Johnson, *Partisan Rangers*, 349; *Evansville Daily Journal*, Sep. 24, 1862, 2; Aug. 20, 1871, 2.

partisans. His men took a few prisoners, as some riders lost all ability to control their mounts and they consequently galloped behind the Confederate lines. The whole thing had almost been too easy. Is this the best the Yankees could muster? Was this their strategy? If that was the case, maybe Martin could change his defenses.

As the Federals retreated, Martin and Owen rode down the hill and moved to the woods on the western side of the road to scout the enemy formations as they advanced. They moved their horses through the thick brush and trees, keeping an open eye for the Federals. About a quarter mile from Panther Creek, they spotted the Legion column and its Federal colors. The artillery piece was in front, the infantry close behind. Martin did not see any sign of the cavalry they had just sent running. As the column marched southward, Martin and Owen could not resist taking a shot, an indication of their naïveté as officers. They were not afraid of consequences due to the thick foliage protecting them from return fire. The two officers drew their pistols and each man fired, expecting a swift and large reaction. But no return shots came. The column kept marching with eyes front as if nothing had happened.[15]

Disappointed that there was no reaction, the two men rode back to the Sutherland Farm to prepare their men for the coming Union attack. Martin arrived at the top of the hill and began shouting orders to his officers. The twenty-two-year-old commanded about half his men to move to the bottom of the hill into a field and take position behind a stake-and-rider fence that ran parallel to the ditch of the Livermore Road. He left his 4-lb gun on top with a few troopers. Every eighth man rode to the rear side of the hill with the mounts of the others. As the battle would disclose, Martin and the other partisan officers lacked the proper tactical knowledge to place their forces to repel the Union attack.[16]

If the Legion was going to make an advance up the hill, then the defensive line from the lower level could decimate the Federal infantry, and possibly allow the Rangers to chase down and capture the Yankee gun. With another gun, and a bigger one at that, it would make the 10th Kentucky a force with which to be reckoned throughout the theater of operations. Moreover, there would be the extra bonus of securing the weapons and supplies left by the fleeing infantry and the dead and wounded.

Martin swung the left half of his line back 90 degrees up the hill, facing north. Evidently, the company that Wood had sent to engage the Confederate left had at least made its presence known enough for Martin to take precautions. James Munday described the layout of Ranger forces in his diary: "The regiment was then

15 Johnson, *Partisan Rangers*, 349.

16 Ibid.; Munday, *Diary*, 7.

Modern view of Sutherland's Hill from the initial Union line. The road running across the background is the old Livermore Road, now Highway 431. A few modern homes dot the northern slope, but the rest of the hill remains farmland. *Author*

formed in a meadow on the front left of the house. Beginning some distance from the lane," Munday explained with geometric precision, "our line was extended through to low ground parallel with the gravel road and then hurried on the left at right angles, a portion facing the cornfield and the woods on the left and extending to the hillside on which at some distance to the rear in the angle formed by the extension of the lines the cannon was placed."

The shots from the west did not interfere with the Indianans' march. It would be a waste of ammunition to try to hit a moving target through that much brush. In addition, they didn't want to give the enemy any indication of how close they were. The rest of the march toward the Sutherland Farm took about 15 minutes. Their muskets were loaded, and as they proceeded south, they could see the end of the trees where the gravel road opened into fields on both sides and the farm lane. By making a right turn at the opening of the trees, the farm lane went all the way up to the top of Sutherland's Hill.[17]

The men could hear hooves quickening their cadence as the horses pulling the cannon began to increase their speed. The Union cannoneers had a lot to do when they reached the field. They would need to unlimber the gun, put it into position, move the horses and limber chest back to safety, and then fire and reload before too much return fire came their way.

The Legion men gripped their muskets tighter as they prepared themselves for the baptism of fire that was soon to come. For most of the men in the ranks, this

17 *Evansville Daily Journal*, Sep. 24, 1862, 2.

was the first battle in which they had ever fought. Wood gave orders for Crooks to double-quick the infantry and form on the gravel road parallel to the hill on which he presumed the Confederates were positioned.[18]

Wood gave the signal, and the plan went into motion. He stayed with the brass gun while the infantry passed behind it and filed into line from the column. The crash of Rebel guns and the boom of the Confederate cannon was almost instantaneous. The canister of the Clarksville Belle blew pieces of lead through the trees like a hundred angry hornets. Luckily for the Legion, the Southern gun was far out of range for improvised canister.

Crooks gave the command "On the right by file into line" while the men moved out of the lane at the double-quick. He ran ahead to set the right flank of his line while the men ran in column formation. When he made it to that point he yelled, "March!" and the line immediately began to shift from the column of fours to a battle line on the road. The militiamen performed this maneuver as if they were veteran soldiers serving with their comrades in Mississippi or chasing Bragg further east. The weeks and months of drill were paying its dividends, and the discipline of the Legion made it evident that they were not the poorly trained recruits or ill-led forces with which the Partisan Rangers had previously dealt.[19]

While the infantry moved, the cannon advanced into range. When the gun was ready, Wood calmly lit his cigar and ordered, "Boys, wheel about that cannon, facing the enemy!" The gun was turned and Wood placed his cigar on the vent of the gun, setting off the round of canister toward the Confederates. The sound of the Federal gun intensified the sound of battle as gunners on both sides vied with each other to send death and destruction toward their enemy.[20]

Colonel Crooks's infantry began to march toward the Confederates in the ditch. After covering nearly two-thirds of the 700 yards toward the Confederates in the road, the Rangers opened fire on the Legion. The Indiana soldiers immediately halted and returned fire and the duel ensued. For nearly an hour, the two lines traded volleys, though perhaps not well aimed.[21]

By now, Munday had finally retrieved his horse. As he mounted, he could hear the rattle of musketry swelling louder than before. The thunder tones told him the battle had begun, and he was nowhere near the action. He rode hard toward one of the troopers holding the horses in the rear, dismounted, and handed off the reins.[22]

18 *Evansville Daily Journal*, Sep. 24, 1862, 2.

19 Indiana Legion Collection, Indiana State Archives, Box 2.

20 Truman, *At War With Ourselves*, 22.

21 *Evansville Daily Journal*, Sep. 24, 1862, 2; Sep. 27, 1862, 2.

22 Munday, *Diary*, 7.

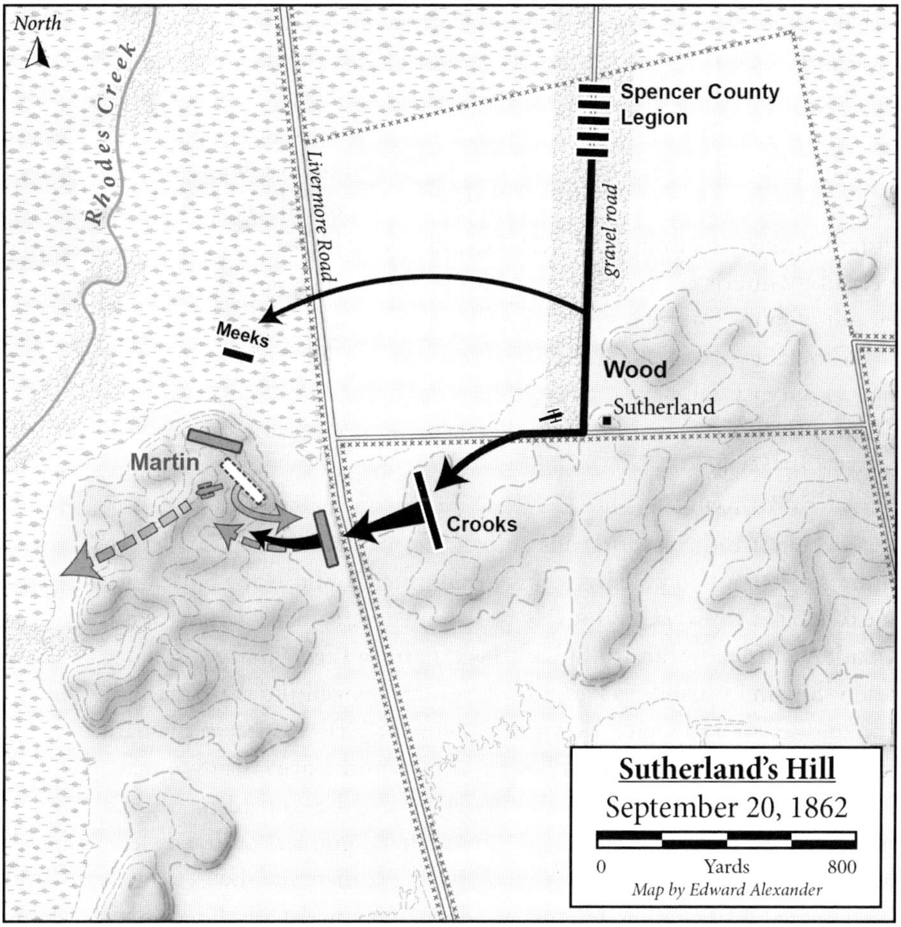

The sound of battle was now a continuous roll as nearly a thousand men engaged in combat. As he ran toward the top of the hill, Munday could see rising smoke, and the Clarksville Belle firing as fast as the gunners could load. Given the density of the smoke and confusion of the attack, he could not find his company. It had moved toward the bottom of the hill near the road. Even if he wanted to rejoin it, the smoke kept him from distinguishing one group of Rangers from another. The scene from the top of the hill stunned him. From this point, he could see the whole action. He recognized men from the first company and fell in to fight with them. By this time, everyone was dismounted and firing their pieces at the Federals.[23]

23 Ibid.

View from the top of Sutherland Hill looking toward the area of the Union advance. The elementary school is partially on the path of the advancing line. The Legion's right flank rested on the road on the left. *Author*

Crooks steadily assured his soldiers from behind their battle lines, giving firing orders and confidence to his Legion men. Solid balls, buckshot, and even musket balls whistled by him as the Confederates held their ground. Colonel Charles Fournier of the 5th Indiana Legion, from Perry County, imitated Crooks's leadership and walked back and forth behind his wing of the battalion, shouting confidence, even though his own men were not participating in the fight.[24]

During the fight, Capt. Al Fowler, commander of Company I, may have used some interesting language in the presence of the reverend-turned-Confederate officer, Major Scobee. In a biographical sketch in Johnson's book, Fowler is depicted as urging his men to keep up their firing, "Damn them, boys, give them hell!" Noticing Scobee nearby, he apologized for the language he used in the Major's presence. Undaunted, Scobee apparently replied, "Captain, if it does you any good let them have it."

The "Clarksville Belle" fired its loads of bagged musket balls at irregular intervals. Munday loved the sound of the gun and how its roar excited his fellow partisans. However, it seemed to overshoot the Yankees every time. Lack of proper ammunition and training limited its effectiveness.

From atop the hill, Munday and his fellow troopers kept up a steady fire with their ineffective guns. Few of the troopers carried the new Enfields, or even Belgian muskets. The newer recruits, like Munday, still bore their squirrel rifles and shotguns from home. Munday was positioned with the left flank, so he likely fired on the lonely company of the Indiana Legion sent to distract the left. Some of the muskets taken from Newburgh in July were now firing at the troops to

24 Indiana Adjutant General, *Indiana Legion Reports*, 35, 39.

whom they had been originally issued. It is hard to imagine men with the newer Enfield muskets not causing more casualties than they did. It is possible, with Merriwether's company at the fence, that the better-armed men found themselves positioned in the wrong portion of the line.

A few men of the Legion began to fall and Crooks ordered his men forward. They could not stay in this open and exposed position long without taking more casualties. Right now, distance aided them as many of the Confederate shots missed their targets. However, they could not sustain this rate of fire and hope to end the day in victory. A fence stood not far into the field bordering the Livermore Road, and if he could push the Rebels out and away from it, it would provide good cover for his line. He wanted to avoid exhausting the ammunition from this distance, so it was imperative that the battalion only fire when he commanded. This would explain Munday's observation that the Federal fire appeared to have slackened before the end of the battle.[25]

Wood observed the battle from his position near the gun, still smoking his cigar. He had been in many fights before in Missouri and Arkansas, and this was no different. As a minister, he seemed to conduct himself as though death held no terrors for him. From the gun position, he could direct its fire and the movements of the infantry. The first two rounds had been canister, but he ordered the gun to fire a solid ball for the third shot. The men loaded the gun and when Sgt. Finch gave the order to fire, the gun exploded. The force knocked the old iron gun off its trunnion caps and rendered it useless for the remainder of the day. Wood wasted no time in ordering the gun off the field and back down the gravel road to safety. Finch directed the gunners to assemble the team of horses and limber the cannon for withdrawal.[26]

With their artillery piece disabled, the Union battle plan would need to change. Over the crash of the muskets, Crooks consulted with Wood. They decided that the best option was to close in with the infantry and push the enemy out of the ditch towards the hill. They continued firing controlled volleys at the Rebels and waited for an opening to move forward. The Legion was about to make the very first advance in its history.[27]

After ordering the men to cease firing, Crooks and Wood assumed their positions in front of the battalion. Wood yelled as loud as he possibly could, "Battalion! Forward, March!" The Legion began to move forward in a steady battle line.[28]

25 Terrell, *Report of the Adjutant General of Indiana*, vol. 1, 292-293.

26 *Evansville Daily Journal*, Sep. 27, 1862, 2.

27 Ibid.; Munday, *Diary*, 8; *Owensboro Messenger*, Jan. 27, 1903, 3.

28 *Evansville Daily Journal*, Sep. 27, 1862, 2; *Owensboro Monitor*, Sep. 24, 1862, 2.

Sutherland's Hill as seen from the ditch along the Livermore Road. The Confederate cannon's position was near the part of the hill near the road. *Author*

Munday on the left of the Confederate line watched the Hoosiers advance toward the field where his missing company deployed. The rising smoke from the corn obviously gave him a sense of their position, but the firing ceased as hundreds of men began to fall back toward the hill in the face of Legion bayonets. At this moment, Meeks's company must have applied the necessary pressure on the Confederate left that helped force its gradual withdrawal toward the hill. An anonymous writer to the *Evansville Daily Journal* recalled nearly nine years later, "At this juncture Captain John Meeks, of Newtonville, was detached with his company of sharpshooters to make a short detour to the right of the cornfield and take the enemy in flank which was done in excellent style. Soon the enemy's line began to waver and give way."[29]

Smoke no longer rose from the cornfield in the Legion's front as the troops continued forward. As the line neared the fence just before the cornfield, Crooks took notice of a ditch made from the throwing up of the Livermore Road just before the fence. It would be a natural trench, and the fence would provide additional cover.[30]

Crooks and Wood ordered their men into the ditch and gave the order to fire a volley at the retiring Rebels. They were much closer now, and the cornfield did not prove to be a hindrance to finding targets and shooting down the enemy. Several of the men placed their muskets through the slits in the wood of the fence and took careful aim at each command to fire. Crooks was pleased with the efficiency

29 *Evansville Daily Journal*, Aug. 20, 1871, 2.

30 Terrell, *Report of the Adjutant General of Indiana*, vol. 1, 292-293; *Evansville Daily Journal*, Sep. 27, 1862, 2.

his men exhibited in their shooting. It was if they were back home hunting game, their aim true, steady, and unerring.[31]

More minutes passed as the two sides continued to trade fire, the better of which was given by the Legion. Its cover and superiority in arms and discipline was beginning to have effect, even given the struggles of the novice Legionnaires. One veteran of the fight remembered that another man oftentimes bit too far down the cartridge and lost much of the powder. The lack of proper Confederate drill and weapons outpaced the mistakes of the Legion troops, however, whose pressure continued to show results.[32]

Sergeant Munday fired his piece as quickly as he could but noticed his ammunition beginning to run low. Given the fight the day before, and now this heavy engagement, the regiment would not be able to stand its ground much longer. Rangers were already falling back on the right. By this point, they no longer held their line near the road and the cornfield and tried to establish new positions on the lower slope of the hill. They continued to fire, but broke suddenly for the crest, apparently having exhausted their ammunition. The retreat had begun, and there was nothing any Confederate officer could do to stop it.[33]

To Wood, the Rebel right appeared vulnerable and he instantly saw his opportunity to sweep them off the hill. When the Confederates fell back to the slope on the lower portion of the hill they attempted to make a stand, but the Hoosiers instantly cut them down in the exposed position. It was, as one soldier remembered, like shooting hogs. The Union fire forced them up to the crest of the hill as the Rebel line began to fall apart.[34]

Wood emerged in front of the battalion, sword drawn, and gave the order to charge. As the Legion moved forward, the Federal colors waved in the morning light and the smoke of the muskets and the Rebel cannon hovered over the ground. A few vulnerable paces in front, Wood led a steady advance. The militiamen heard his voice over the roar and crash of battle, "Come on my brave Indianans, right here we shall conquer or die!" The Hoosiers raised such a cry of enthusiasm that they continued to push further, even as men around them fell from Rebel bullets. It was a small tidal wave, impossible to stop.[35]

As Wood began his ascent up the hill, a Confederate bullet struck his sword, forcing it out of his hand. In the process, Wood lost his balance and fell to the

31 Terrell, *Report of the Adjutant General of Indiana*, vol. 1, 292-293.

32 *Rockport Journal*, Aug. 28, 1879, 2.

33 Munday, *Diary*, 8.

34 *Evansville Daily Journal*, Sep. 24, 1862, 2; Sep. 27, 1862, 2.

35 *Owensboro Monitor*, Sep. 24, 1862, 2.

ground. A soldier named John Hicks believed that Wood was dead and exclaimed so loudly. No sooner had Hicks cried out when the lieutenant colonel leaped back to his feet. His blood was up as he said, "No, I ain't! But kill that damn Rebel!" He pointed toward the crest of the hill at a certain Confederate and his men instantly began firing in that direction. Without a sword, he picked up a musket and bayonet from a wounded Legion man as the line halted to return fire. Again, the Southerners fell back, this time to the very top of the hill. A partisan defeat was near.[36]

By now the Yankee fire was murderous. Several Confederates fell just below the crest of the hill, being totally exposed to the Legion bullets. Munday remarked in his diary, "[H]ere several fell and were carried bleeding from the field and down the hill." Many of the wounded men were carried to their horses, some placed in wagons, and some taken to one of the farm buildings. To keep the Rebel gun from falling into the hands of the Hoosier militia, the partisans quickly moved it toward the back of the hill away from danger.[37]

Munday joined a group of about 300 men who continued to stave off the Federal advance, but it was soon apparent their attempt was futile. With ammunition nearly depleted, they turned and ran to their mounts. Munday regretted leaving bleeding comrades behind, but he had little choice. He could either try to bring off a wounded comrade and risk capture or escape to fight another day. Most of the Partisan Rangers chose the latter.[38]

The Legion continued its charge, shooting Confederates as they fell back. They, too, could sense the impending victory, and probably did not need much urging to move forward. James Wilson, of the 26th Kentucky, who was home recruiting, fell in with the Legion that day and fought with his Henry repeating rifle. Just days before a group of Confederates had attacked him near his home in Rumsey. As he moved with the battalion to the top of Sutherland's Hill, he killed six Rebels and likely wounded a few more.[39]

With raised musket and bayonet, Wood led his men beyond the crest. He wished they had been able to capture the Rebel gun, but the Confederates had already begun moving it down the rear slope of the hill. Scores of Confederate dead and wounded lay about the top of the hill, but the Legion continued its relentless

36 *History of Daviess County, Kentucky*, 164-165; *Evansville Daily Journal*, Sep. 22, 1862, 2.

37 Munday, *Diary*, 8.

38 Ibid., 8.

39 *Evansville Daily Journal*, Sep. 24, 1862, 2; U.S., Compiled Service Records of Volunteer Union Soldiers Who Served in Organizations from the State of Kentucky, 1861-1865, James Wilson Service Record, "List of Absentees at Special Muster," M397, Roll 0383, National Archives.

push. Wood noticed some of the Rebels run into a farm building and immediately charged in that direction. He leveled his bayonet and burst through the door, running his steel through one of the defenders. The sight of such a gruesome death terrified the others inside, all of whom immediately surrendered.[40]

The Rebels brought the Clarksville Belle down the rear side of the hill to a thicket of woods that lay just beyond. After falling back from the hill, Munday and others located their horses and quickly mounted. Martin came riding through and ordered Munday's company to escort the gun while they retreated. Munday wrote, "Our company with another was ordered to bring off the artillery and waiting we fell in the rear of the famous piece." Once they limbered the gun and moved off, his company fell in behind it and kept up with its irregular speed through old country roads and fields.[41]

When Crooks reached the top of the hill, he was elated with his Legion. The Southerners were in full retreat. He always had confidence in his men but now that confidence was boundless. They had fought just as well as any veteran regiment down south and completely whipped the enemy. Everywhere about him, Confederate supplies lay scattered. Saddles and bridles, possibly commandeered from Owensboro, lay where their users had abruptly left them when the fight started. Blankets, pistols, muskets, and other supplies were everywhere on the ground. In some places, it was easy to tell where individual Rebels had been sleeping, while other areas denoted the hasty Confederate battle lines.[42]

Crooks watched the guerrillas escape to a distant wood with the cannon. He immediately thought of the cowardly retreat by some of Netter's recruits. Had they returned and fought with the infantry, they could have bagged more prisoners and the gun. Holmes later stated that he had wanted to chase down the retreating Confederates but Wood would not allow him to do so. Neither Wood nor Crooks mention of this, but one anonymous writer who went by the penname "Quill" speaks of the want of a couple companies of cavalry. He complained later that they could have captured the entire enemy force had they been present.[43]

The lack of cavalry was key in this situation. Wood had already proved by his actions in Missouri and Arkansas that he would often pursue a retreating enemy with his cavalry, bagging more prisoners and supplies and inflicting more casualties.

40 *Evansville Daily Journal*, Sep. 24, 1862, 2.

41 Munday, *Diary*, 8.

42 *Evansville Daily Journal*, Sep. 27, 1862, 2; Terrell, *Report of the Adjutant General of Indiana*, vol. 1, 292-293.

43 *Owensboro Messenger*, Dec. 16, 1902, 12; *Evansville Daily Journal*, Sep. 24, 1862, 2; Etter, *Indiana Legion*, 87.

The Partisan Rangers retreated down this side of Sutherland's Hill and away from the advancing Indiana Legion. *Author*

Since Netter's recruits either could not get their mounts to cooperate or refused to re-enter the fray after being scattered, there was no cavalry to be had to chase down the retreating Confederates. If the cavalry had been present, it is possible they may have been able to capture the enemy gun and more prisoners.

The dust undoubtedly kicked thick clouds into the Confederates' faces while they rode southwest toward the Green River, looking back constantly for enemy pursuit. Munday's company held back every now and then at the beginning of the march and the Federals only followed on foot for about half a mile. One Owensboro teenager present in the Confederate camp, whose name has been lost to history, claims that he did not participate in the battle but approached the field once the firing had largely ceased. He wrote to the *Owensboro Monitor*: "The Federals were drawn up in line of battle on the hill on which the guerrillas encamped the night before. I could see the dead and wounded scattered over the field of action, but could not tell which there were most of. I rode up to the Federal Surgeon and asked him if the affair had terminated, but just then some of the guerrillas showed themselves near where I was standing, and the Federals fired a volley at them and I disappeared for fear that I might get hurt. I could hear the sharp whistle of the bullets as they passed me."[44]

After riding roughly twenty miles, the Rangers reached the Green River near Ashbyburg, free of further pursuit. Here they proceeded to ford the river. Munday was surprised at not finding the enemy waiting. In his diary he recorded, "[A] rough ride brought us opposite Ashbyburg where somewhat to our surprise we finished the crossing of the river rapidly and without dispute." Some of the men let their horses swim, while they crossed in a dilapidated boat. The young diarist, however,

44 Munday, *Diary*, 8; Johnson, *Partisan Rangers*, 349; *Owensboro Monitor*, Dec. 17, 1862, 2.

did not trust his horse's safety to swimming across on its own, and instead rode on its back while it swam through the water. It was apparently quite enjoyable to him for he records in his diary how he and his horse swam and re-swam the river. Once across, the Rangers felt once again secure. The Green River was between them and pursuers that might be coming from Owensboro. They made camp below the hill where the Federals had entrenched the previous winter to guard the river crossing. The village of Ashbyburg was nearby, and Munday and his compatriots settled in for much needed rest. "Here at Ashbyburg as if in perfect security we halted and encamped for the night in the low ground near the now dilapidated breast works thrown up last winter by the enemy," he wrote.[45]

* * *

Crooks surveyed the scene after the shooting had stopped. Three of his Legion men were dead. 21-year-old Curtis Lamar was all that his financially poor mother had left. Some years earlier, Curtis's father had abandoned the family and the responsibility of providing for them fell on his shoulders. Now she did not have her son, and she did not have a means of income.[46]

Corporal Isaac Varner lay mortally wounded and would die soon. Varner was in Company C, Captain Meeks's company. Varner, 24, left behind a widowed wife and a fatherless daughter, Mary. It was not long before he took his last breath. Another one of the many who gave their all for the Union, and so close to home.[47]

A third man, Simpson Palmer, also made the ultimate sacrifice. Legion men loaded his body onto one of the carts brought to remove the wounded and captured supplies. They were going to need as many wagons as they could get.[48]

The Federals ascertained that they had 35 men wounded. These men needed attention back in Rockport as quickly as possible. Dr. J. S. Houghland, who accompanied Crooks and the Legion on the march, began immediately tending to the wounded. Crooks, a trained civilian physician, likely also helped tend to the wounded as well.[49]

45 Munday, *Diary*, 8.

46 James Curtis Lamar Mother's Pension Application, Case Files of Approved Pension Applications of Widows and Other Veterans of the Army and Navy Who Served Mainly in the Civil War and the War with Spain, compiled 1861–1934, National Archives.

47 Isaac Varner Pension Application, Case Files of Approved Pension Applications of Widows and Other Veterans of the Army and Navy Who Served Mainly in the Civil War and the War with Spain, compiled 1861–1934, National Archives.

48 *Evansville Daily Journal*, Sep. 27, 1862, 2; Terrell, *Report of the Adjutant General of Indiana*, vol. 1, 292-293.

49 Terrell, *Report of the Adjutant General of Indiana*, vol. 1, 292-293.

The Legion captured 16 partisans, along with multiple pistols, muskets, shotguns, saddles, sabers, blankets and several horses and mules. In his official report submitted later that December, Crooks stated that his men recovered over 130 firearms left on the field by the Confederates. Surely, some of these weapons had once been a part of the stockpiles taken during the Newburgh raid, or even Clarksville and Uniontown.[50]

Wood ordered the Rebel dead and wounded counted as well. Along with the 16 prisoners, 36 Confederates lay dead on the field, plus 30 wounded men left behind. A farmhouse just south of the battlefield became the gathering point for some of the Rebel wounded, while others ended up at neighboring farms. The discrepancy in killed and wounded between the two sides is quite large, especially since the Indiana Legion was the attacking force. It is likely that most of the Confederate casualties occurred while they retreated up Sutherland's Hill while exposed to the mass fire of the Legion. Additionally, the ditch and fence concealed the Legion for a good portion of the fight. Crooks credited the fence and ditch "for our comparatively small loss."[51]

The *Owensboro Monitor* reported that citizens from McLean County passed the Partisan Rangers on their retreat to Green River. They claimed they spoke with Major Scobee who admitted that the Confederates had been badly whipped and lost 70-80 men. This would stand in stark contrast to later Confederate reports of only a few killed or wounded. The *Monitor* published a column refuting the Confederate claim and explained, "The very fact that 400 well mounted men after a fight of an hour and a half had left six dead and seventeen wounded on the field proves they had a great many more to carry away." In October, the *New Albany Daily Ledger* reported that six more of the wounded Confederates had since died, and that "The total number of rebel dead in the battle, therefore, is fifty-four." None of the accounts agree, but the official reports by Crooks and Wood both put the Confederate casualties at about the same number, which tends to confirm the alleged comment by Scobee.[52]

It is safe to assume that the battle produced well over 100 casualties, no matter the size of the forces. With the Confederates removing at least some of their wounded, and possibly some of their dead, it is impossible to know exactly how many Southern men fell that morning. With over 1,000 men fighting as long as they did, the overall casualty numbers tally nearly 10 percent, a telling bit

50 Ibid.

51 Terrell, *Report of the Adjutant General of Indiana*, vol. 1, 292-293; *Owensboro Messenger*, Sep. 24, 1939, 13.

52 *Owensboro Monitor*, Sep. 24, 1862, 2; *New Albany Daily Ledger*, Oct. 8, 1862, 2.

of information. Historian Paddy Griffith's theory on the effectiveness of musket fire, smoothbore or rifled, comes into play here. Weapons of the Civil War era mostly "fell a long way short of perfection. The sequence of actions required to load and fire a rifle musket was still extremely complex and difficult to follow correctly in the heat of combat," Griffith has explained. Additionally, the notion that most men of the middle 19th century, especially Southerners, were experts with firearms is patently false. Even if a soldier considered himself a proficient hunter, "the huntsman who loads carefully and then stalks his inoffensive prey is surely in a very different state of mind from the soldier who has to fire forty rounds in double-quick time against an enemy regiment which is busy returning the compliment." Maintaining an effective rate of fire was difficult under the best circumstances, more difficult still when units possessed neither the ammunition nor the time for extensive drill. The Partisan Rangers did not have enough powder and ball to conduct target practice, and the Indiana Legion possessed little more in their county arsenal.[53] These deficiencies help explain why the two sides did not inflict more damage on each other, even when they closed to within a few yards at Sutherland's Hill.

The number of Rebels involved in the fight also became a source of debate between the two sides. The Confederates left behind one of their surgeons to care for the wounded and he informed Wood that there had been 800 raiders. The Confederates consistently claimed their numbers were less than 400 or 500. The Union argument generally placed the number higher, toward 800, and never below 500. If Wood told the truth about the Rebel surgeon then why would the Confederates lie about the size of the regiment? Would claiming a higher number of men be cause for a more humiliating defeat?[54]

Crooks was very pleased with his men. For an hour and a half, they had traded blows with a force larger than their own, a force that had the advantage of topography, artillery, and mobility. They had fought like "veteran tigers," driving the enemy in their front and clearing Daviess County of Confederates for the time being. Wood led like the brave and accomplished officer he was, just as he had many times elsewhere. The *Evansville Daily Journal* also commended the Legion by writing, "It was decidedly one of the most brilliant skirmishes of the war."[55]

Not all heroes of the day were grown men. The *Louisville Daily Democrat* wrote of one fifteen-year-old boy, George W. Swint, an apprentice in the *Rockport*

53 Griffith, *Battle Tactics of the Civil War*, 85, 87.

54 *History of Daviess County*, 164; *Owensboro Monitor*, Sep. 24, 1862, 2.

55 Terrell, *Report of the Adjutant General of Indiana*, vol. 1, 292-293; *Evansville Daily Journal*, Sep. 22, 1862, 2.

Memorials and monuments marking the location of the battle. The UDC dedicated the small marker in the 1930s, while the base of the Confederate monument that formerly stood on the Daviess County Court House lawn was moved to this location in 2022. *Author*

Democrat newspaper office. The paper reported that he killed three men, as did the proprietor of the paper, Cal Jones.[56]

Not all Union accounts were as glowing. "Quill" began the northward march back to Owensboro and the Ohio River with the rest of the Legion. His actual identity is unknown, but he provided readers in Rockport, Evansville, and Owensboro with his account of the fight and the aftermath. One thing that is certain is that he was greatly disappointed in the conduct of the Kentucky men, save a few. He complained, "There were no more than twelve in the fight [Kentuckians]. The cavalry officers and men, with a few exceptions among the *men*, acted in the most cowardly and shameful manner."[57]

One such post-battle incident that annoyed him and other members of the Legion was the conduct of one Federal officer. "Quill" mentions that as the victorious column marched back to Owensboro, a Union officer with the rank of major approached them. The man went to one of the companies that had carried colors through the fight. He asked the Indiana men if he could carry the victorious flag, and whomever carried it allowed it. What they did not expect was the officer

56 *Louisville Daily Democrat*, Sep. 23, 1862, 2.

57 *Evansville Daily Journal*, Sep. 24, 1862, 2.

to ride over a mile in front of the column to the crowds of civilians, especially ladies, as if he had carried the flag through the fight. "Quill" states that the man had told the people, "There was the flag *we* didn't let go down!" Offended by this scene of stolen valor, "Quill" offered some choice words for "the pusillanimous popinjay [who] was not in the fight at all." However, it seems "Quill" did this particular officer a favor by not revealing the major's name.[58]

After some hours collecting items from the battlefield, assisting the wounded, and caring for the dead, the Legion finally arrived back in Owensboro that afternoon. Colonel Crooks and some other men made their way to what used to be Netter's Camp. An occupying Union force made up of hundreds more Indiana Legionnaires from Warrick, Vanderburgh, and Spencer Counties, plus a few companies of Owensboro Home Guard, now guarded Owensboro and the surrounding area. The steamer *Ben South* had been busy ferrying men across during the late morning and early afternoon. Some of the Warrick men were even mounted, but no effort was made to send them out and track down the Rangers. They would have been very useful had it been possible to have them there earlier.[59]

Sometime after the close of the battle, Crooks experienced intense pain behind his eyes. Occipital neuralgia can cause sharp and jabbing pain that often feels like an acute migraine and Crooks frequently suffered from its effects. Quill noted that Crooks was nearly blind because of the severe discomfort. After resting for some time in the Union camp, he approached one of the Federal officers to obtain a pass to retire to his home early. The officer, only known as Freeman, was not happy about the request. According to "Quill," this officer swore and blustered considerably before giving his consent. However, that was not the end to Freeman's behavior. Crooks also requested one of his men, a friend, to accompany him home in case he needed assistance due to the neuralgia. Freeman exploded saying, "By God, sir, if you talk that way you shall not go. I'll order you back." It is not known why Freeman acted the way he did, or what authority he held over Crooks. Perhaps he was afraid of another Rebel attack and thought he needed every man at hand. Perhaps he was merely being contemptuous. Either way, Crooks did not take it lightly. He responded emphatically: "I have 400 Indianians in town, and I will send for them and they will come down and take you and your whole damned camp." This strong language caused a change in the demeanor of the officer. "You never saw a dirty coward more obsequious," quipped "Quill." Freeman took Crooks at his word and preferred not to quarrel with a man who had just returned from battle. "Quill" remarked that the man acted like a "whipped spaniel," and he made

58 Ibid.

59 Ibid.; *Owensboro Monitor*, Sep. 24, 1862, 2.

the passes himself. This quarrel would not be the last between men of Spencer and Daviess County. That would continue through the following days and weeks.[60]

In camp, the men of the 4th Indiana Legion fell to their bedrolls, exhausted. In 24 hours, some of them had marched nearly 40 miles, defeated a larger enemy force, and all of this on very little sleep. The men were tired, hungry, and thirsty. The Warrick County Legion, or 3rd Indiana Legion, under Col. Daniel F. Bates, had arrived in town during the day and learned about the "beautiful thrashing" the 4th had given the enemy. Naturally, the Warrick County men received much of the adoring attention since they were the closest Legion men to most of the citizens, even though they were not in the fight.[61]

The Spencer County men of the 4th Legion began to feel unappreciated and forgotten. "Quill" stated that all they had was one bucket to fetch water for the three or four companies encamped there, and not only that, but they had to fetch the water themselves. To eat they were furnished only "bakers raw ham from the camp, and crackers and cheese from some German citizens. But I suppose that was good enough for common men, who had gone there to drive the enemy from their town." Evidently, "Quill" felt that they had protected a people that did not want them there and used the newspaper to voice his frustrations.

The *New Albany Daily Ledger*, however, printed a contradiction to such slanders, calling it a "Wicked Falsehood." That paper wrote:

> We are informed by a highly respectable citizen of Louisville, who was at Owensboro at the time, that the correspondent's story is a gross falsehood; that as soon as opportunity offered[,] the citizens of Owensboro provided liberally for the Spencer county boys, giving them all they could eat, and much more, and treating them in the most cordial and hospital manner. We make this statement as an act of justice to the citizens of Owensboro.[62]

60 *Evansville Daily Journal*, Sep. 24, 1862, 2; *Owensboro Monitor*, Oct. 8, 1863, 3.

61 Indiana Adjutant General, *Indiana Legion Reports*, 31; *Owensboro Monitor*, Oct. 8, 1862, 3; *Evansville Daily Journal*, Sep. 24, 1862, 2.

62 *Evansville Daily Journal*, Sep. 24, 1862, 2; *New Albany Daily Ledger*, Oct. 18, 1862, 2.

Chapter 15

"Again the same quiet, again the same burst"

Colonel W. E. Hollingsworth of the 2nd Indiana Legion in Evansville had been sent an urgent message with a request to reinforce Owensboro. Evansville had its own problems, and after the Newburgh raid in July, he could not leave it bare of organized fighting men. There were numerous reports of large numbers of guerrillas pillaging across the Ohio in Henderson County who might turn their attention to Evansville. These rumors proved to be false, but Hollingsworth had to take a threat to Evansville seriously.[1]

A few hours after receiving the request, Hollingsworth received an updated report from Colonel Bates in Newburgh. It said that the enemy had retreated some miles south of Owensboro and that the Spencer County boys had given them quite the thrashing. If the Rebels were retreating to get away from Owensboro, they may be heading for the Green River. The south and west side of that river had always been their safe area where they could blend in with the population and disappear, only to reappear and wreak more havoc. If the Partisan Rangers planned to do that, the safest and closest place for them to cross between Henderson and Calhoun would be the ferry at Ashbyburg.[2]

Hollingsworth sent a dispatch to Colonel Foster. In it, he suggested that Foster intercept the Rebels with a force of cavalry, artillery, and infantry. It was hoped that this force would cut them off and finally destroy the irregular threat in the area.[3]

1 Morton Telegraphs, Morton telegram book, no. 8, 237-238.

2 John W. Foster to Governor Oliver P. Morton, Sep. 23, 1862, Morton Telegraphs.

3 Indiana Adjutant General, *Indiana Legion Reports*, 25-26.

Foster was more than ready to crush the Rebels on the Green River. Back in July, they had narrowly slipped through his fingers after the Newburgh Raid, and he did not want that to happen again. To catch them, he would need to move quickly. If the news was true, then the Confederates had lost some of their strength and expended much of their ammunition at Sutherland's Hill. Foster had a decent force to pursue the Confederates. Some of the 65th Indiana was still in Henderson and a portion of the 8th Kentucky Cavalry, which had engaged Johnson's force at Geiger Lake three weeks previous, was also available. Because of Shackelford's foot wound, Maj. James Holloway commanded in the field. Unfortunately, for Foster, the rest of the 8th's companies were in Russellville, Kentucky, about 90 miles distant. The 4th Indiana Cavalry was still having supply problems and was not yet ready for the field as had been demonstrated the month before on the approach to Madisonville. He would have to move on Martin with only portions of both regiments.

Foster put into motion a plan like what he had sought to do after Newburgh. He would use a boat to steam upriver and get behind the guerrillas with infantry. While doing so, the men of companies A–D of the 8th Kentucky, with artillery, and with Major Holloway in command, would engage the Rebels in the front. The Southerners would essentially be pinned against the Green River, with the steamer prohibiting the Rebels from escaping across the Green. That was Foster's aim, but like most plans in the Civil War, it would not survive contact with the enemy.[4]

Foster intended for the cavalry and the steamer to work together during the attack. The cavalry would advance south at a pace where the steamer could move up the Ohio River, then up the Green and meet somewhere near Ashbyburg. The battalion from the 8th Kentucky would mostly be moving due south, with only a slight turn east just before Ashbyburg. The steamer would have a much longer journey. To move the 28 miles and hit the Confederates sometime Sunday morning, the cavalry and its accompanying artillery would have to move out early. This the troopers did and coordinated their movements with the steamer perfectly. The Confederates would be very surprised.[5]

For the Rangers, the morning after the battle seemed like it might be an easy day of rest and recuperation. Martin ordered the regiment drawn up into a hollow square formation so he could address them. It felt like an obvious defeat, but Martin and Scobee complimented them on their conduct. Ammunition went low, the proficiency of their training was nowhere near that of the Legion, and it would

4 *Henderson Weekly Reporter*, Sep. 25, 1862; *Evansville Daily Journal*, Sep. 24, 1862, 2; Morton Telegraphs, John W. Foster to Governor Oliver P. Morton, Sep. 23, 1862.

5 *Evansville Daily Journal*, Sep. 24, 1862, 2; *Henderson Weekly Reporter*, Sep. 25, 1862, 2.

have been foolish to stay on the field. Those Yankees fought like veteran infantry and it was obvious they had been drilling for some time. Many of the Rangers were new at this.[6]

Scobee then proceeded to close his eyes and open his mouth with prayers over the Rangers. And then the alcohol appeared. It was the first time the Rangers had "passed around the whiskey." The whiskey preceded, it should be noted, the replenishment of much needed ammunition from their stockpiles in the region.

Once the necessary resupply was accomplished, the men received permission to go down the road to Ashbyburg to get food for their horses. Their mounts were undoubtedly hungry as the previous few days had been quite busy for man and beast. As Munday and some of the other men returned, the pickets came rushing back to camp. Yankees were on the way. Lots of them.[7]

Foster and his infantry aboard the steamer moved along the Green River, in hopes of passing the Rebels in the entrenchments on the heights at Ashbyburg where the ferry was located. As they neared the Confederate positions, the boat unexpectedly ran aground and could go no further. Seeing the smoke from the steamer, the Federal cavalry had begun to engage the Confederates as originally planned. However, the Rebels' vantage from the heights, and the open and flat ground that would need to be traversed to reach their position, made surprise impossible. Foster was stuck on the boat for more than two hours, unable to complete the encirclement. Those two hours would prove crucial.[8]

* * *

For the Rangers' horses, it looked like another defrayed meal as the men quickly mounted and repositioned behind the large hill that dominated the surrounding countryside. They immediately dismounted and each man positioned himself in the old, dilapidated rifle pits. There they watched and waited for the enemy to approach. If an attack came from the front and rear, it would be the end of the Rangers, and quite possibly James Munday's short military career. The general feeling of the men on top of the hill was "anxious."[9]

A cannon roar broke the silence. The Yankees were already closing in on their front, but Munday could not yet see them. As soon as the cannon had pierced the silence with its boom, the silence returned. To the left, they could see some of the Federals skirting through the woods in the distance. They were trying to tighten

6 Munday, *Diary*, 8.

7 Ibid.

8 *Evansville Daily Journal*, Sep. 24, 1862, 2; *Henderson Weekly Reporter*, Sep. 25, 1862, 2.

9 Munday, *Diary*, 8.

the noose. The Rangers remained quiet, readying themselves by laying behind the works and expecting an attack at any moment. A second roar of the cannon again pierced the anxious silence. This time, the shell whizzed over their heads and the hill, and crashed into the woods on the other side of the river. Then silence returned. Munday recorded, "Again the same quiet, again the same burst and a ball fell in front of the embankment." It appeared the Federals were getting their aim down. But then a longer silence. Munday remarked that it was a painful stillness.[10]

Martin watched and waited like the rest of his men for the impending Yankee advance. He ordered men to begin withdrawing off the hill and mount up. He would use one portion of the regiment to hit the Federal force in the flank, while the rest made a break for Slaughtersville.[11]

A deeper roar followed. A second Federal gun came alive. Its shell whistled over the top and crashed beyond the river. They expected enemy steamers to appear, but for some reason they had not. The Rangers took the opportunity to break out of the still-forming Yankee circle. One by one, Confederates quietly and slowly filed down the backside of the hill to where their horses awaited them. They mounted just as the Union attack on the hill began. The Clarksville Belle came alive amid the muskets of the men remaining on the hill. The Federals advanced as the Rangers boldly and defiantly replied in kind.[12]

The Federals moved toward the rifle pits, and the cannon and muskets erupted into a sheet of flame and lead. The Federals did not stand it long and fell back out of range. During this brief respite, the remainder of the partisans pulled out with the Belle. Company A covered the retreat against the Union cavalry trying to encircle them. The break was on.[13]

Munday sat on his mount and waited for the rest of his company in the woods behind the hill. The cannon was brought down as the rest of the men in the pits also descended and mounted their horses. They made a long circuitous ride to evade the enemy and eventually made it to Slaughtersville after a 9-mile journey.[14]

Though another plan to capture the partisans had failed, Foster and Holloway had at least forced the Rebels from the area. They brought a few prisoners with them back to Henderson, along with horses and supplies. Foster was obviously frustrated when he wrote to Oliver Morton: "The whole party could have been taken if information had reached me in time as it was I attacked the guerrillas after

10 Munday, *Diary*, 8.

11 Johnson, *Partisan Rangers*, 349-350.

12 Ibid.; Munday, *Diary*, 8.

13 Johnson, *Partisan Rangers*, 349-350.

14 Munday, *Diary*, 8.

they crossed Green River." Foster also reported that they had killed a number of men and captured five prisoners. The *Henderson Reporter* stated that two citizens of Henderson County had been captured, Cortez R. Priest and J. C. Hicks.[15]

Not only had the guerrillas been, in Foster's words, "scattered . . . in great confusion," but the Union forces had given the Rebels a bloody nose over the course of three days of fighting. Johnson and Martin's summer campaign had gone very well up to this point. Casualties were light, and most of the skirmishes had been victories. This would be the last time the Partisan Rangers operated independently in western Kentucky.[16]

After escaping Ashbyburg and reaching Slaughtersville, the regiment came once again to friendly territory. The Yankees did not seem as if they were going to follow, and the population was not only politically friendly but gave freely of food and supplies. Since the distance from Ashbyburg was no more than a few miles, Munday and the rest of the men only stayed for a few minutes. Here they received provisions and then continued their march until sunset. Once it became too dark to keep moving, they bivouacked for the night.[17]

Over the next few days, the Rangers continued to move south, passing though Nebo, Madisonville, and eventually on to Hopkinsville. On the road to Hopkinsville, Munday would ride through a very pro-Union area. He thought the locals rude and ignorant, and without the slightest appearance of thrift.[18]

Before making it to the town, the Rangers rode through the Confederate camps of the previous winter. The long rows of rough looking huts, nearly all of them destroyed in some way, were a brutal reminder that the war had not gone in their favor. The haunting scene where many Confederate soldiers died of disease did not help their morale.

Upon reaching Hopkinsville, Munday thought the town was a beautiful place, though not as grand as it was before the war. It had endured occupation by both sides, including Johnson's surprise capture of the place the month before. They continued through town and encamped near the grounds of Bethel College, the former school for girls turned Confederate hospital.

The next day would bring them 12 miles east of Hopkinsville, nearly halfway between that town and Russellville in Todd County. The Rangers stayed at this place, Colemans Spring, for nearly two weeks. During this time, Munday became

15 John W. Foster to Governor Oliver P. Morton, Sep. 23, 1862, Morton Telegraphs; *Evansville Daily Journal*, Sep. 24, 1862, 2; *Henderson Weekly Reporter*, Sep. 25, 1862, 2.

16 John W. Foster telegraph to Governor Oliver P. Morton, Sep. 23, 1862, Morton Telegraphs.

17 Munday, *Diary*, 9.

18 Ibid., 9.

frustrated at the lack of regular drilling, and when they did drill, it was never enough. The camp became a place of idleness, but not for much longer.[19]

19 Johnson, *Partisan Rangers*, 349-350.

Epilogue

In Evansville, Gabriel Netter's family laid his body to rest. One of the steamers, the *Delaware*, which had been shuttling Legion soldiers to and from Owensboro, brought his remains to Evansville for burial. Netter's sister, Pauline, and her husband, John Fournier, had lived in Evansville since coming to America several years before. Fournier was at the time a hat maker. Upon receiving the news of his brother-in-law's death, he traveled to Owensboro to collect the body.[1]

Evansville paid tribute to a man widely respected and esteemed. Just weeks before, Netter had been presented with a sword and sash as a gift from his friends in the city, including Colonel Hollingsworth. In an accompanying letter, Hollingsworth wrote:

> Some of your old friends and citizens of Evansville, appreciating your services and approving your courage and zeal in the cause of our country, desire to present you a sword and sash accompanying this letter. Although but a slight testimonial, they feel assured you will prize it and will continue to persevere in the prosecution of the glorious undertaking until the last of our country's enemies shall be put down.
>
> You will, then, accept this token of their approbation for past services and assurance of kind regards.

Just a few days after receiving the gift that he probably carried during his death, Netter responded:

1 *Evansville Daily Journal*, Sep. 22, 1862, 2.

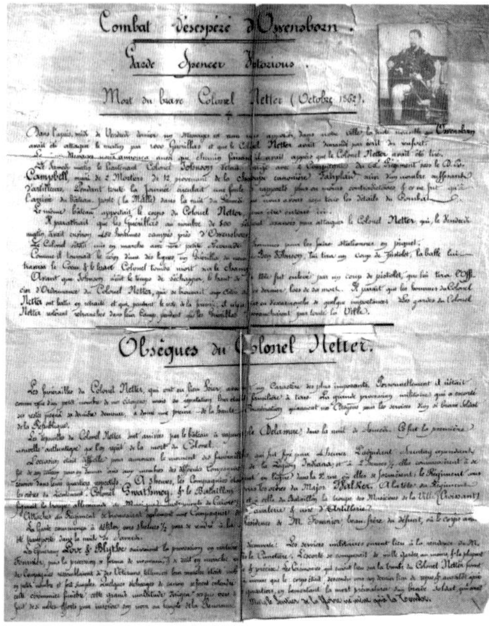
Combat désespéré d'Owensboro.

Garde Spencer Victorieux.

Mort du brave Colonel Netter (Octobre 1862).

Obsèques du Colonel Netter.

The translated copy of the story from the *Evansville Daily Journal* sent to Netter's family in France. *Courtesy of the French side of the Netter family*

The handsome sash, beautiful sword, and so very kind letter, presented to me by yourself and others of your true, loyal and generous townsmen, came all duly to hand to-day.

With my heart only, not with words, can or will I thank you. Such an encouragement from my countrymen is a compliment to be remembered to the last.

May God grant me to show and prove myself worthy of your generosity and kindness—worthy of taking my humble share in the war for the redemption of our country.

May He grant me, if I fall, to fall with my face to the foe, my last breath expending itself in a kiss to the fine blade you presented me with, my last prayer to be listened to by the Almighty, for the speedy success of our noble and holy cause.

Believe me, sir, forever,

Your true friend,

GABRIEL NETTER,

Lt. Col. Comm'g.

> P. S.—To my friends, please be patient. I have got a great deal to contend with. I was sent to this place without a man or a gun and have been much neglected since; but I will get ready, by the by, nevertheless.
>
> G. N.

Netter's wish came true as his dying breath was in defense of the cause for which he fought, with that very blade drawn against the enemy.

As Netter's funeral procession moved to Oak Hill Cemetery, a regiment and battalion of the Indiana Legion followed the procession with their respective bands accompanying each unit. The regiment had its German brass band, and the Crescent City Band followed the battalion. After the burial, Fournier translated into French the article from the *Evansville Daily Journal* describing Netter's death and mailed it along with a photograph of Netter to the family in France.[2]

Netter's Battalion

Netter's Avengers, or so they called themselves after those fateful days in September 1862, would not stay in Owensboro for long. Colonel Quintus Shanks, the Federal officer who competed for recruits in nearby Cloverport, Kentucky, arrived in town with his regiment, the 12th Kentucky Cavalry. His regiment grew with the incorporation of Netter's men. The recruits of Netter's regiment, whether they would have been designated the 15th Kentucky Cavalry or the 38th Kentucky Mounted Infantry, would not hold that designation for long. Though they were now officially soldiers in the 12th, they still called themselves the Netter Battalion. The 12th initially received training in a new campground further west from Owensboro. While there, the regiment frequently conducted anti-guerrilla operations in the area east of the Green River. Later in the fall of 1862, the 12th relocated to southwest Kentucky, and participated in many more actions over the course of their three years of service.[3]

Private W. C. J. Adams, the recruit who shot Netter's killer, was actually a member of the 26th Kentucky. In March, he deserted shortly after enlisting but before officially mustering in. He then enlisted with Netter, a former captain from his former regiment. Adams would not become a member of the 12th Kentucky Cavalry. Instead, he rejoined his old outfit and eventually rose to the rank of first corporal in Company G of the 26th Kentucky. He would survive the war.[4]

2 Ibid.

3 *Owensboro Monitor*, Oct. 8, 1862, 3.

4 W. C. J. Adams Service Record, U.S., Compiled Service Records of Volunteer Union Soldiers Who Served in Organizations from the State of Kentucky, 1861-1865, National Archives, M397, Roll 0374.

Sergeant C. B. Mitchell continued to serve as a non-commissioned officer in the 12th Kentucky. Within a year he received a promotion to lieutenant and was wounded at Fair Garden, Tennessee, forcing him to miss several weeks of duty to recuperate. Mitchell served until the end of the war.[5]

The men of Netter's battalion, though only serving with him for a few weeks, had grown to admire and love him as their commander. C. B. Mitchell later wrote about a reunion of sorts in the 1880s. One of Mitchell's comrades was able to communicate with Netter's nieces still living in Evansville, Indiana. Receiving the veterans as visitors, the ladies showed the men the sword and sash Netter had worn at the time of his death, as well as the photograph of him in his uniform. The men escorted Netter's nieces to his gravesite at Oak Hill Cemetery. Mitchell related, "after a short address by Colonel John H. McHenry, formerly colonel of the 17th Kentucky Infantry, who knew him well and appreciated his worth, we proceeded to place our floral offerings on the mound that marked the place where slept our honored dead. With sad hearts, awakened by the memory of the loss of one whom we loved so well, we silently and reverently took our departed from the hallowed spot and left him alone in his glory." The recruiting animosities between McHenry and Netter had by this time long been forgotten.[6]

Southern Indiana After the Battle

After the Battle of Sutherland's Hill, Rockport and Spencer County had dozens of wounded men to care for. In a letter to her husband dated September 20th, local homemaker Minerva Thomas wrote:

> Colonel Wood was In Recruiting he Joined them In a short time with his recruits Netters men & all those that voluntarily Joined chaced them eight miles from Owensborough there they commenced fiting of our men there was three killed & a bout 40 wounded a mong the killed was one of the Garnars James Nany & Anderson Carney had Each an arm badly Broken George Sheed tells me they were all Brought to town last night there was many seemed to be suffering severely from their wounds the loss of the Rebels is supposed to be one hundred killed & wounded they counted 30 Eight killed they had twice the number we had.

On September 25th she continued:

5 C. B. Mitchel Service Record, U.S., Compiled Service Records of Volunteer Union Soldiers Who Served in Organizations from the State of Kentucky, 1861-1865, National Archives, M397, Roll 0119.

6 Bernheim, *Settlement of the Jews*, 46-47.

> I heard the roar of Canon & musketry In the direction of Owensbourough which lasted for an hour I can not tell with what result but the fireing was very rapid It commenced a bout 9 o'clock this morning
>
> In the other affair that took place among the wounded was John Scammahorn Joel Shrusbery Anderson Carney he will loose his arm
>
> as far as I know the most of them are getting better our whole country Is In a state of confusion all the Business houses are closed at 2 o clock every day for the purpose of Drilling they have been getting anew suply of Arms & are still looking for more I will enclose a scrap of paper which will give you a more minute account of the Battle I will send you some papers but I believe they do not often get through the mails.[7]

The Legion of Spencer County suffered over 30 wounded men, but most of the wounds were not serious. In his report, Colonel Crooks listed each wounded man and the type of wound they received. Moving into the small trench during the battle apparently shielded them from torso wounds.[8]

While the partisans retreated south, Owensboro saw a heavy Union presence. Legion men from Spencer and Warrick Counties, Owensboro Home Guard, the 12th Kentucky Cavalry, and even the men from the still-forming 91st Indiana were present at some point over the following days and weeks. If any Confederate guerrillas, partisans, or cavalry appeared, a serious Union force would meet them.[9]

According to Colonel Hollingsworth's report, Colonel Wood sent another urgent request for reinforcements on September 22nd. Rumors reached him that the Confederates were regrouping, reinforcing, and riding for Owensboro. Such rumors were baseless; the Rebels were actually going in the opposite direction. No one wanted to take the chance of another disaster along the Ohio River, however.[10]

In response, Hollingsworth led five companies of the Vanderburgh County Legion to Owensboro. The men traveled on the steamers *J. T. McCombs* and *Gillium*. During the trip upriver, the *Gillium* ran aground on the Scuffletown bar, near the same location from which Johnson had launched his raid on Newburgh two months before. Hollingsworth had his men from the *Gillium* transferred to the *J. T. McCombs*, and the crammed steamer made it to the opposite side

7 Minerva Thomas to George Thomas, Sep. 25, 1862, Thomas Family Letters, University of Notre Dame Rare Books and Special Collections, https://rarebooks.nd.edu/digital/civil_war/letters/thomas/5014-21.shtml, accessed Dec. 11, 2017.

8 Terrell, *Report of the Adjutant General of Indiana*, vol. 1, 292-293.

9 *Owensboro Monitor*, Sep. 24, 1862, 2; Oct. 8, 1862, 3.

10 Indiana Adjutant General, *Indiana Legion Reports*, 26.

of Owensboro by 3:00 that afternoon and landed the men the next morning. Hollingsworth disembarked and met with Wood. By this time, Wood had received reliable information that the threat to the city and camp was gone. Hollingsworth had orders to return to Evansville to guard that place once he dealt with the Rebels in Owensboro. After they had been fed breakfast "by the *good* citizens of Owensboro," Hollingsworth ordered his men back to the *McCombs.*[11]

On the return trip, an unfortunate event took place aboard the boat. A gunshot broke the easy mood of the boat. The shot did not come from a Rebel guerrilla on land, but from one of the Legion men. Sergeant Mierhoff of the 2nd Indiana Legion carelessly dragged his musket while moving about the boat and accidentally shot himself in the head. The bullet entered below his left eye and exited the top of his head. It then passed through one of the cabins on the boat and out through the roof. He died instantly. The Legion buried Mierhoff the next day in Evansville and collected $200 for his family.[12]

Indiana Legion of Spencer County

The 4th Indiana Legion remained on high alert for many weeks after its victory at Sutherland's Hill. Patrols along the river and the occasional visit to Owensboro during times of rumored attack continued. This occurred less often as other Federal regiments took on the role of guarding the town.[13]

Just a little over two weeks after the fight at Sutherland's Hill, Owensboro again called on Crooks for assistance. By now, the 12th Kentucky Cavalry encamped only a few miles west of town, but the call for help still went to Crooks. His men seemed to be growing tired of helping a town where half of the population seemed to be against them. It was also time for the tobacco harvest, one of Spencer County's most profitable crops, and that required heavy attention. Crooks's men would undoubtedly have crossed if ordered, but he listened to their grumblings and found some merit in their complaints. He and his men did not cross.[14]

Owensboro had turned out very little help to fight the Confederates on September 19th and 20th. Why waste time crossing the river and fight when he could fire on the town from the Indiana side of the river? On October 6th, rumors circulated that Owensboro was about to be attacked once again. Crooks sent a message to the town that he would not cross but would help defend the place from

11 Ibid.

12 Ibid.; *Evansville Daily Journal*, Sep. 24, 1862, 2.

13 Indiana Adjutant General, *Indiana Legion Reports*, 37.

14 Ibid.

1861 image of the Marine Hospital in Evansville that served sick and wounded Union soldiers throughout the war. *Darrel Bigham Collection, University of Southern Indiana*

the Indiana side of the river with two pieces of artillery. He said that if Rebels took Owensboro, he would commence shelling it once the women and children were out. This reply seemed to put a stop to many of the rumors that still floated around the area that fall.[15]

In the summer of 1863, the 4th Legion once again entered active service when Gen. John H. Morgan led his Confederate cavalry across the Ohio and began moving through Indiana, with Adam Johnson among his brigade commanders. Morgan crossed at Mauckport, Indiana, in Harrison County, just three counties to the east. The Spencer Legion constituted a part of a continuous, multicounty picket line on the Ohio River that stretched from Evansville to New Albany after the Confederates had crossed, but it did not see any action during the raid.[16]

In the spring of 1864, Crooks resigned his commission as commander of the Legion due to his rapidly deteriorating health. He died shortly thereafter on May 1, 1864, and was buried at Sunset Hill Cemetery in Rockport. Command of the 4th Legion fell to Col. William N. Walker who commanded the unit for the next few months, but the remainder of the war was quiet for the 4th Legion.

15 Ibid.

16 Colonel John W. Crooks Resignation, Box 25 and 26, *Indiana Legion Papers*, Indiana State Archives; Etter, *Indiana Legion*, 103-104.

It never again fought battles on Kentucky soil and most of its men returned to peaceful lives in Spencer County.[17]

Owensboro Post Battle

Owensboro saw its fair share of drama in the months and years following September 1862. Federal units continued to pass through as they moved south and occasionally some units stayed for extended periods. Recruitment of United States Colored Troops occurred in town and the 100th, 109th, and 118th United States Colored Infantry as well as the 5th and 6th United States Colored Cavalry went on to perform admirable service. Owensboro also saw the recruitment of an anti-guerrilla regiment, the 35th Kentucky Mounted Infantry, a one-year regiment.[18]

Smaller raids occurred as well, such as one led by former Partisan Ranger Capt. Jake Bennett in August 1864. Bennett rode into Owensboro with less than 30 men and attempted to rob the bank. The only person who could open the vault had escaped town, so Bennett attacked an unsuspecting riverboat laden with Union supplies, which resulted in the murder of several soldiers of the 108th Colored Infantry.[19]

Captain Bill Davison, a former officer in the 17th Kentucky Infantry, turned outlaw more than Confederate, raided the city on January 4, 1865. He subsequently burned the town's beautiful courthouse to the ground since the city had tolerated the recruitment of black soldiers. He allowed the authorities to remove all the records and important papers before putting the torch to the building.[20]

Though shocking and destructive, the town would never again see the likes of Netter's death or the Legion's victory at Sutherland's Hill, probably to the relief of Owensboro's citizens. Instead, intense guerrilla activity, by the Rebels and the Union guerrilla hunters, persisted in the county until the end of the war.

17 Colonel John W. Crooks Resignation, Box 25 and 26, *Indiana Legion Papers*, Indiana State Archives; Etter, *Indiana Legion*, 37.

18 *Owensboro Monitor*, July 6, 1864, 2; Aug. 31, 1864, 2; Randy Mills, "Confederate Raider . . . Criminal . . . Hero: Jake Bennett's Civil War," *Journal of the Indiana Academy of the Social Sciences* (2012) vol. 15, Issue 1, 46.

19 *History of Daviess County*, 176-177; *Owensboro Monitor*, July 6, 1864, 2; Aug. 31, 1864, 2; Mills, "Jake Bennett's Civil War," 46.

20 Stuart Sanders, "The Radicalization of 'Bloody-Handed' Bill Davison: How a Union Soldier Became a Pro-Confederate Bushwhacker," *The Register of the Kentucky Historical Society* (2018) vol. 16, no. 2, 201.

Adam Johnson, Robert Martin, and the 10th Kentucky Partisan Rangers

In the weeks following the Battle of Sutherland's Hill, Martin and the 10th Kentucky Partisan Rangers retreated to the opposite end of the state. Just days before, they were on the banks of the Ohio River; now they were just a stone's throw from the Tennessee border. They were also without their cannon, the Clarksville Belle. After the retreat from Ashbyburg, they decided they ought to hide the cannon to move faster and retrieve it the following year. The Confederates hid it in a wooded lot on land owned by a certain W. H. Jackson. However, the gun would not stay there for long. The next day, the Rangers learned that one of Jackson's slaves had seen the hidden weapon. Afraid that the piece would fall into enemy hands, a small band of men returned to the hiding place. They covered the cannon with a wagon sheet and hauled it by hand through the fields to a place near the head of Deer Creek, near Slaughtersville. There, the Rebels buried their prized weapon with the hope that they could retrieve it during the spring campaigning season. The Partisan Rangers would never again fire their prized Belle.

About a year after its burial, Union soldiers learned of the hidden cannon in the Slaughtersville area. They interrogated William Wilkerson, one of the men who buried it, and he apparently gave up its location. The Federals dug up the gun and carried it back to Owensboro as a prize. It was fired over 100 times on the one-year anniversary of Netter's death, until it exploded, severely wounding one of the gunners.[21]

Johnson never made it to Richmond as planned and returned to the regiment shortly after its defeat at Owensboro and Sutherland's Hill. He wrote that he received orders from Gen. Braxton Bragg to aid in the Kentucky Campaign, the Confederate army's invasion of the Commonwealth. Unfortunately for Johnson, the Confederate invasion failed, and his regiment's only accomplishment was a few burned bridges. He complained, "I was left in an isolated, critical situation, overpowering forces were sent against me, and I was compelled to resort to my old tactics of disbanding my men to scatter all over the country." The great fight Johnson sought between the two armies at Green River did not occur. When Bragg's army returned to Tennessee, the regiment received orders to join the main army there, while Johnson traveled to Richmond, this time successfully, to meet with President Jefferson Davis.[22]

21 Munday, *Diary*, 9; Johnson, *Partisan Rangers*, 350-351; *Owensboro Monitor*, Sep. 23, 1863, 3.

22 Johnson, *Partisan Rangers*, 125-126.

The problem with Johnson's claim during the Kentucky Campaign is that it does not fit the timeline. Colonel John T. Wilder surrendered Munfordville to Bragg on September 17th, while the Union army entered Louisville on September 24th. On the 19th and 20th, Martin and the Partisan Rangers were engaged at Owensboro, and then again at Ashbyburg on the 21st. The hope for a decisive battle at the Green River disappeared as soon as Bragg vacated the Munfordville area for Bardstown near the same time. Perhaps his fading memory in old age had Johnson confused with his 1864 exploits in the war when he again tried to recruit men in the western part of the state. Another possible explanation could be that Johnson received Bragg's orders, but the situation changed once he was able to return to his men.

Generally, the Confederate government in Richmond struggled with controlling partisan ranger regiments. Johnson's appears to be one of the exceptions. When he received orders, such as Bragg's order to operate to his west when the Confederate Army of Mississippi advanced into Kentucky, he obeyed. Later, when orders arrived for him to join the army in Tennessee, he also obeyed. Though other partisan ranger outfits devolved into mere guerrillas and bandits carrying on a brutal total war, these men did not. Johnson's regiment may be one of the better examples of the ways in which a partisan ranger regiment was supposed to operate and behave.

The summer of 1862 was, by all accounts, a very successful campaign for Adam Rankin Johnson's 10th Kentucky Partisan Rangers. The small band had begun with only Johnson and Martin, and had swelled to the size of a full regiment recognized by the Confederate government. In that time, they had caused panic in the Union occupation forces, captured a Northern town, forced a veteran regiment to surrender, paroled hundreds of prisoners, and become a force that would go down in legend for its exploits. All this happened without losing more than a handful of men. That is until September 19th and 20th, 1862 in Owensboro, Kentucky.

The lightning campaign waged by Johnson and Martin that summer took a dramatic turn after Owensboro. With the heavy casualties of September 20th, the Rangers were considerably weakened. The day after Sutherland's Hill, the Partisans would have been annihilated at Ashbyburg had Foster's steamboat and infantry made it to the planned location on the Green River. They lost their prized gun, the Clarksville Belle, and suffered nearly 100 casualties all because of the events that spanned those three days. Netter's refusal to surrender was the wrench thrown into the machinery that sent the Rangers' campaign to ruin. Even upon Johnson's attempt to resurrect his prospects by raiding shipping along the lower portions of the Ohio, the Union had learned how to deal with his particular style of warfare.

When Johnson finally reached Richmond, he met with the son of Gen. Albert Sidney Johnston, Col. William Preston Johnston. The son of the fallen general presented him to President Davis and he reported on the actions of his command over the previous months. Johnson wrote that Davis "expressed his pleasure and satisfaction." In this report, Johnson claimed:

> Nine cities had been captured . . . over a million dollars worth of Federal stores had been destroyed. . . . During this occupation I lost fewer men, killed, wounded and captured than any other command of the same number in the Confederate service. . . . I had penetrated the Federal lines and began an open warfare with a single recruit, and soon magnified the number so as to overawe the Federal forces that occupied the surrounding towns.[23]

Davis asked what he would do to protect his men from Federal mistreatment as prisoners. Johnson answered that he had bluffed and threatened to retaliate in the same manner, but confessed, "I hardly know what I would in an extreme case." Davis cautioned Johnson, "Don't retaliate in kind, Johnson; think what it would lead to; the war is horrible enough as it is. . . . The war would become brutal and barbarous and sanguinary beyond conception. No, never shall we come to this." Johnson assured him he would obey his wishes and departed for his men, his regiment finally official.[24]

On his return, Johnson believed that Bragg wanted to absorb his command with the intention to dismount the Partisan Rangers and transfer them to the infantry since they were an independent regiment and not brigaded with any of the army's cavalry brigades. John H. Morgan, a fellow Kentuckian, offered to make the 10th Kentucky Partisan Rangers one of the regiments of his command. Johnson quickly took the offer and commanded a brigade the following year. He also requested a small battery of two guns, but the army refused. Johnson assumed that this happened because Bragg, "probably [thought] mine was a 'paper battalion.' I sent for my command, and shortly four hundred manly fellows came riding in to confront him as a pledge to care and protection of that battery." Though Johnson was proud of these 400 men that arrived shortly after the battle of Hartsville, Tennessee, it was a far cry from the full regiment he had in September. Less than 50% of his original command was in camp with the rest of Morgan's men, mostly because many of the shirkers only felt the need to serve if the fight was near their homes. Basil Duke, Morgan's second-in-command, noted years later that the regiment "was very strong upon the rolls, but from losses by capture and other causes had been reduced [to] less than four hundred effective men. It was a fine body of

23 Ibid., 127-128.

24 Ibid., 131.

General John H. Morgan
LOC

men and splendidly officered." Such was the problem with many partisan ranger units.[25]

Under Johnson's command, the 10th Kentucky Partisan Rangers returned to Kentucky to participate in Morgan's famed Christmas Raid in 1862, and the disastrous Indiana and Ohio Raid in the summer of 1863. During the latter, Morgan led Johnson to believe that once the division reached the Ohio River, he could take his men west toward the Green River region where he had seen so much success the previous year. However, once at the river, Morgan reneged on the promise and ordered Johnson to remain with the division. Union forces captured most of the Partisan Rangers during the expedition, destroying the regiment for the remainder of the war. Johnson managed to escape with a few hundred men into Virginia during the disastrous battle of Buffington Island. During the ill-fated raid, LeRoy Fitch again met Johnson as his gunboats closed off a large portion of the Ohio River to Morgan's men trying to cross back to the southern shore of the Ohio.[26]

Johnson eventually received a promotion to brigadier general and ventured again back into his home state to recruit more men and try to replicate his previous success. Though causing some trouble, he never gained the spotlight as he had in 1862. Willing men were not as plentiful and the Union army had learned how to contain him. On August 21, 1864, near Princeton, Kentucky, one of Johnson's own men accidentally shot him in the face during a skirmish at Grubb's Crossroads. After capturing several Federal soldiers, another Confederate believed them to be armed and fired upon the now-Brigadier General Johnson. In his memoirs, Johnson recalled, "One of the balls struck me in the right eye, and coming out the left temple, cut both my eyes." This wound cost him his sight for the rest

25 Ibid., 132; Duke, *Morgan's Cavalry*, 229.

26 Lynn, *Company K*, 17; Johnson, *Partisan Rangers*, 131-132; Bern Anderson, *By Sea and by River: The Naval History of the Civil War* (New York, 1963), 154-155; B. Kevin Bennett, "Morgan's Luck Runs Out: The Battle of Buffington Island," *Blue and Gray Magazine* vol. 15 no. 4, 12, 14.

Lieutenant LeRoy Fitch
Naval History and Heritage Command

of his life. Badly wounded, his men left him at a friendly home where he finally fell into the hands of Union soldiers who sent him on to Fort Warren, Massachusetts. He remained a prisoner until the end of the war.

Once peace came, Johnson returned to his wife in Texas where he became a wealthy man and leader of his community, Marble Falls. Considered the father of the town, one newspaper called the place "Blind Man's Town." Johnson's plans for the community were realized though he was never able to see it himself. As he moved from military officer to civic leader, Johnson's idea of harnessing the power of the Colorado River became reality as he invested and led the construction of a mill on the site that brought the railroad to Marble Falls. The railroad brought prosperity. One Texas newspaper wrote that "during his period of darkness he has exercised the best faculties of a shrewd man in full possession of his senses." The paper continued, "He planned it all himself. Every detail that slowly unfolded itself in reality was born first in his imagination. He walks the streets of Marble falls today with the picture of it printed on his mind, but he will never see more plainly than he did before one stone was set upon another." Johnson died in 1922 at the age of 88.[27]

Robert Martin eventually moved away from the unconventional military operations he was accustomed to since the start of the war and suffered a much more dramatic ending than his friend, "Stovepipe" Johnson. After serving for some time as colonel of the 10th Kentucky, a severe chest wound forced him out of action, as did a foot wound a year later. He led the remnants of the Partisan Rangers against Wilder and Minty's mounted forces in the opening actions of the battle of Chickamauga under Forrest. After recuperating from his foot wound, he traveled to Canada to plan the burning of New York. He had a group of ten men that he commanded but the plot failed. Martin "became convinced that this service was of little benefit to the cause of the Confederate States" and rejoined the

27 Johnson, *Partisan Rangers*, 174-176; *The Refugio Review*, Mar. 9, 1900, 2.

Adam Rankin Johnson later in life.

Courtesy of the Texas State Library and Archives Commission

remnants of Basil Duke's command in Virginia. Martin claims to have been a part of the escort for President Davis while he fled south. He surrendered himself in Washington, Georgia, and began his journey home to Kentucky.[28]

While passing through Bowling Green on his way home, Martin was recognized. Federal troops followed him to Greenville and arrested him at his father's home in late 1865. Charged with treason, Union troops brought Martin to the prison at Fort Lafayette in New York. While in prison, he even mentioned knowing John Wilkes Booth, including details of the Lincoln assassination and the plan to kidnap the vice president. Eventually, Martin reconsidered his defiance as he took advantage of the amnesty proclamations issued by President Johnson. He wrote in October 1865, "I now accept the result achieved by the arms for the Government of the United States, and in good faith, & all sincerity, pledge myself to abide by the constitution and laws, in like manner with every citizen of the country. Pardon & release. I most earnestly and respectfully petition." President Johnson pardoned him in 1866, sparing him from the firing squad or hangman's noose.[29]

Released from prison months later in 1866, Martin returned to the Green River region but not to his home in Kentucky. Ironically, Martin settled in Evansville, Indiana, the city that hated his kind during the war and was the nerve center for anti-guerrilla operations in the summer and fall of 1862. In Evansville, Martin began his post-war life in the tobacco business. Martin made and lost many fortunes through tobacco and other business ventures over the years. He spent the majority of his post-war life in Evansville, 14 years in New York City, and finally settled down in Louisville.[30]

Due to his financial success, Martin frequently traveled. While onboard the ship *Oceania*, he met a girl from Murfreesboro, Tennessee, named Caroline Wardlaw. They married shortly thereafter and had a daughter named Ocey, after the boat on which they had met.[31]

28 Rothert, *History of Muhlenberg County*, 324; *Murfreesboro Post*, Feb. 1, 2009; Mike West, "The Man Who Would Have Burned New York City," *Murfreesboro Post*, Feb. 1, 2009; Headley, *Confederate Operations*, 449-450; Eric J. Wittenberg, *Holding the Line on the River of Death: Union Mounted Forces at Chickamauga, September 18, 1863* (El Dorado Hills, CA, 2018), 101-102.

29 Rothert, *History of Muhlenberg County*, 324; Headley, *Confederate Operations*, 451; R. M. Martin, Oath, 12 October 1865, Office of the Governor, Thomas E. Bramlette: Governor's official correspondence file, petitions for pardons, remissions, and respites 1863-1867, BR16-171 to BR16-173, Kentucky Department for Libraries and Archives, Frankfort, KY. Accessed via the *Civil War Governors of Kentucky Digital Documentary Edition*, discovery.civilwargovernors.org/document/KYR-0001-004-2604.

30 Headley, *Confederate Operations*, 461.

31 Rothert, *History of Muhlenberg County*, 324-325.

In the final years of his life, the chest wound caused him much discomfort, and probably contributed to his death. Martin returned to New York for special medical treatment, only to pass away there shortly after he arrived on January 9th, 1901. The Kentucky Confederate was buried in Greenwood Cemetery in Brooklyn.

At the time, many believed Martin's cause of death was natural, but recent scholarship has opened the possibility that Martin was the victim of murder at the hand of his wife. The suspicious deaths began when Martin's son mysteriously fell down a flight of stairs in 1900, which proved fatal. Caroline collected a sizable insurance policy on her son. Caroline also stood accused of murdering her own daughter, Ocey Snead, in 1909. Allegedly, after she killed her daughter, Caroline arranged Ocey's body to appear as if she had committed suicide, ostensibly overcome with grief at the death of her own child, Caroline's grandchild. Though foul play was not initially considered after Martin's passing, it was suspected in Ocey's, as large life insurance policies had been taken out on her just before her tragic death. Her apparent murder became a national story in papers across the country and was regarded as the crime of the century at the time. Caroline spent time in prison but died of heart disease in 1913 while in an asylum.[32]

Overview

By late 1862, the *Evansville Daily Journal* seemed to gloat about the fact that Johnson and the other irregulars no longer operated in the Green River area. In November, the paper reported:

> We learn that the guerrillas have nearly all disappeared from that country, and that the responsible citizens have determined that there shall [be] no more plundering. . . . The present disposition of the Federal troops in the Green river country renders the operations of the thieves who have held such long immunity, a rather dangerous affair, and hence they are migrating to a more Southern clime. Col. Shanks' cavalry have become as much a terror to the rebels on the east side of the Green river as Col. Foster's command has on the west side. . . . Cols. Bruce and Shackelford now hold Hopkinsville, and the troops at Madisonville cut off the line of rebel communications between the Green river county and the south. Adam Johnson has left for parts unknown, and most of his gang of thieves have followed. The remainder are being gathered in by Cols. Foster and Shanks, and Major

32 Kelley Ewing, "More Dreadful than the Most Gruesome of Tales: Newspaper Coverage of the East Orange Bathtub Mystery," *Fit to Post: Dispatches From the Virginia Newspaper Project at the Library of Virginia* (2016): http://www.virginiamemory.com/blogs/fit-to-print/2016/06/03/more-dreadful-than-the-most-gruesome-of-tales-newspaper-coverage-of-the-east-orange-bathtub-mystery; Rothert, *History of Muhlenberg County*, 324-325; West, "The Man Who Would Have Burned New York City"; Mike West, "Fearless Confederate died mysteriously in NYC," *Murfreesboro Post*, Feb. 15, 2009.

> Holloway, who is operating in the vicinity of Russellville. So that we hope this entire region is now about free, forever from guerrilla outrages.[33]

Indeed, guerrilla and partisan activity drastically changed in western Kentucky. Though the Partisan Rangers had been defeated at Sutherland's Hill and driven from the region, the impact they had on the Green River area remained for the rest of the war. Their success at capturing isolated Federal garrisons, harassment of Union supply lines, and the disruption of river traffic, all had a direct consequence on the war in that part of the state, and even further south. Emergency regiments that could have been used in Buell's army to stem the Confederate invasion, or even Bull Nelson's ill-fated Army of Kentucky at the battle of Richmond, were kept back to safeguard the Ohio River border and its tributary, the Green. In so doing, they prevented the number of Union forces from growing in the deeper South.

In western Kentucky, General Boyle ordered the Union regiments spread throughout the region to make sure a major irregular threat could not materialize. Seven companies of the 65th Indiana and four companies of the 4th Indiana Cavalry garrisoned Henderson, with two more detached companies of the 4th moving there from out of the region. Caseyville would be held by six companies of the 12th Kentucky Cavalry along with the 87th Illinois in support at Shawneetown. The remaining six companies of the 12th Kentucky stayed in Owensboro. An entire brigade commanded by Col. Sanders Bruce would operate between Hopkinsville and Clarksville. Boyle reasoned, "These forces [ought] to be ample to secure all that portion of the State from the raids of the enemy, and from the depredations and outrages of guerrillas, and, if kept on the alert, will no doubt prove to be so." Though these numbers may not have filled an entire division, it still meant that the Union armies had to find other means to protect their own immediate supply lines. When cavalry regiments roamed Kentucky to hunt Johnson, they were not reconnoitering or screening the main armies. When infantry regiments found themselves stationed at important towns and sent into the interior on patrols, they were not able to fill brigades for much needed attacks or defenses and weakened an army's punching power on the battlefield. When the Indiana farmer or machinist was kept on extended duty with the Indiana Legion, essential civilian occupations behind the lines and on the home front went unattended. Johnson's actions in the summer and fall of 1862 might not appear significantly consequential to the overall war at first glance, but when the details of his operations are taken into consideration, the effect of his Partisan Rangers becomes much more apparent.[34]

33 *Evansville Daily Journal*, Nov. 21, 1862, 2.

34 *OR* 20, pt. 2, 62-63.

Union authorities raised well-armed and well-trained cavalry and mounted infantry regiments for the sole purpose of driving out guerrillas and other irregulars. Infantry could defeat them when Johnson's partisans paused to give fight, but the only way to destroy them was with a sufficient cavalry force that could equal their speed and maneuverability. The successes of conventional raiders such as John H. Morgan and Nathan Bedford Forrest in 1862 ground the advances of the Union Army of the Ohio/Cumberland to a halt and pushed the Federal high command to rethink its occupation strategy in the rear of its armies. For example, in December 1862, Clarksville was garrisoned with an entire brigade commanded by Kentuckian Sanders Bruce. His garrison consisted of the 17th and 28th Kentucky, the 102nd Ohio, two battalions of Shackelford's 8th Kentucky Cavalry, and artillery from the 1st Tennessee Battery. Nearly 3,000 men controlled Clarksville and the surrounding area compared to the handful of companies from the 71st Ohio a few months earlier. By late winter, Bruce reported that "the country is clear" with enemy activity amounting to only minor guerrilla actions while nothing compared to the events of the late summer and fall of 1862.[35]

The style and allure of Partisan Ranger warfare resulted in many small independent commands, usually only at company level, sprouting up all over western Kentucky by 1863. Rebel-minded guerrillas would not be able to organize into sizable units as Johnson had done the previous year, and it became apparent as 1863 dragged into 1864 that these small bands would not take part in the greater strategic roles they envisioned for themselves. Some of the men leading these small outfits were former Partisan Rangers, who sought to fight the war in an even less conventional way than Johnson, and usually that meant more brutality as raiders operated outside the rules of war that bound regular army units, North and South. Some of these irregulars found themselves growing increasingly discontented with the original causes for taking up arms, relegating themselves to common bushwhacking and thuggery.[36]

When such bands did spring up in western Kentucky, specialized regiments for fighting guerrillas, such as the 35th Kentucky Mounted Infantry, were able to respond quickly and drive them out. This regiment routinely made a show of force by parading through cities like Owensboro. The *Owensboro Monitor*

35 Sutherland, *A Savage Conflict*, 146; Michael R. Bradley, *Tullahoma: The 1863 Campaign for the Control of Middle Tennessee* (Shippensburg, PA, 2000), 10; Cooling, *Fort Donelson's Legacy*, 190-191, 214.

36 Mills, "Jake Bennett's Civil War," 4; Scott A. Tarnowieckyi, "Descent into Anarchy: The Evolution of Irregular Warfare in the Lower Green River Country of Kentucky," in *Border Wars: The Civil War in Tennessee and Kentucky*, Kent T. Dollar, Larry H. Whiteaker, and W. Calvin Dickinson, eds. (Kent, OH, 2015), 54.

reported on the one-year anniversary of Netter's death and the fight at Sutherland's Hill: "The 35th Kentucky regiment of cavalry marched into town preceded by the same cannon that, with which the guerrillas one year before had startled the quiet citizens of Owensboro." The 35th patrolled the area between the Green and Cumberland Rivers, with companies stationed in different locations. Learning from the mistakes of 1862, regiments like the 35th chased guerrillas, supported by other Union regiments and state militia troops that held the vital towns, such as the multiple United States Colored Troops units that frequently moved through the region. Though not entirely successful in their mission, mostly due to other units constantly moving south to the armies, the 35th showed that mounted and well-armed forces could deal irregulars a crippling blow. Ella Johnson, the young girl from Owensboro, remembered the long blue lines marching through her city and the impact it made on many of its citizens. "There were days when every one went about with hushed movements while rows and rows of marching blue-coats went thought the street. We watched them furtively through jalousies, as all the houses were closed, shuttered and deserted-looking. Some one, my aunt, perhaps, said: 'The whole Union army must be going by,' and someone replied, 'This isn't a drop in the bucket.'" Even with the Federal success against irregulars in late 1862 and 1863, the Union army emptied Kentucky for the campaigns of 1864, once again leaving the state open to irregular fighters, and the violence returned on a more brutal scale.[37]

37 Thomas Speed, *Union Regiments of Kentucky*, 596-598; *Owensboro Monitor*, Sep. 23, 1863, 3; Johnson, *Granny Remembers*, 14; L. L. Valentine, "Sue Mundy of Kentucky: Part 1," *The Register of the Kentucky Historical Society*, Vol. 62 no. 3, 180; Tarnowieckyi, "Descent into Anarchy," 45-46.

Bibliography

Primary Sources

Manuscript Materials

Filson Historical Society, Louisville, Kentucky:

Benjamin T. Field Memoir.

James A. Munday Diary.

Indiana State Archives, Indianapolis, Indiana:

Indiana Legion Papers.

J. L. Tinsly letter to Governor Oliver Morton, September 1861.; J. L. Tinsly letter to Governor Oliver Morton, October 1861. Box 25 and 26, Indiana Legion Papers.

Company Muster Rolls of the 4th Indiana Legion Regiment, Box 25 and 26, Indiana Legion Papers.

Bentley Historical Library, University of Michigan, Ann Arbor, Michigan:

Thomas D. Henderson Letter of September 7, 1862.

Ohio History Connection Library, State Library of Ohio, Columbus, Ohio:

Rodney Mason, Et al., *Testimony by Rodney Mason to Abraham Lincoln,* 1863.

Vigo County Historical Society, Terre Haute, Indiana:

Ransom Hawley Letters.

Robert T. Ramsay Jr. Archival Center, Wabash College, Crawfordsville, Indiana:

The Wabash Magazine, 1863.

University Library, Indiana University-Purdue University Indianapolis, Indianapolis, Indiana:

Governor Oliver Morton Telegraph and Slips Book.

Cornelius D. Waldron Letter to Mother and Sister, June 3, 1862, "Spared and Shared," https://sparedshared9.wordpress.com/2015/05/15/1862-cornelius-d-waldron-to-mother/.

"Thomas Letters—September 20, 1862." 2018. *Rarebooks.Nd.Edu*. Accessed December 11 2017. https://rarebooks.nd.edu/digital/civil_war/letters/thomas/5014-21.shtml.

Published Sources

Books

Admire, Jacob V. *Memoranda : Company E, 65th Regiment, Indiana Infantry Volunteers,* Osage City, Kansas: Osage City Free Press, 1888.

Duke, Basil. *Morgan's Cavalry,* New York: The Neale Publishing Company, 1906.

Dyer, John Will. *Reminiscences, or, Four years in the Confederate Army: a history of the experiences of the private soldier in camp, hospital, prison, on the march, and on the battlefield, 1861 to 1865.* Evansville, Indiana: Keller Printing and Publishing Company, 1898.

Foster, John W. *War Stories for my Grandchildren*. Washington, D.C.: The Riverside Press Cambridge, 1918.

Grant, Ulysses S. *Personal Memoirs of Ulysses S. Grant*, New York: De Capo Press, 1982.

Johnson, Adam R. *Partisan Rangers of the Confederate Army*, edited by William J. Davis. Louisville, Kentucky: George G. Fetter Company, 1904.

Nannie Haskins Williams. *The Diary of Nannie Haskins Williams: A Southern Woman's Story of Rebellion and Reconstruction, 1863–1890*, Minoa D. Uffelman, Ellen Kanervo, Eleanor Williams, Phyllis Smith (Knoxville: University of Tennessee Press, 2014).

Government Documents

Dictionary of American Naval Fighting Ships. Volume 1, Navy Department, Office of the Chief of Naval Operations, Naval History Division: University of Virginia, 1964.

Gabriel Netter to George D. Prentice, 21 August 1862, Office of the Governor, James F. Robinson: Governor's Official Correspondence File, Military Correspondence, 1862-1863, R2-22 to R2-23, Kentucky Department for Libraries and Archives, Frankfort, KY. Accessed via the *Civil War Governors of Kentucky Digital Documentary Edition*, discovery.civilwargovernors.org/document/KYR-0001-027-0015, (accessed March 11, 2018).

Iowa Adjutant General's Office. (1908-1911). *Roster and record of Iowa soldiers in the war of the rebellion, together with historical sketches of volunteer organizations, 1861-1866.* Des Moines: E. H. English, state printer.

John W. Finnell to Nathaniel Gaither, Jr., 25 July 1862, Office of the Governor, Beriah Magoffin: Governor's Official Correspondence File, Military Appointments, 1859-1862, MG7-9, Kentucky Department for Libraries and Archives, Frankfort, KY. Accessed via the *Civil War Governors of Kentucky Digital Documentary Edition*, discovery.civilwargovernors.org/document/KYR-0001-018-0391, (accessed July 27, 2018).

Martin, Robert M., R. M. Martin to President Andrew Johnson, Oath, 12 October 1865, Office of the Governor, Thomas E. Bramlette: Governor's official correspondence file, petitions for pardons, remissions, and respites 1863-1867, BR16-171 to BR16-173, Kentucky Department for Libraries and Archives, Frankfort, KY. Accessed via the Civil War Governors of Kentucky Digital Documentary Edition, discovery.civilwargovernors.org/document/KYR-0001-004-2604, (accessed March 6, 2020).

Official Records of the Union and Confederate Navies in the War of the Rebellion. 31 Vols. Washington, D.C.: Government Printing Office, 1880-1901.

Terrell, William H. H. *Report of the Adjutant General of the State of Indiana*, Vol. 3, 1866.

The War of the Rebellion: A Compilation of the Official Records of the Union and Confederate Armies. 128 volumes in 3 series. Washington, D.C.: United States Government Printing Office, 1889.

Periodical Collections

Badger, Mary Elizabeth. "Thrilling Heroism by Confederates," *Confederate Veteran*, vol. 8, 1900.

Bently, James R. "The Civil War Memoir of Captain Thomas Speed," *The Filson Club Historical Quarterly*, Vol. 44, 1970.

Martin, Robert M, "Service by Kentucky Cavalry," *Confederate Veteran,* vol. 19.

W. Williams. "A Reminiscence of Clarksville, Tenn," *Confederate Veteran Magazine*, Vol. 2 No. 1, January 1893.

Newspapers

Athens Post (Athens, Tennessee)

Austin State Gazette (Austin, Texas)

The Boonville Enquirer (Booneville, Indiana)

The Boonville Standard (Booneville, Indiana)

Cannelton Reporter (Cannelton, Indiana)

Cincinnati Commercial

Cleveland Daily Leader

Daily Nashville Patriot

Detroit Free Press

Evansville Daily Journal (Evansville, Indiana)

Henderson Weekly Reporter (Henderson, Kentucky)

Houston Tri-Weekly

Indianapolis Star

Indianapolis State Sentinel

Louisville Daily Courier

Louisville Daily Democrat

Louisville Journal

McArthur Democrat (McArthur, Ohio)

Nashville Daily Union

National Tribune (Washington, D.C.)

New Albany Daily Ledger (New Albany, Indiana)

Owensboro Messenger (Owensboro, Kentucky)

Owensboro Monitor

Owensboro Twice-A-Week Messenger

The Refugio Review (Refugio, Texas)

Rockport Weekly Democrat (Rockport, Indiana)

Richmond Dispatch
Richmond Weekly Platinum
Steuben Republican (Angola, Indiana)
The Standard (London, England)
Urbana Union (Urbana, Ohio)
Washington Telegraph (Washington, Arkansas)

Secondary Sources

Books

Anderson, Bern. *By Sea and by River: The Naval History of the Civil War*. New York: Da Capo Books, 1962.

Arms and Equipment of the Confederacy. United States: Time-Life Books, 1991.

Arms and Equipment of the Union. United States: Time-Life Books, 1991.

Barnes, Dr. James J. and Patience P. Barnes, eds. *500 Strong: Wabash College Students in the Civil War*. Carmel, Indiana: Hawthorne Publishing, 2013.

Bergemann, Kurt D. *Brackett's Battalion: Minnesota Cavalry in the Civil War and Dakota War*. Nepean, Ontario, Canada: Borealis Books, 2004.

Beringer, Richard E, Herman Hattaway, Archer Jones, and William N. Still, Jr. *Why the South Lost the Civil War*. Athens and London: The University of Georgia Press, 1986.

Bernheim, Isaac W. *History of the Settlement of Jews in Paducah and the Ohio Valley*. Paducah, Kentucky, 1912.

Bradley, Michael R. *Tullahoma: The 1863 Campaign for the Control of Middle Tennessee*. Shippensburg, Pennsylvania: Burd Street Press, 2000.

Coggins, Jack. *Arms and Equipment of the Civil War.* Mineola, New York: Dover Publications, Inc., 1990.

Cooling, Benjamin Franklin. *Fort Donelson's Legacy: War and Society in Kentucky and Tennessee, 1862-1863*. Knoxville: University of Tennessee Press, 1997.

Coons, John W. *Indiana at Shiloh: Report of the Commission*. Indiana Shiloh National Park Commission, 1904.

Daniel, Larry. *Days of Glory: The Army of the Cumberland 1861-1865*. Baton Rouge: Louisiana State University Press, 2004.

Davis, William C. *Breckinridge: Statesmen, Soldier, Symbol*. Baton Rouge: Louisiana State University Press, 1974.

Dollar, Kent T., Larry H. Whiteaker, and W. Calvin Dickinson. *Border Wars: The Civil War in Tennessee and Kentucky*. Kent, Ohio: Kent State University Press, 2015.

Etter, John P. *The Indiana Legion: A Civil War Militia*. Hawthorne Publishing, 2006.

Finck, James W. *Divided Loyalties: Kentucky's Struggle for Armed Neutrality in the Civil War*. California: Savas Beatie, 2012.

Griffith, Paddy. *Battle Tactics of the Civil War.* New Haven, Connecticut: Yale University Press, 1989.

Hattaway, Herman and Archer Jones. *How the North Won: A Military History of the Civil War*. Chicago: University of Illinois Press, 1983.

Headley, John W. *Confederate Operations in Canada and New York*. New York: Neale, 1906.

History of Daviess County: Together with Sketches of its Cities, Villages and Townships, Educational, Religious, Civil, Military, and Political History; Portraits of Prominent Persons, Biographies of Representative Citizens, And an Outline History of Kentucky. Chicago, Illinois: Inter-State Publishing Company, 1883.

History of Warren, Spencer, and Perry Counties, Indiana: From the earliest time to the present; together with interesting biographical sketches, reminiscences, notes, etc. Chicago, Illinois: Godspeed Bros. and Co. Publishing, 1885.

History of Union County, Kentucky: A complete account of the settlement, organization and government of the county, together with facts and figures concerning the society, professions, commerce, industries, agriculture, coal, railroads, education, religion, and other institutions and resources of the county, and biographical sketches of its leading citizens. Evansville, Indiana: Courier Co., Printers, Binders and Engravers, 1886.

Johnson, Ella H. *Granny Remembers*. Macon, Georgia: The J.W. Burke Company, 1928.

Jones, Archer. *Civil War Command and Strategy: The Process of Victory and Defeat*. New York: The Free Press, 1992.

_____. *Confederate Strategy from Shiloh to Vicksburg*. Baton Rouge, Louisiana: Louisiana State University Press, 1961.

Kolakowski, Christopher L. *The Stones River and Tullahoma Campaigns*. Charleston, South Carolina: The History Press, 2011.

Lynn, Stephen D. *History and Roster of Company K, Tenth Kentucky Cavalry, C.S.A.* **

Mackey, Robert R. *The Uncivil War: Irregular Warfare in the Upper South, 1861-1865*. Norman, Oklahoma: University of Oklahoma Press, 2004.

Masters, Daniel A. and L.M. Strayer. *Echoes of Battle: Annals of Ohio's Soldiers in the Civil War, 1861-1861 Volume One: Philippi to Perryville*. Perrysburg, Ohio: Columbian Arsenal Press, 2022.

Meacham, Charles. *Meacham's History of Christian County Kentucky: From Oxcart to Airplane*. Evansville Indiana: Unigraphic, 1974.

Minnesota in the Civil and Indian Wars, 1861-1865.

Powell, David. *Failure in the Saddle: Nathan Bedford Forrest, Joe Wheeler, and the Confederate Cavalry in the Chickamauga Campaign*. El Dorado Hills, California: Savas Beatie LLC, 2010.

Prokopowicz, Gerald J. *All for the Regiment: The Army of the Ohio, 1861-1862*. Chapel Hill: The University of North Carolina Press, 2001.

Reid, Richard J. *4th Indiana Cavalry Regiment: A History*. Fordsville, Kentucky: Sandefur Offset Printing, 1994.

Rothert, Otto Arthu. *History of Muhlenberg County*. Louisville, Kentucky: John P. Morton and Company Incorporated, 1913.

Rowell, John W. *Yankee Cavalrymen: Through the Civil War with the 9th Pennsylvania Cavalry*. Knoxville, Tennessee: University of Tennessee Press, 1971.

Scott, Sean A. *A Visitation of God: Northern Civilians Interpret the Civil War*. Oxford University Press; Reprint edition, 2012.

Smith, Timothy B. *Shiloh: Conquer or Perish*. Lawrence, Kansas: University Press of Kansas, 2014.

_____. *Grant Invades Tennessee: The 1862 Battles for Forts Henry and Donelson*. Lawrence, Kansas: University Press of Kansas, 2016.

Starling, Edmund Lyne, *History of Henderson County, Kentucky: Comprising History of County and City, Precincts, Education, Churches, Secret Societies, Leading Enterprises, Sketches and Recollections, and Biographies of the Living and Dead.* Henderson, Kentucky, 1887.

Stewart, Martin. *Redemption: The 71st Ohio Infantry in the Civil War*. Troy, Ohio: Self Published, 2012.

Sutherland, Daniel E., *A Savage Conflict: The Decisive Role of Guerrillas in the American Civil War.* Chapel Hill: The University of North Carolina Press, 2009.

Thompson, Ed Porter. *History of the Orphan Brigade*. Louisville, Kentucky: Lewis N. Thompson, 1898.

Truman, Arthur C. *At War with Ourselves, 1861-1865: A Military History of the Daviess County, Kentucky Area*. Owensboro, Kentucky: McDowell Publishing, 1994.

Speed, Thomas. *Union Regiments of Kentucky*. Louisville, Kentucky: Courier-Journal Job Printing Company, 1897.

Vogel, Susan Carter. *Germans in the Civil War: The Letters They Wrote Home*. Edited by Kamphoefner, Walter D. and Helbich Wolfgang. Chapel Hill: The University of North Carolina Press, 2006.

Wittenberg, Eric J. *Holding the Line on the River of Death: Union Mounted Forces at Chickamauga, September 18, 1863*. El Dorado Hills, California: Savas Beatie LLC, 2018.

Woodworth, Steven E., *Nothing But Victory: The Army of the Tennessee 1861-1865*. New York: Knopf Doubleday Publishing Group, 2005.

Periodicals

Allison, Young E. "An Account of the Terrible Kentucky Guerrilla of the Civil War Times." *The Register of the Kentucky Historical Society* 57, no. 4 (1959).

Bennett, B. Kevin. "Morgan's Luck Runs Out: The Battle of Buffington Island." *Blue and Gray Magazine* 15, no. 4 (1998).

Canup, Charles E. "Conscription and Draft in Indiana During the Civil War." *Indiana Magazine of History* 10, no. 2 (1914): 70-83.

Chyet, Stanley. "Ohio Valley Jewry During the Civil War." Bulletin of the Historical and Philosophical Society of Ohio, Volume 21, No. 3 (1963).

Crane Jr., Michael J. "The Demise of Slavery on the Border: Federal Policy and the Union Army in Henderson, Kentucky." *The Register of the Kentucky Historical Society*, 113, no. 4, 2015.

Dew, Aloma Williams. "'Between the Hawk and the Buzzard': Owensboro During the Civil War." *The Register of the Kentucky Historical Society* 77, no. 1, 1979.

_____. "Little Ado About Much- Life on the Homefront in Civil War Owensboro." *Daviess County Historical Quarterly*, April 1984, Volume II Number 2, 38.

Ewing, Kelley. "More Dreadful than the Most Gruesome of Tales: Newspaper Coverage of the East Orange Bathtub Mystery." *Fit to Post: Dispatches From the Virginia Newspaper Project at the Library of Virginia* (2016): http://www.virginiamemory.com/blogs/fit-to-print/2016/06/03/more-dreadful-than-the-most-gruesome-of-tales-newspaper-coverage-of-the-east-orange-bathtub-mystery/.

Fialka, Andrew. "Guerrillas in the Archive: Kentucky's Irregular War through the Governor's Eyes." *The Register of the Kentucky Historical Society*, 2014.

Gildrie, Richard P. "Guerrilla Warfare in the Lower Cumberland River Valley, 1862-1865," *Tennessee Historical Quarterly* 49, no. 3, 1990.

Martin, James B. "Black Flag Over the Bluegrass: Guerrilla Warfare in Kentucky, 1863-1865." *The Register of the Kentucky Historical Society* 86, no. 4, 1988.

Mills, Randy. "Confederate Raider . . . Criminal . . . Hero: Captain Jake Bennett's Civil War." *Journal of the Indiana Academy of the Social Sciences*: 15, no. 1, 2012.

Sanders, Stuart. "The Radicalization of 'Bloody-Handed' Bill Davison: How a Union Soldier Became a Pro-Confederate Bushwhacker." *The Register of the Kentucky Historical Society*, Vol. 116 No. 2, 2018.

Snepp, Daniel W. "John W. Foster, Soldier and Politician." *Indiana Magazine of History* 32, no. 3, 1936.

Sutherland, Daniel E. "Guerrilla Warfare, Democracy, and the Fate of the Confederacy." *The Journal of Southern History,* Vol. 68, No. 2, 2002.

Tarnowieckyi, Scott A. "'Branded by the Lincolnites as Guerrillas:' Adam Rankin Johnson and Guerrilla Identity, and Irregular Warfare in the Lower Green River Valley in 1862." *The Register of the Kentucky Historical Society,* Vol. 113 No. 4, 2015.

Trudeau, Noah Andre. "Fields Without Honor: Two Affairs in Tennessee." *Civil War Times Illustrated* 32, no. 3, 1992.

Valentine, L. L. "Sue Mundy of Kentucky: Part 1," *The Register of the Kentucky Historical Society*, Vol. 62 no. 3, 1964.

Weissbach, Lee Shai. "Kentucky Jewry During the Civil War." *The Register of the Kentucky Historical Society* 110, no. 2, 2012.

West, Mike. "The Man Who Would Have Burned New York City." *Murfreesboro Post*, February 1, 2009.

Kenneth H. Williams and James Russell Harris. "Kentucky in 1860: A Statistical Overview." *The Register of the Kentucky Historical Society* Vol. 103, No. 4, 2005.

Wilson, Don. *The Boys from Calhoun: The story of Camp Calhoun and its contribution to the Civil War.* Self-Published, 2008.

Yonkers, Charles E. "The Civil War Transformation of George W. Smith: How a Western Kentucky Farmer Evolved from Unionist Whig to Pro-Southern Democrat." *The Register of the Kentucky Historical Society* 103, no. 4, 2005.

Index

About the Author

Derrick Lindow teaches 8th grade United States history in Owensboro, Kentucky. He graduated from Kentucky Wesleyan College (2010) with a BA in history and holds an MA in Education from the University of the Cumberlands. In 2023, he earned his MA in history from Western Kentucky University. He is the 2015 Dr. Tom and Betty Lawrence National History Teacher Award recipient from the National Society of the Sons of the American Revolution and the 2019 James Madison Fellow for the state of Kentucky. Derrick is the creator and co-administrator of the Western Theater in the Civil War website, which brings together authors and historians to write about that crucial area of the war. The Kentucky native is married to his lovely wife Allie and is the father of two boys, Ezra and Owen.